W9-BVS-132

habnf   HED
364.163 TELFE

Telfer, Tori, author
Confident women
33410017043409   02-25-2021

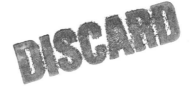

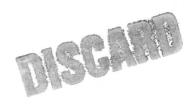

Hebron Public Library
201 W. Sigler Street
Hebron, IN 46341

CONFIDENT WOMEN

ALSO BY TORI TELFER

Lady Killers

CONFIDENT

WOMEN

**SWINDLERS, GRIFTERS, AND SHAPESHIFTERS OF THE
FEMININE PERSUASION**

TORI TELFER

An Imprint of HarperCollins*Publishers*

Portions of "The Spiritualists" chapter originally appeared in "The Female Persuasion" in *The Believer* and are reprinted by permission.

CONFIDENT WOMEN. Copyright © 2021 by Tori Telfer. All rights reserved. Printed in the United States of America. No part of this book may be used or reproduced in any manner whatsoever without written permission except in the case of brief quotations embodied in critical articles and reviews. For information, address HarperCollins Publishers, 195 Broadway, New York, NY 10007.

HarperCollins books may be purchased for educational, business, or sales promotional use. For information, please email the Special Markets Department at SPsales@harpercollins.com.

FIRST EDITION

Designed by Jamie Lynn Kerner

Library of Congress Cataloging-in-Publication Data

Names: Telfer, Tori, author.
Title: Confident women / Tori Telfer.
Description: New York : HarperCollins, 2021. | Includes bibliographical references. | Summary: "Why do we love stories about scammers so much? Journalist Tori Telfer dives into the stories of historical female con women and explains why we are so enamored by their tricks"— Provided by publisher.
Identifiers: LCCN 2020025856 (print) | LCCN 2020025857 (ebook) | ISBN 9780062956033 (paperback) | ISBN 9780062956040 (epub)
Subjects: LCSH: Swindlers and swindling. | Swindlers and swindling—Biography. | Women—Psychology. | Women in popular culture.
Classification: LCC HV6691 .T425 2021 (print) | LCC HV6691 (ebook) | DDC 364.16/309252—dc23
LC record available at https://lccn.loc.gov/2020025856
LC ebook record available at https://lccn.loc.gov/2020025857

ISBN 978-0-06-295603-3 (pbk.)
ISBN 978-0-06-306513-0 (library edition)

21 22 23 24 25 LSC 10 9 8 7 6 5 4 3 2 1

TO CECIL

In a twisted way, she resembles the skier or the mountain climber.
One imagines her asking, "Will I make it again this time?"

—DR. WILLIAM A. FROSCH

CONTENTS

INTRODUCTION

CHARMING

In 1977, the New York *Daily News* published an article about a beautiful young con woman named Barbara St. James. (At least, that was one of her names.) "If you meet her, you will like her," ran the article. "She will draw out your life story, your troubles and triumphs. She appears wealthy, a woman of substance and class. She drips with sincerity."

Appears was the second-most important word in the paragraph, but the first was *like*. *You will like her.* Beautiful Barbara's life story has long been forgotten, but that line could be used to describe almost every con woman before and after her. *If you meet her, you will like her.* The con woman's likability is the single most important tool she has, sharp as a chef's knife and fake as a theater mask. Without her likability, she would be nothing. If you like her—and you *will* like her—then her work will be so much easier. It'll all be over quickly. You'll hardly feel a thing.

The fact that we like con artists so much is probably the greatest con of all time. How did they pull it off, these criminals, creating a world in which we call them "confidence artists" while other criminals get unembroidered titles like "thief" and "drug dealer"? Why do we call their crimes "playing confidence tricks," like we're talking about a mischievous toddler? When journalists, lawyers, and lovers spoke about the women in this book, it was as though they were remembering a brilliant performer who had sadly lost her way. "The woman would have been a great human creature had she been highly trained, highly educated," wrote one journalist about a Canadian con woman. The brother of a British con artist insisted that if it weren't for an "unfortunate quirk" in her character, "she would be a wonderful, wonderful person. In fact, she is anyway." The lover of a French con artist said of her, "Without being aware of the danger, I admired this brave spirit that was checked by nothing." The brother-in-law of an American con artist declared, "She's one of the nicest persons I ever met."

There's no point in denying it: the women in this book are extremely charming. Most of them would be fantastic company on a bar crawl. Many had great taste in fashion. The designer handbags! The *fur coats*! Some could do fun accents, others could tell your future. One drove a pink car, while another had a license plate that read 1RSKTKR—Number 1 Risk Taker. The most dangerous one had a habit of giving out $100 bills, just because. Delightful! Clearly these women would have been entertaining to know, assuming that you stayed on their good side. But why do we feel so comfortable admiring them? You can't go around gushing about how your serial-killing sister-in-law is "a wonderful, wonderful person" and a "brave spirit that was checked by nothing," but the internet is choked with articles like "Why We Are All So Obsessed With Scammers" and "How to Dress Up Like Your Favorite Con Artist for Halloween."

A simple explanation for all this adulation is that con artists have a reputation for being nonviolent criminals. Rarely will you find a con artist stashing someone's head in her freezer. Her victims almost never end up dead. Almost never! This makes it awfully convenient for us, because we can dismiss these victims as gullible-but-largely-unharmed idiots and focus all of our fawning attention on what makes the artists—er, criminals—so *fabulous*.

But perhaps there's a darker reason we cheer on the con artist: secretly, we want to *be* her. Most people, especially women, live their lives rattling around inside a thousand and one social barriers. But, through some mysterious alchemy of talent and criminality, the con artist bursts through those barriers like Houdini escaping from one of his famous suspended straitjackets. The con artist doesn't feel the need to use the correct Social Security number, or keep the name her parents gave her, or put her real eye color on her driver's license. She doesn't mind forgery. She's not afraid of a little bigamy. She'll drive a fancy car right off the parking lot or steal a necklace made of 647 diamonds, and she doesn't care who pays the price for her crimes. And though people love to turn her into a metaphor—for entrepreneurship, for capitalist grift, for the American Dream, for America itself, for the Devil, or simply for the average woman's life of mild duplicity—she doesn't give a damn about your figures of speech. The only person she answers to is herself. Isn't it shocking, that sort of naked selfishness? And doesn't it sound sort of delicious?

It's tempting to think that we *could* be her—if we were better at accents and owned a few more wigs and gave in, completely, to our basest social desires: for status, power, wealth, money, admiration, control. These desires may sound crass, but they're inherent to our nature. A recent psychology study found that people crave high social rank not only because it satisfies our aching need to belong, but because it gives us a sense of control, better self-esteem, and even reproductive benefits. (Even animals want to be important. A 2016 study of female rhesus macaque monkeys showed that social climbing actually strengthened their immune systems.) Most of us indulge these desires in milquetoast ways; our tiny, depressing cons just never make the papers. We reinvent ourselves on New Year's Day, we edit our life stories to sound more exciting, and we try our very, very best to be likable—when it benefits us. But we rarely let ourselves go all the way, whether through a sense of morality or social pressure or a good old-fashioned longing to stay out of jail. So when we read about the con woman's hijinks, it's tempting to put ourselves not in her victims' shoes (we're far too smart for that, we think), but in hers. What if we behaved like she does? What if we could charm like that? What if we shucked off morality, and society, and collective responsibility, and just let ourselves . . . *indulge*?

But we could never be her. There's too much standing in our way. Too many rules to follow. Too many social contracts to uphold. This is a good thing, mostly, this following and upholding—a beautiful thing, even, though some of us will hopefully be forgiven for suppressing a small sigh of disappointment at the realization. And maybe that's why the con artist finds it so easy to make us like her. She has to turn on the charm, sure, but we're waiting to meet her with open mouths and shining eyes. As she performs for us, we think, "a great human creature" and "a wonderful, wonderful person" and "what if, what if, what if?" She has us right where she wants us. She's about to make us an offer we can't refuse.

THE GLITTERATI

MISCELLANIA

ONE HOT AIR BALLOON

ONE HOT AIR BALLOON–INSPIRED PRODUCT

EIGHT GRAND PIANOS

647+ DIAMONDS

ONE FAKE QUEEN

TWO FAKE FATHERS

ONE REAL FAINTING SPELL

NUMEROUS FAKE FAINTING SPELLS

ONE SOLDIER WHO LOVES CALLIGRAPHY

ONE ELDERLY MAN DRIVEN TO HIS DEATHBED IN SHOCK

A BATCH OF SWINDLED OLYMPIANS

ONE FAKE MUSTACHE

ONE VERY SIGNIFICANT ROSE

JEANNE DE SAINT-RÉMY

alias: Comtesse de La Motte

1756-1791

ONCE UPON A TIME, THE KING OF FRANCE DECIDED TO BUY HIS lover the most beautiful diamond necklace in the world.

The year was 1772. The king was the shy, awkward Louis XV, and his lover was Madame du Barry, whose flushed cheeks and milky décolletage were the stuff of legends. She needed a necklace worthy of her beauty, and so the royal jewelers got to work, sourcing diamonds from countries as far away as Russia and Brazil. The resulting 647-diamond, 2,800-karat confection was stunning—and a bit ominous. It was designed to circle the wearer's throat and creep toward her bosom, while strands of diamonds poured down the back of her neck. There were a couple of frothy little blue ribbons scattered about the necklace, but they failed to soften the overwhelming effect. The style was called a *collier d'esclavage*: a "slave collar."

It should have been the most coveted piece of jewelry in the world, but Madame du Barry never had a chance to try it on. Before Louis XV could shell out the 2,000,000 livres necessary to buy it—more than seventeen million dollars today—he died of smallpox, leaving his lover without her bauble and the panicked jewelers without a dime. For a while, the jewelers trudged around Europe, waving the necklace under various royal noses, but no one was charmed by its malicious twinkle, and even if they were, they couldn't afford it anyway.

So the jewelers returned home to try one last option. There was a new girl in town. A young queen from Austria, famous for her elegant neck. She was said to be a frivolous thing, obsessed with anything that sparkled. Maybe she'd be interested in the piece. After all, what woman wouldn't want to get her hands on something so . . . precious?

✳

SIXTEEN YEARS EARLIER, A SCRAPPY LITTLE GIRL WAS BORN INTO A world without diamonds. Her father was a drunk, her mother beat her with sticks, and her family had squandered their pathetic fortune generations ago. But her name! Her name was Jeanne de Saint-Rémy, proud descendant of the House of Valois, and her name meant *everything* to her. Jeanne's father was technically the great-great-great-grandson of Henry II, who ruled France in the mid-1500s as the tenth king of the House of Valois. But her father was an illegitimate great-great-great-grandson, descended from Henry II's mistress, and so while his forefathers had gotten *some* royal favor, his descendants suffered. For generations, Jeanne's bastard ancestors had lived as poachers and thieves in a dilapidated country home outside the village of Bar-sur-Aube in Champagne. Gradually, most of their land was sold to absolve various debts, and by the time Jeanne and her three siblings came along, there was no Valois glitter left. In fact, the kids were so thin and feral that locals found them difficult to look at. There was a little hole in the wall of the shack where they lived, and the locals would shove food through the hole at the children, so as not to see their starving faces.

But Jeanne grew up believing that there was Valois money waiting in the wings for her, as long as she could convince someone important to listen. Her parents supported this delusion in their own poisonous ways. When their debts became serious enough, the whole family fled to Paris, where Jeanne's mother forced her to beg, beating her viciously if she didn't bring home enough money. Jeanne would wander the streets, crying, "Pity a poor orphan of the blood of the Valois!" In Paris, her father died of alcoholism, and Jeanne claimed that his last words to her included the exhortation, "Let me beg you, under every misfortune, to remember that you are a VALOIS!"

When she was eight years old, her cry caught the ear of a generous lady called the Marchioness de Boulainvilliers, who scooped up Jeanne and her siblings, scrubbed them behind their ears, and sent them off to boarding school. (By this point, Jeanne's mother had run off with another man.) The marchioness even managed to get the children's Valois heritage authenticated, and wrangled a small royal pension for them, the equivalent of about $8,000 annually today. This should have been a huge deal for Jeanne— royal acknowledgment that she was who she said she was—but the ambitious girl was practically insulted by the gesture. She wanted real money. She wanted the Valois country home back. She wanted people to look at her in awe.

Though France was crumbling internally—pouring money into the American Revolution to destabilize their English enemy, and only about a decade away from their own bloody insurrection— the country's upper class was still glamorous enough to dazzle even the most levelheaded young woman. At the center of all that glamour was the young queen Marie Antoinette, who shamelessly overspent her clothing budget, wore huge sculpted hairstyles, kept her own personal chocolate maker on call, and hired someone to make sure that her rooms were always filled with fresh flowers. With a queen like that, who wouldn't want a piece of the glamour for herself? Everyone in the country was striving for more, stepping shamelessly on the heads of those below them in order to rise up another fraction of an inch. And no one in the entire hungry, scrabbling country wanted to climb higher than Jeanne.

✳

CHARLES BOEHMER WAS SURROUNDED BY SO MANY DIAMONDS THAT he wanted to kill himself.

He and his partner, Paul Bassenge, were the royal jewelers who had designed the 647-diamond necklace that, as it turned out, had been the worst mistake of their professional lives. The thing was cursed. Cursed! They'd spent the last ten years begging Marie Antoinette to take the necklace off their hands, and the queen had yet to express the slightest interest in it. At one point, Boehmer flung himself onto the floor in front of her and sobbed that if she didn't buy the necklace from him, he would throw himself into the river. The queen responded coolly that she certainly wouldn't hold herself responsible if he died.

It should have been clear to Boehmer that he was barking up the wrong tree. Marie Antoinette almost never wore necklaces—they distracted from the graceful simplicity of her long neck. But he was too deeply in debt to think about aesthetics now. He and Bassenge had bet their entire livelihood on this piece, and for what? It hung around their necks like an albatross. They worried they might carry it forever.

While the royal jewelers pulled out their hair, Jeanne was twenty-three and dreaming of future greatness. Though the marchioness had been awfully kind to her, Jeanne was starting to chafe under her oversight. The marchioness kept trying to turn her into a nice, well-behaved working girl—a seamstress, maybe?—but Jeanne was deeply offended by the implication that she'd be anything other than the greatest lady of all time. Finally, the long-suffering marchioness sent Jeanne and her sister to a nunnery, perhaps spurred on by the suspicion that Jeanne had been seducing her husband. Unsurprisingly, Jeanne had no interest in dedicating her life to poverty and chastity and charity, and by the fall of 1779, she'd had enough of nuns. With a few coins in their pockets, she and her sister scrambled out of the nunnery and ran all the way back to their hometown, hoping to impress the locals who remembered them only as a pair of famished urchins.

Jeanne's homecoming wasn't quite the extravaganza that she'd dreamed of. Some of the locals thought she was a bit of a lunatic, including the woman she was staying with, who called her a "demon." (It didn't help that Jeanne was seducing *her* husband, too.) But others were taken in by her charms. For all her alarming qualities, Jeanne had three notable traits: her smile, her bright eyes, and her persuasiveness. She wasn't well educated, but she had an instinctive understanding of how society worked—and she wasn't afraid to break society's rules when she felt inconvenienced by them. "Without being aware of the danger, I admired this brave spirit that was checked by nothing," wrote a young lawyer named Jacques Beugnot, who'd fallen desperately in love with her. He found it charming that Jeanne "contrasted so curiously with the timid and narrow character of the other ladies in the town."

Jeanne was interested in Beugnot more for his legal help than his love, thinking that he could help her get her Valois fortune back. For love, she looked elsewhere, and by the time she was twenty-four, she'd found another man: a talentless army officer named Antoine de La Motte. When she got pregnant, the two of them scrambled to get married in order to save face. (Jeanne wasn't afraid to break society's rules, but only when it benefited her, and being an unwed mother might have hindered her social climbing.) At midnight on June 6, 1780, they were wed, and promptly started calling themselves Comte and Comtesse de La Motte—Count and Countess. There were actually some noble La Mottes, of no relation, living elsewhere in France, and Jeanne and Antoine must have figured they could simply ride their coattails. *Fake it till you make it* had always been Jeanne's policy, after all.

Unfortunately, it was impossible to fake the timeline of her pregnancy. One month after the wedding, Jeanne gave birth to twin boys, who died a few days later. She hardly had time to mourn them. The newlyweds had been living with Antoine's aunt, who now realized that Jeanne had clearly gotten pregnant out of wedlock and, scandalized, kicked them out. Suddenly Jeanne and Antoine needed money. And housing. And support. A bit of power wouldn't hurt, either.

By September 1781, Jeanne learned that her old benefactress, the marchioness, was staying with a very important person: Cardinal Prince Louis de Rohan, from one of France's best and oldest families. *Interesting*, thought Jeanne. Rohan was full of potential. He was a handsome, tall, white-haired man of almost fifty, who spent money like it was going out of style (which, in 1780s France, it was). His gardens were massive, his palace was the jewel of the surrounding countryside, and he owned fifty-two English mares.

But Rohan wasn't as elegant inside as he was on the outside. "Weak and vain, and credulous to a degree; anything but devout, and mad after women," one historian scoffed. He was hopelessly in debt, and Marie Antoinette herself couldn't stand him. Being disliked by the queen was a social and professional death sentence; Rohan had convinced himself that her disapproval was the only thing standing between him and his goal of being prime minister. So he tried desperately to win her love—once, he even put on a disguise and tried to sneak into one of her parties—but nothing worked. He was growing desperate. He would have given anything for the queen to like him. *Anything.*

When Jeanne met Rohan, she saw a man consumed by a single, obvious desire. And as Jeanne knew well, desire made people defenseless. Desire was a crack in the armor. An opportunity. A little door, just begging to be walked through.

✳

WHETHER OR NOT JEANNE AND ROHAN ACTUALLY SLEPT TOGETHER is up for debate, but Jeanne seduced him masterfully. Whenever he was around, she wore her best gowns and always made sure that the smell of her perfume filled the room. She charmed, teased, and flattered, and he lapped it all up, rewarding her with lavish gifts and a promotion for her husband. She was so convincingly delightful that she even conned Rohan's own personal con man: a swindler named Count Alessandro di Cagliostro who lived at Rohan's palace, employed as a sort of life coach. Cagliostro was famous for his supposed knowledge of the occult and had charmed plenty of Parisians with his séances and love potions. But thankfully for Jeanne, he wasn't good enough to sniff out a fellow grifter. In fact, while Cagliostro was a flashier trickster, Jeanne was the better artist. Sure, Cagliostro could always break out an "Egyptian Elixir" or speak grandiose nonsense about "columbs" and "demonic Masonries," but at the end of the day, he dealt in smoke and mirrors—sometimes literally. Jeanne's area of expertise was much more impressive: the endlessly vulnerable human heart.

With a new benefactor at her beck and call, the world was Jeanne's oyster. She and Antoine rented rooms in both Paris and Versailles, and Jeanne began pretending to be much richer than she actually was. She blew her pension on extravagant outfits. She bought expensive silverware to impress her guests—and then pawned it the very next day. She was trying to creep closer and closer to the center of all wealth: the king and queen of France, who could fulfill all her dreams with just a snap of their fingers. Queen Marie Antoinette was famous for her charity, and Jeanne was sure that if she could just explain the whole Valois situation to her, the queen would restore her and her family to their old glory.

The problem was that everyone else at Versailles was on a similar mission. You couldn't throw a brick at the palace without braining a noble who was dying for an audience with the queen. So in order to attract Marie Antoinette's attention, Jeanne had to get creative. She started lurking around Versailles, hoping to "accidentally" run across the queen in one of its many hallways. Then she began dramatically fainting in front of various noblewomen, thinking that word of the poor, starving Valois orphan would reach the queen's tender ears. Nothing worked. The only thing she gained was a reputation as a nuisance—a strange, bright-eyed nuisance who was always inexplicably fainting.

By the beginning of 1784, Jeanne and Antoine were nearly broke, and Jeanne had to come up with a new plan. If Versailles was already a rumor mill, she thought, why not take advantage of it? Her scheme was simple, but daringly genius: she started telling people that she and Marie Antoinette were friends. *Best* friends, really. In fact, she said, Marie Antoinette had taken a *personal* interest in her situation, and the two of them were now unburdening their souls to each other during secret nighttime meetings.

To make this narrative seem more believable, Jeanne struck up an acquaintanceship with the gatekeeper at Marie Antoinette's private Versailles estate, the Petit Trianon. Late at night, Jeanne would make sure people saw her creeping out of the gate, as though she'd just come from an intimate late-night hot chocolate with her royal pal. From there, the gossipmongers did the rest of the heavy lifting. Soon enough, nobles were actually coming to see Jeanne herself, begging her to use her influence over the queen to help them. Jeanne would nod graciously, accept the money that they pressed into her palm, and promise to see what she could do. It wasn't long before Rohan heard the rumor and thrilled to it. How convenient for him that his best friend Jeanne was so close with his future best friend, Marie! He begged Jeanne to ask the queen to give him another chance.

Like a shark scenting blood, Jeanne smelled Rohan's desperation from a mile away. She told him that she'd talk to the queen, and then returned with the greatest news in the world: Marie Antoinette was open to reconciliation. In fact, she wanted Rohan to send her a letter . . .

※

THE LETTERS THAT STARTED TO FLY BETWEEN CARDINAL ROHAN and "the queen" were warm, friendly, and a little bit sexual. (Rumor had it that he called her "master" and referred to himself as "slave.") Sometimes the queen wrote to him on paper edged with blue flowers, sometimes on paper decorated with gold. Her letters often mentioned, offhandedly, that Rohan should give Jeanne a little something to thank her for bringing them together. Rohan did so, happily. Before long, Rohan was imploring the queen to let him visit her, but the queen kept responding that it wasn't the right time . . . yet.

Rohan would have died of shame if he'd known that the let-

JEANNE DE SAINT-RÉMY   13

ters weren't being written by Marie Antoinette at all, but by a shifty soldier with a penchant for calligraphy. Jeanne had teamed up with an old army buddy of her husband's named Rétaux de Villette, who was both her lover and her official forger. She would dictate the missives to Villette, and he'd write them down dutifully and sign them with a flourish. His handwriting looked nothing like the queen's, but Rohan was too starry-eyed to notice.

For a while, the letters satiated Rohan, but Jeanne couldn't put him off forever with her *not now my darling* responses. He insisted so strongly on meeting the queen in person that Jeanne realized she'd have to produce a queen. So she sent her husband out to trawl the streets for someone who could pass as Marie Antoinette, and he came back with a pretty, naive sex worker named Nicole le Guay. Jeanne told Nicole that she was friends with the queen and that the queen wanted Nicole to do a favor for her in exchange for a nice little reward. Jeanne then told Rohan that the queen would meet him at midnight, in the Park of Versailles, where she would hand him a single rose. The whole thing was painfully erotic: the nighttime, the secrecy, the flower and all that it might possibly signify. Rohan was in heaven.

When the fateful night came, Jeanne hid in the bushes and watched. A very nervous Nicole clutched her rose and trembled inside a frothy white gown called a *gaulle*—exactly the sort of slightly scandalous summer dress that Marie Antoinette loved to wear. It was dark when Rohan entered the garden, and as he moved through the gloom, he saw the faint outline of a woman, dressed in white. She handed him a rose, and he was pretty sure he heard her say, "You may believe that the past will be forgotten."

The whole thing was a blur, a glorious blur, and it was over much too fast, because suddenly Jeanne was at his elbow, saying that they needed to scatter before they were found out.

It was the illusion of the century. Nicole really did look like the queen, especially in the darkness, and Rohan was so blissed-out that he went home and named one of the walks at his summer palace the "Promenade of the Rose." And Jeanne? Jeanne was at the top of her game. Sure, a professional swindler like Cagliostro could use candles and scarves to conjure up visions, but little Jeanne from nowhere had just conjured up the queen of France herself. She was powerful now, in Rohan's eyes—and she used it. In letters, "the queen" started asking to borrow larger and larger sums of money, and Rohan obliged happily. Jeanne took the money and treated herself to a country house in the village where she grew up. Whenever she was there, she put on her finest gowns and threw lavish dinner parties. *Look at me*, she seemed to be saying to the villagers who knew her when she was just a kid, scrawny and wild and infinitely hungry. *I told you I was special.*

*

THANKS TO THE GOSSIPS OF VERSAILLES, THE RUMORED FRIEND-ship between Jeanne and the queen eventually reached the royal jewelers, and their ears pricked up. Maybe *they* couldn't convince Marie Antoinette to buy an eye-wateringly expensive piece of jewelry—but Marie Antoinette's *best friend* certainly could. So one day, the jewelers brought the necklace itself over to Jeanne, and asked her if she could find it within her gracious heart to help them sell the damn thing.

Jeanne looked at the necklace: the most beautiful, burdensome thing in the world. She saw the perfectly round diamonds, sourced from all around the globe. The frilly little ribbons, a desperate attempt to soften the dreadful weight of the piece. The massive teardrop-shaped diamond at its center, gorgeous and inscrutable as the heart of a queen. Marchionesses and cardinals and con men had all been easy for her to fool. But this? This was a challenge worthy of her intellect, her courage, her Valois blood. And so she agreed to help them.

In short order, "Marie Antoinette's" letters to Rohan began hinting that she could really use his help with a sensitive matter. It was, she wrote, "a secret negotiation which interests me personally, and which I am unwilling to confide to anyone except yourself." Rohan would have to be *extremely* discreet, because, well, there was this necklace, and though she couldn't be *openly* involved in the purchase, the trinket was so *beautiful*, so suited for her long neck, that she simply *had* to have it. Would Rohan be a dear and arrange the purchase for her? She'd pay him back, of course. Eventually.

Somehow, this request didn't strike Rohan as suspicious, probably because the real Marie Antoinette was infamous for running up huge debts. Still, Rohan was deeply in debt himself, and the necklace was staggeringly pricey. He visited the jewelers and agreed on a discount and a payment plan: 1,600,000 livres, to be paid in four installments. The jewelers didn't feel like they needed a contract—who needs a contract when your buyer is the queen?—but Rohan insisted on one. So Jeanne pretended to deliver a contract to the queen, and brought it back with *Marie Antoinette de*

France scrawled on the bottom. This was an amateur mistake—the queen only ever signed papers as *Marie Antoinette*—but everyone was too excited to notice. And just like that, after thirteen years of agony, the necklace was sold.

Rohan brought the necklace to Jeanne's apartment. Jeanne promised that she'd deliver it to the queen as soon as she could. But when she and her husband were finally alone with the glittering thing, they took out a knife—and began to hack the necklace apart.

For the next couple of days, Rohan and the jewelers waited on pins and needles. Every time Marie Antoinette appeared in public, they panicked. Why wasn't she wearing the necklace? Why wasn't she at least smiling at them in a knowing fashion? Boehmer sent her a treacly letter about how happy he was that the necklace was about to be "worn by the greatest and the best of queens," but it had no effect. (Marie Antoinette had no idea what he was talking about, and told her lady-in-waiting, "That man is born to be my torment; he has always some mad scheme in his head.") Finally, Jeanne soothed the men by saying that the queen simply didn't feel comfortable wearing the necklace until she'd paid for it in full, especially since the country was so wracked with debt. And so the men settled down to wait, as Jeanne sent her husband to London with a bag of loose diamonds to sell.

Meanwhile, people noticed that Jeanne was suddenly a lot richer than before. Her gowns were better, she was buying nonsensically extravagant objects like a mechanical bird that could actually fly, and her new carriage was shaped like a hot air balloon. (Hot air balloons were very trendy at the time. One newspaper called it "balloon mania.") In fact, she was blowing through more money than most of France's nobles spent in a year, though she tried to explain it away by saying that she'd, um, won a lot of money at the horse races. But the clock was ticking. Jeanne knew that it was only a matter of time before the jewelers demanded their first payment, or Rohan contacted Marie Antoinette directly to ask why she wasn't clinging to his neck in gratitude for helping her purchase the necklace, or both.

So as usual, Jeanne decided to go on the offensive. She met with Bassenge and told him, solemnly, that Marie Antoinette's signature on the contract had been forged. Rohan had enemies, Jeanne said, and someone was using the necklace to try and destroy him. In other words: the whole thing was a con—a con masterminded by somebody else, of course. She told the shocked jeweler that the best thing to do would be to ask Rohan for the whole payment *now* in order to keep things quiet.

It was a chess move so audacious that it could have worked. Rohan might have swallowed his pride and paid up, simply to avoid scandal and humiliation. But there was just one problem: the gossips. Boehmer heard from one of Marie Antoinette's ladies-in-waiting that the queen had never purchased the necklace after all. Rohan saw an example of Marie Antoinette's actual handwriting and realized with a shock that *his* letters from the queen looked completely different. Finally, the anxious jewelers went straight to the queen for an explanation. Had she purchased the necklace?

No, said the queen. Just like that, Jeanne's elaborate ruse was punctured, and the whole thing deflated with sickening speed, like a hot air balloon falling from the sky.

＊

ON AUGUST 17, 1785, JEANNE WAS AT A FANCY DINNER NEAR HER hometown when she heard that Rohan had been arrested moments after leaving an audience with the king. "There is talk of a diamond necklace he was to have bought for the queen, and did not buy," said the man who delivered the news—no one knew, just yet, how much more complicated the transaction had really been. Jeanne's old lover, Beugnot the lawyer, was there at the table, watching her. He saw her face turn white. She dropped her napkin. She said she had to go. He took her home, where she began burning her papers. After years of trying and failing to get the queen's attention, she never imagined that the queen would actually pay attention now.

The next morning, Jeanne was arrested and taken to the Bastille. Rohan was already there; during his arrest, he'd managed to slip a note to a friend, begging him to race home and burn every letter that was written on paper edged in gold or blue flowers. The two of them were soon joined by Nicole and Villette, the fake queen and the forger. Jeanne, always on the offensive, declared that the conjurer Cagliostro and his wife were the ones responsible for the plot, so they were arrested, too. The only one who wasn't arrested was her husband, Antoine, who was still in England, distracted by the daunting task of selling 647 diamonds.

Five months later, the trial was underway. The central question was this: Who was the *real* guilty party? Was the whole affair masterminded by Rohan, attempting to undercut the queen's reputation for his own nefarious political gains? Or was Rohan himself—a man from one of France's most powerful families—actually the *victim* here? Was it possible that the real mastermind behind this audacious scheme was this former street urchin, this nobody with pretty eyes, this . . . *woman*?

Nicole and Villette testified about the scandalous nighttime meeting in the garden, which supported Rohan's insistence that he had truly believed he was corresponding with the real queen. Their testimony made Rohan look like an idiot—but an innocent idiot. In response, Jeanne tried every trick in the book to bolster her case. When Nicole testified, Jeanne winked at her to try and get her to change her story. During Cagliostro's testimony, she hurled a candlestick at his head. She laughed if she thought it would help her; she wept when weeping seemed more appropriate. She denied that she had ever claimed to be Marie Antoinette's best friend. She said that the only reason she and her husband had been selling loose diamonds was because Rohan had given her some old jewelry. She bit her jailor on the arm. She hid naked under her bed to avoid being taken into court. And she argued her case with the vigor of a thousand lawyers. How crazy did they think she was, she cried, to try and pull off such a crazy swindle?

Outside the courtroom, the people of France could not believe what they were hearing. The whole affair was so wonderfully sleazy. It was delicious—*delicious!*—to see people like pompous old Rohan and materialistic Marie Antoinette implicated in such a sordid scheme. And at the center of it all, a diamond necklace: no longer just a pretty bauble that rich ladies wore around their throats, but a sinister weapon that smacked of ambition, greed, status, sex, and ruin. As the trial progressed, an entire cottage industry of Jeanne-themed merchandise sprang up on the streets. Vendors sold plates painted with pictures of the necklace and images of Jeanne having sex with Rohan, or Jeanne having sex with Villette, or Rohan having sex with the queen. Jeanne may have been locked up in jail, penniless and busily biting people on the arm, but she'd achieved at least one of her childhood goals: her name was on everybody's lips.

Though Marie Antoinette was truly innocent here, the whole affair damaged her reputation more than Jeanne could have ever anticipated. Her reputation had been fragile before the necklace went missing, but now it was being dragged through the dirt. People whispered about how Rohan really *had* seduced her in the bushes of Versailles, how he had promised her the necklace in order to access what was underneath her frothy *gaulle*. Pornographers went wild, with one pamphlet called *The Royal Bordello* snarking that Rohan was actually the father of some of Marie Antoinette's children. Even though the queen's entire role in the affair had been conjured up by Jeanne, much of France was now convinced that their queen was a diamond-addled slut—and that their monarchy was a joke, and should be destroyed.

❇

MARIE ANTOINETTE COULDN'T STOP CRYING WHEN SHE HEARD that Rohan had been set free.

"Come and weep with me, come and console my soul," she wrote to her friend, the Duchess of Polignac. "The verdict which has just been given is a frightful insult. I am bathed in tears of grief and despair." By letting Rohan go, the French court was admitting that Rohan could have conceivably believed the queen would be willing to meet with him in the bushes. In other words: her reputation was already so terrible, so *trashy*, that poor Rohan's only mistake was buying into it. In retaliation, Marie Antoinette exiled Rohan from her court, but it didn't relieve the sting of his verdict. Later, her own lady-in-waiting looked back at the affair with horror, writing in her memoirs, "At this juncture came to an end the happiness of the queen."

Cagliostro and his wife went free, too. Nicole was released due to lack of evidence. Villette was banished. Antoine, who had never shown up for the trial, was sentenced to the galleys for life in absentia. But the main punishment was reserved for the scrappy little girl from nowhere, the one who had been identified as the true mastermind of what was becoming known as the Affair of the Necklace. All of Jeanne's property was seized by the king. She was flogged. She was branded with a V on each shoulder— for *voleuse*, "thief"—though she writhed so much during the branding that the sizzling metal missed one shoulder and landed on her breast. She was then imprisoned for life.

None of this agreed with the self-described *comtesse*, who seemed to think that she would be declared innocent and sent back into high society in a golden carriage. She reacted to her sentencing with fury, screaming, "It is the blood of the Valois that you outrage!" But she didn't have to endure prison for very long. Within a year, Jeanne began receiving anonymous messages from someone who wanted to help her escape, and by June of 1787, an almost thirty-one-year-old Jeanne scrambled out of jail, disguised as a man. Nobody knows who, exactly, helped her, but it was likely someone who hated the queen. For those who despised the monarchy, a free Jeanne was a useful Jeanne. Who knew what that impudent woman would say once she was back on the streets again?

To Marie Antoinette's horror, Jeanne had a *lot* to say. She fled to England to join her husband, and from a safe distance, she announced that she was going to publish her memoirs. This news was greeted in Versailles with trepidation—or glee, depending on whose side you were on. Once Jeanne started writing, she couldn't stop. She wrote so much that she even wrote a sort of meta-memoir *about* her memoirs, titled *An Address to the Public Explaining the Motives Which Have Hitherto Delayed the Publication of the Memoirs of the Countess de Valois de la Motte.* Her actual memoirs were stuffed to the gills with furious capital letters, dramatic italics, and grandiose declarations of her own innocence—e.g., "The public must at length pronounce between HER MAJESTY and *the atom she has crushed.*"

Jeanne was no atom, but she was far from invincible, either. In August 1791, when she was thirty-four, she was visited by men who frightened her so much that she actually jumped out of a window to escape them. The papers reported that the visitors were bailiffs, come to arrest her for a small debt, perhaps linked to her husband's gambling. Her husband says, in *his* memoirs, that Jeanne believed that the visitors were sent by the queen to drag her back to prison. Whoever they were, Jeanne fled from them in terror—and landed on the pavement with her thigh splintered, her arm fractured, and an eye knocked out of her head. She never recovered. Two months later, local papers reported, "The noted

Countess de la Motte, of *Necklace Memory*, and who lately jumped out of a Two-pair of Stairs Window, to avoid the Bailiffs, died on Tuesday Night last, at Eleven o'Clock, at her Lodgings near Astley's Riding School."

Just like her birth, the circumstances of her death were sad and inglorious, but at least the papers used the title she'd given herself on her wedding day: *Countess*.

✳

THE FRENCH REVOLUTION BEGAN IN 1789, THREE YEARS AFTER Jeanne's trial and two years before her death. As aristocratic heads began to roll, contemporary scholars like Johann Wolfgang von Goethe and Edmund Burke took a cold, hard look at Jeanne's scheming and concluded that the whole business with the diamonds had played an important role in bringing down the monarchy. (Just like Marie Antoinette, Jeanne's reputation rose and fell over the years; after the Revolution, scholars began to downplay her role, but by the 1980s they were starting to notice her again. "A catalyst of the French Revolution," one historian called the affair in 2003.) Even Napoleon knew who Jeanne was—and blamed her for at least some of the chaos. When asked for his thoughts on the Affair of the Necklace, he responded, "The queen's death must be dated from then."

Nobody who dealt with the necklace ended up happy. Nicole, the fake queen, died young. Rohan died poor. Villette went to Italy and was eventually hanged there for some other crime, according to rumors. Cagliostro died in prison for practicing freemasonry. Antoine popped in and out of prison and finally expired, miserable, in 1831. Boehmer and Bassenge died without ever being paid in full for their work. (The necklace was finally paid off by the Rohan estate in the 1890s, over a hundred years after it was created.) And two years after Jeanne's death, Marie Antoinette found herself driven through hordes of her screaming subjects in a dirty cart. She was interrogated in front of a scornful all-male tribunal, who asked her—among other things—about Jeanne. The queen said, for the last time, that she never knew the woman, that she had nothing to do with the whole scandal. It didn't matter. She had touched plenty of other jewels. On October 16, 1793, the guillotine blade came down on that famous bare neck.

It's hard to imagine that Jeanne could have predicted how her con would end. She had simply meant to restore her family's honor, and instead contributed to one of history's biggest, bloodiest plot twists. Then again, maybe she wouldn't have been surprised by any of it. If there was ever someone who believed in their own extraordinary destiny, it was Jeanne. She was a Valois, after all. She was born to play with diamonds.

CASSIE CHADWICK

born: Elizabeth Bigley

alias: Madame Lydia De Vere, Florida G. Blythe, Mary D. Laylis, Maxie De Laylis, Lydia Brown, Lydia Cingan, Lydia D. Scott, D. C. Belford, Mrs. Bagley, Mrs. Scott, Mrs. Wallace, Alice M. Bestedo, Elizabeth Springsteen

1857–1907

WHEN AMERICA WAS STILL YOUNG AND GRIFTERS ROAMED free through its streets with their pamphlets promising a gold rush or an oil rush or a railroad rush out West, there was a time when everybody secretly wanted to be like a plain-looking middle-aged swindler named Cassie Chadwick. She wasn't even an American herself, and yet the country loved her. People put her face on fake $20 bills and replaced the motto *E pluribus unum* with "Cassie's motto": *I need the money*. A druggist sold bottles of "Cassie Chadwick Nerve Tonic," designed to give the buyer Cassie's level head, her steady hands, her nerves of steel. She was proof that the most ordinary woman could become someone truly memorable if they just bluffed hard enough. Who wouldn't want to bottle up her incredible spirit and drink it down?

Cassie Chadwick was born Elizabeth Bigley in 1857, in a small Canadian village near Woodstock, Ontario. She had six siblings and poor parents who never learned to read. She had hearing problems and a lisp and a strange habit of staring into space for hours on end. She had no dowry, no inheritance, no particular hope for the future. But she was intelligent, in her own odd way. She was gutsy. And though she was hardly a beauty, she had one physical trait that people would comment on for decades: her eyes. They seemed to possess their own strange power, and when she stared at someone . . . especially a man . . . especially a *banker* . . . that someone often found himself going weak at the knees.

From a young age, it was obvious that Cassie—or "Betty," as she was known back then—enjoyed the finer things in life. Her father could never afford to buy the clothing and jewelry that she longed for, and so she realized that she'd have to come up with the money for clothing and jewelry herself. This desire for cash became one of the central tenets of her character—a formative drive, an obsession. Decades later, when Cassie was famous and dead, her sister refused to talk to reporters, except to tell them that Cassie "had been possessed of a mania from childhood to acquire great wealth quickly."

There was the old, traditional way of acquiring wealth—work hard for a long time and hope that someday you'll be rewarded—but then there were newer, faster, more modern ways. And Cassie was nothing if not a modern woman. At the age of twenty-one, she strolled into a barbershop and asked the barber to chop off her hair, which was an unusual request for a young woman of the time. He complied, but got nervous when she asked him for a fake mustache, and when she pulled out her father's golden watch and tried to pawn it off on him, he panicked at the thought of what this strange young woman might be plotting—and called the police. Cassie's father had to show up and take his wild daughter home, where he gave her a "sharp scolding."

Unfazed, Cassie plunged into a new scheme. She typed up a letter from her uncle's "lawyers" declaring that her uncle had died and left Cassie a massive inheritance. The letter was so convincing that even Cassie's own parents believed her, especially when she printed up a batch of calling cards that read, "Miss Bigley, heiress to $15,000." Cassie was young, but she'd already absorbed an important lesson: official-looking paperwork is half the battle.

But small-town Canada wasn't the ideal place for grift. People talked, stared, noticed. Before long, Cassie was arrested for purchasing several items—including an organ—with fake banknotes. She was tried for forgery, but took pains to act "eccentric" in court and was declared not guilty by reason of insanity. In lieu of being sent to an asylum, she was sent home to be watched by her mother.

The experience was a close call for Cassie, but even worse, it was a *drag*. It must have been clear to her that she needed a bigger stage. She needed a country obsessed with finding the next great thing, a country that couldn't help being impressed by heiresses, a country where the lines between dreams and scams were continuously, thrillingly blurred. So she packed her bags, set off for

America, and settled in Cleveland to live with her married sister, Alice.

It wasn't long before Alice realized she'd made a huge mistake. Cassie was—it had to be said—*trouble*. When Alice left on vacation, Cassie took it upon herself to mortgage Alice's furniture, calling herself "Alice M. Bestedo" and pretending that she owned all of her sister's ottomans and armoires. Before long, her brother-in-law discovered the ruse and threw Cassie out, so she moved from rooming house to rooming house for a while, continuing her furniture-mortgaging scam and running up all sorts of debts. Alice—the real Alice—started to worry about her sister, and would try to pay Cassie's bills whenever she could. "At that time," said Alice, "I began to think she was unbalanced."

The furniture mortgaging was an effective con, but it was ultimately a petty one. How much could you *really* get for a mortgaged ottoman? To increase her income, Cassie began eyeing Cleveland's wealthiest men, and before long she was engaged to a doctor named Wallace S. Springsteen. She told him all about her various troubles—real or imagined, who knows—and then explained that she was about to come into a *lot* of money. It was the perfect tactic for snagging a husband: a sob story undercut with promises of great wealth, calculated to soften the heart and inflame the greed. The two of them were married at the end of 1883. Twelve days later, when Dr. Springsteen discovered that Cassie was lying about absolutely everything, they were divorced.

As usual, Cassie landed on her feet. She moved home, wrote letters to all her friends about how "Elizabeth Springsteen"—her married name—had died, and then returned to America, determined to get rich quick.

✳

In Erie, Pennsylvania, Cassie told everyone that she was dying and desperately needed money for a doctor. She had learned to make her gums bleed on command—the technique itself has been lost to history, though one source said she would prick her gums with a needle—and so she would wander around, bleeding from the mouth like a deranged vampire, saying that she was having a "hemorrhage of the lungs." When sympathetic locals lent her money, she would disappear without paying it back, lungs and gums in perfect working order. In Buffalo, New York, she told everyone that she was a clairvoyant named "La Rose" and spent some time filching cash from people desperate to know what the future held. Eventually, she ended up back in Cleveland, where she set up a cryptic establishment that one journalist later described as "some kind of demi-social, dubious resort where men, possibly influential citizens, came and went."

Was this just an oblique way of describing a brothel? Maybe. People have whispered for decades about Cassie's sex life, wondering if she slept with her victims in order to better con them. She certainly had a strange influence over men, an influence so palpable that her contemporaries seriously debated whether or not she had hypnotic powers. But her cons always involved costumes, simulacra, fake backstories, and false fronts. She was never one to go for the obvious solution. And sex was so . . . *obvious*. Regardless, no matter what happened at her "dubious resort," the business enabled her to rub elbows with powerful men, listen to their secrets, and learn to dislike them. It was there, the same journalist writes, that Cassie began to feel an "utter contempt for men and for their weaknesses and vanities." Whether or not she slept with them, she "felt her intellectual superiority . . . over them." All of her scams, up until this point, had taught her a simple, powerful lesson: "To her no man was great, and most men were fools."

Speaking of men, she zipped through several more husbands around this time and gave birth to a boy named Emil (rumor had it that his father was a prominent Cleveland politician). By the time she was in her early thirties, she'd landed in Toledo, Ohio, working as "Madame Lydia De Vere"—fortune-teller, clairvoyant, mesmerist, medium. Along with traditional fortune-telling, Madame De Vere offered a more unusual service: for an extra fee, she'd give out stock market tips. Her clients were educated men, bankers, and doctors, but their training was no match for Madame De Vere's spellbinding eyes. When she asked for loans, they'd lend willingly; when she faked rich men's signatures, the banks accepted them. Before long, she'd racked up a cool $40,000 in forged notes.

Unfortunately, this line of work landed Cassie in court for the second time, and though she tried to weasel out of trouble with an elaborate story about how she was really an heiress named Florida G. Blythe, the judge was unconvinced. She was charged with forgery and given nine years at the Ohio state penitentiary. Behind bars, she turned out to be a model prisoner, sewing clothes for the male inmates and glibly telling fortunes. Even the warden wanted Cassie to look into his future, which she did, informing him he would lose $5,000 in a business deal and then die of cancer. Unhappily for the warden, both of her predictions came true.

After only two years, Cassie was paroled for good behavior, but not before the penitentiary wrote down a detailed description of her looks: five feet five and a half inches tall, pierced ears, high forehead, "arched and approaching" eyebrows, ears that were "large and stand out," medium straight nose, "small and round" chin, and a scar on her right elbow. This description, along with the accompanying mug shot, was really nothing more than a few pieces of paper shoved into a drawer somewhere. But paperwork— as Cassie knew well—was often far more important than it seemed at first glance. Now, no matter where Cassie roved, there was a dangerous little file in Ohio with her face inside it.

✳

BACK IN CLEVELAND, CASSIE WAS FREE AND SINGLE AND READY TO settle down for good. And it didn't take her long to meet her favorite sort of man: wealthy, well-meaning, and susceptible to a pair of mesmerizing eyes.

People disagree about how, exactly, Cassie met Dr. Leroy S. Chadwick, the widower. The more salacious tales say that they met in her Cleveland brothel. Dr. Chadwick, however, always insisted that Cassie had not seduced him. He had a nagging problem with his leg, he said, and Cassie suggested that he try massage. When he took her advice and found relief, he also found himself falling in love with her. Either way, the Chadwicks were one of Cleveland's most venerable families, and so everyone was shocked when, in 1896, Dr. Chadwick suddenly showed up with a brand-new bride. Who in the world was this Cassie creature? What in the world did Dr. Chadwick see in her? She was nearing forty, and rather plain. Local gossips simply couldn't pinpoint her appeal—well, except for her eyes. Everyone was in agreement about those eyes.

If Cassie had dreamed of riches as a young girl, she was now officially living her dream. Dr. Chadwick had gobs of money and didn't seem to care if Cassie spent it like a maniac. So, with a ring on her finger and a fancy new last name, Cassie began to shop. She bought a huge pipe organ for her music room. She bought a set of golden chairs that sang when guests sat down on them. She bought dishes of silver, decorated with rubies. She bought emeralds, ermine, ninety pairs of gloves, $1,200 worth of handkerchiefs. Other ladies bought jewels by the piece, but Cassie bought them by the entire tray. Cleveland merchants learned to love the sight of Cassie and her servants walking down the street toward them. She wore ropes of pearls around her neck. She never asked what anything cost. "She had a mania for fancy clocks," one merchant remembered fondly.

She was as extreme in her generosity as she was in her consumption. If high-society Cleveland wouldn't accept her, she would *buy* her way into their hearts. So she ordered eight grand pianos and had them delivered to eight of her friends. Another time, she took twelve young society girls to Europe and paid for their entire trip, treating them to the best of everything, including tiny portraits of each girl painted on porcelain and framed in solid gold. Her generosity wasn't just a form of social climbing, either. She bought her maid an entirely new wardrobe; she gave her cook a sealskin coat; she ordered tailor-made suits for the local butcher's boy. (Later, when things got grim, her adoring servants would stick by her until the end.) She bought toys for every orphan in the local orphanage, and she overwhelmed poor families with gifts and food. She'd known what it was like to be poor, and all the golden chairs in the world wouldn't make her forget it. As one reporter wrote, "No beggar was ever turned away from her door."

Her shopping was so over-the-top that it seemed like a compulsion. She bought far more than made sense, far more than she could ever use. She bought an "Old Master" painting and never hung it up. She bought a Steinway piano and kept it in storage. She shopped like she'd been holding her breath for her whole life and now she could finally breathe. One Christmas Eve, she took her husband out on a date, and when they returned home, he was shocked to find that the house had been completely redecorated. Every rug, every stick of furniture, every painting, every tiny piece of bric-a-brac was now replaced by something newer and more fabulous. "This is your Christmas gift," she declared—and then handed him a fur-lined overcoat worth $1,100. Another time, she took herself on a road trip around the country, selling her car at each stop and buying a new one, just for fun.

"She had everything she wanted," her sister Alice remembered. But still she wanted more.

✳

EVEN THOUGH SHE WAS HAPPILY MARRIED TO A VERY RICH MAN, Cassie continued to swindle bankers. And so she'd burst into local banks wearing her finest Parisian dresses, playing the part of the silly little rich wife. She would cry with fake embarrassment, saying that she'd been a bit reckless with her husband's checkbook and desperately needed a loan so that her husband wouldn't find out. In return for the banker's gentlemanly discretion, she'd be happy to give him a large bonus. To convince him, she'd pull out a stack of official-looking paperwork: notes from important men swearing that her assets were real, papers saying that she was an heiress to millions of dollars, piles of bonds. The effect of the paperwork may have been a bit overwhelming, a bit dazzling, but the banker knew one thing: a woman with paperwork like this would definitely be able to pay back a loan.

In reality, the notes were forged, the inheritance didn't exist, and the bonds were mostly imitations sandwiched between two legitimate ones. But when bankers heard her story, they saw two things: a woman who *looked* like she had money, and a woman who was offering them an easy way to *make* money. Classist assumptions wiped away the first half of their misgivings. Greed took care of the rest.

For a while, Cassie amused herself by taking out loans this way, but by 1902, when she was forty-five, she decided to increase the stakes of her swindles. She wanted more—more money, and perhaps more of a challenge. So she gave herself a new backstory. And since she was Cassie, the type of woman who never bought a single piano when she could buy eight, she decided to tell people that she was the daughter of Andrew Carnegie, one of the wealthiest men in the entire world.

In certain ways, Andrew Carnegie and Cassie Chadwick were

similar. Both of them were immigrants who'd come to America in rags and ended up surrounded by riches. Carnegie was a boot-strapping Scottish entrepreneur who'd made a fortune in steel; in fact, he had just sold his company one year earlier, which made him even richer. His name alone was worth a thousand pieces of forged paperwork, and none of his assets were imaginary. Cassie knew that there wasn't a banker in America who would refuse Andrew Carnegie's daughter.

The problem was that Andrew Carnegie only had one daughter, and she was five years old. So Cassie had to come up with a believable story to explain why no one in the world knew that she was a Carnegie, too. And then she had to get other people to spread the story *for* her—and they had to do it subtly, so that Carnegie himself wouldn't find out. It was a challenge, but Cassie was up for it. Batting her hypnotic eyes, she "accidentally" told a prominent Cleveland lawyer that she was Carnegie's illegitimate child, and that he had given her a trust worth $11 million. She even brought the lawyer along to "visit" her "father" in New York City, explaining that he should probably stay in the carriage while she ran into Carnegie's mansion to say hello.

Suitably intrigued, the lawyer watched Cassie waltz into Carnegie's house like she owned the place. She emerged half an hour later with a package full of impressive paperwork, including two notes signed by Carnegie himself that were worth tens of millions of dollars. The lawyer was stunned: The woman really *was* a Carnegie! He had no idea that the paperwork was all forged and that Cassie had been carrying it with her when she entered the house. He didn't know that she hadn't seen Andrew Carnegie at all; she'd just stayed in the foyer, making small talk with his housekeeper. All the lawyer knew was what he had seen with his own two eyes, and—as Cassie had known for years—aesthetics mattered far more than reality. Bleeding gums made you look sick. Parisian dresses made you look wealthy. And walking out of Andrew Carnegie's house with an air of daughterly confidence made you look like you were Andrew Carnegie's daughter.

As Cassie had anticipated, the whole story was far too sensational for the lawyer to keep to himself. Before long, every mogul in Cleveland knew that Cassie was the secret love child of the steel tycoon. Of course, no one would dare to ask Carnegie if the scandalous story was actually true, which meant that Cassie was safe in her lie. In fact, the men who heard her story tended to feel a bit defensive of Cassie, the poor little unacknowledged rich girl. As one banker said, gallantly, "I deemed it my duty to protect her in the story of her birth as she had given it to me."

That gallant, naive banker was a man named Iri Reynolds, and one day, Cassie asked him if she could deposit a package in his bank vault. She even showed him the contents of the package: a stack of deeds and notes signed "Andrew Carnegie," all demonstrating that she was worth millions and millions of dollars. As Reynolds watched, Cassie slipped the paperwork into an envelope, sealed the envelope with wax, placed the envelope in the vault, and then handed Reynolds a list of everything that the envelope contained.

Later that afternoon, Reynolds received a frantic call from Cassie. She'd forgotten to make a copy of the list herself! Would he mind terribly sending her a copy of *his* copy? Reynolds was happy to do so. He copied out the list of Cassie's assets onto an official piece of bank paper and signed it. And just like that, Cassie had proof that she *was* good for millions and millions of dollars. She had a list of her fake assets written out on real bank paper and signed with a real banker's signature. With it, she could head to any bank in America and take out a massive loan. It was the ultimate piece of official-looking paperwork because, for once, it *was* official. Her Carnegie assets were imaginary, but she had leveraged them into something tangible, using her most valuable asset of all: her nerve.

✳

THE ONE BIG FLAW IN CASSIE'S PLAN WAS THAT IT COULD NEVER GO on forever. Banker A would eventually want his loan repaid, so she'd have to steal from Banker B to do it, and then when Banker B wanted *his* money back, she'd have to pay a visit to Banker C. The good news was that she was excellent at this sort of delicate finagling. The bad news was that one of her bankers was starting to crack.

This particular banker was a sweet elderly man named Charles T. Beckwith, president of the Citizens National Bank of Oberlin. He trusted Cassie completely. There was no one in the entire country who was more convinced that Cassie was indeed Andrew Carnegie's daughter. But Beckwith had lent Cassie thousands and thousands and *thousands* of dollars, and as the months dragged on, he wasn't any closer to being repaid. His wonderful friend Cassie always had an excuse for why the money wasn't available. Sometimes she'd cry and tell him that Carnegie wasn't letting her spend her trust fund at the moment because she'd been a bit too reckless with it. Sometimes she'd yell at him. At one point, Beckwith actually fainted at her feet, and when he woke up, he told Cassie that he was going to kill himself if the situation continued. Cassie replied sharply that suicide wouldn't fix anything.

When it came to keeping her creditors at bay, Cassie had a whole bag of tricks, and most of them involved an extravagant show of riches. Sometimes, she'd pick up irritated bankers in her expensive carriage and bring them to her golden house, where their faith in her assets would be renewed. She'd invite suspicious lawyers to her hotel room, where she'd make sure that her jewelry was scattered around, and the lawyers would see the gems and conclude with relief that Cassie was obviously rich enough to be a Carnegie. She'd throw parties for worried businessmen where she'd dress up her servants and claim that they were rich local wives, and the businessmen would stumble out of there, murmuring happily that Cassie was so well connected that she simply couldn't be scamming them. Once, when one of her victims was really upset, she hired an actor to play Andrew Carnegie's representative and reassure him.

Cassie herself must have known that the bubble of her swindles would eventually burst, because she was working on a backup plan. She made plans to flee to Belgium, a country where she'd be safe from extradition if her crimes were ever discovered. And she was so close to getting away with it all. By 1904, she'd sent her husband on to Brussels, Belgium's capital, and she was about to head overseas herself.

But Cassie never knew when to stop. She couldn't buy just

one pair of gloves; she had to buy ninety. She couldn't buy a nice piece of jewelry; she had to have the entire tray. And she couldn't help sneaking in one last con. She was still in America, trying to scam $500,000 from a couple of Pittsburgh businessmen, when one of her many victims finally snapped. It wasn't Beckwith, surprisingly. It was an irate businessman named Herbert B. Newton, and on November 22, 1904, he sued Cassie for the $190,000 that she owed him.

The lawsuit made the papers. Cassie's other victims looked at the papers in horror. And the city of Cleveland—as one article put it—"woke up."

✳

THE MEN IN CASSIE'S LIFE WERE IN A STATE OF PANIC. WHAT HAD just happened? Who was that woman in the ropes of pearls? And why did they feel so light-headed?

"Oh, this is awful, awful, awful," said Dr. Chadwick, who'd learned about his wife's arrest by reading a paper in Brussels.

"Torture and transactions and transactions and torture," said poor Charles T. Beckwith.

"Every time she looked at me I became dizzy," said a sheriff.

"I know nothing of the woman or her dealings," declared Andrew Carnegie.

As soon as the story of Cassie Chadwick hit the papers, the entire country turned out to watch it unfold. Herbert B. Newton and his lawyers began digging into Cassie's past, where they found something awfully interesting: the elegant Mrs. Chadwick looked a lot like a common swindler named "Madame Lydia De Vere" who'd served a couple of years in the Ohio state penitentiary in the early 1890s. Though Cassie denied the rumors indignantly—the *nerve* of some people!—the similarity between Madame De Vere's mug shot and her own formal portraits was hard to ignore. Plus, there was that detailed description, courtesy of the penitentiary files: *five feet five and a half inches tall, pierced ears, high forehead, "arched and approaching" eyebrows* . . .

In Cleveland, high society reeled. Surely the rumors couldn't be true: Cassie Chadwick of the golden chairs and the respectable doctor husband was a *fraud*? Cassie, who'd given them grand pianos, who'd been so kind to orphans, who took those twelve sweet girls to Europe and paid for everything herself? If Cassie was a fraud, who *could* you trust? Your neighbor? Your husband? Your local bank? As more of Cassie's cons were revealed, nervous locals tried to make a run on their banks, and fourteen bank presidents had to put out an "anti-panic proclamation" to keep Cleveland's entire financial infrastructure from crashing to the ground. Poor Beckwith took to bed in shock as his bank closed down, and on the streets, businessmen started asking each other, "How much did she get of you?"

Cassie faced the commotion like a real lady. She acted calm yet mildly offended, and made sure that important people saw her walking into the office of Andrew Carnegie's lawyer, as though she were paying him a casual visit in order to straighten out those silly rumors. (She never actually met with the lawyer. Instead, she dashed up to the sixth floor, crawled out a window, and leaped onto the next building's roof in order to escape.) As the newspapers filled with ever-more-outrageous rumors, like a story that

Cassie had killed herself, she responded coolly with statements like, "Please deny reported suicide, and further say I have no intention of committing any such act." Those who weren't financially affected by her cons found themselves amused and even impressed by her. One paper suggested that Andrew Carnegie should stop his current philanthropic work and instead give Cassie a medal: "for nerve."

Unfortunately for Cassie, her nerve could no longer save her. On December 7, 1904, she was arrested in New York City. She remained in character until the last possible minute. The marshal who arrested her found her lying in bed, bolstered by two pillows, clad demurely in a white lace dressing gown.

✳

AFTER HER ARREST, CASSIE WAS TAKEN BACK TO CLEVELAND AND held in the county jail as she awaited her trial. An intrepid Canadian journalist named Kit snuck into the jail to interview her, and found that though Cassie was refusing to talk about her case, she simply could not help talking about money. "It was odd how the mind of the woman ran to figures," Kit wrote. But the most notable thing—the thing that Kit herself couldn't help talking about—was Cassie's eyes. In practically every other paragraph of her article, Kit returned to them, obsessing over them, unable to get away from them.

"I steadily looked into her hypnotic eyes," wrote Kit, "and I can candidly say, just here, that they are wonderfully beautiful, wonderfully soft, at times searching, at times very appealing, and it is this appeal in the big brown eyes that hypnotizes—if the word may apply. I can quite conceive anyone at all impressionable being affected by the appeal that at times creeps into the eyes of Cassie L. Chadwick." Overall, Kit came away from the interview convinced that Cassie was the possessor of a great—if criminal— talent. She compared Cassie's brow to "that of the inventor, the musician, and the financier."

Cassie may have had the skill of an inventor, a musician, or a financier, but in jail and in the courtroom, she continued to play the role of the wronged rich woman. Upon her arrest, she released a haughty statement: "The time will come when these people will see that I am a very much maligned and persecuted woman. When I think of what I have gone through in the past few weeks I wonder that I am not insane." In the courtroom, she made sure to faint regularly, as though to indicate that the whole process was too overwhelming for her delicate, blameless constitution. At one point, she claimed that her right arm was so badly cramped that she couldn't use it at all—though later that day, she forgot all about the cramp and started waving that same arm around.

Andrew Carnegie himself attended the trial, which must have been awkward for Cassie. He wasn't as furious as some people expected, though; he had no plans to press charges against her, and he told journalists that the whole swindle just proved how good his own credit was. ("Would you not feel glad to know that some one has been able to get $2,000,000 by simply signing your name to a piece of paper?" he chuckled.) Of course, Carnegie hadn't lost a single dollar because of Cassie, but her other victims had, and they weren't chuckling. Only twelve of them came forward, but plenty of people suspected that Cassie had cheated many more men, and that her other victims were simply too embarrassed to admit that they'd been conned by an uneducated woman from small-town Canada. "Undoubtedly [Cassie] allowed for and counted on this," wrote one journalist. "It may never be known how much money she borrowed." No one ever figured out what exactly became of all that money, either. One rumor claimed that she had a million dollars stowed away in Belgium. Or perhaps she'd already spent it all on grand pianos and golden chairs.

On March 11, 1905, a jury quickly found her guilty of conspiring to defraud the United States by banking fraud. Cassie sank down in her chair and sobbed, then got to her feet, walked out of the courtroom with her son and the deputy marshal, and shrieked, "Let me go! Oh, go! Oh my God, let me go! I'm not guilty, I tell you! Let me go!" And then she fainted again, just as the judge was walking by. Her aesthetics were, as usual, quite flawless.

✳

Cassie's sentence was nothing she hadn't heard before: ten years in the Ohio state penitentiary, where she'd been locked up so many years ago. She may have been behind bars, but she was also on the front page of newspapers across the country. Journalists christened her the "Witch of Finance," the "Queen of Swindlers." One paper called her "the most talked of woman in the world." Others emphasized her mysterious ability to influence the menfolk. "Without Education or Beauty, Mrs. Chadwick Fascinated Men," ran one Canadian headline. Another spoke of her "Strange Power" and the "Marvelous Gullibility of Financiers."

In the meantime, other grifters were looking up to Cassie in awe. In New York, a city already bursting with shady deals, the grifters were now being referred to as "Cassies," and just like their queen, they knew the power of a fancy dress or a nice suit. "Good clothes are the tools of the grafters' trade, and the rainment [sic] of the 'Cassies' now crowding the Broadway hotel lobbies would make Solomon envious," ran one article. In Cleveland, a druggist sold "Cassie Chadwick Nerve Tonic," and in Washington DC, grifters used fake $20 bills printed with Cassie's face to trick tourists who didn't know any better. So many of these fake bills flooded the market that the Secret Service had to step in to "suppress" them.

Behind bars, though, Cassie's life was no longer anything to envy. Gone were the ropes of pearls, the fancy clocks, the hotel rooms scattered with jewelry. Instead, she sewed buttonholes, and occasionally pretended that she was sick. And so everyone was skeptical when, three years into her sentence, she fell sick for good—but for once in her life, Cassie wasn't faking it. As her health declined, she surprised everyone in prison by asking to be baptized into the Catholic faith. This was off-brand for Cassie, who had always been more interested in the material realm. "This is the only occasion known that Mrs. Chadwick ever professed an interest in religion," one paper reported. The prison doctor blamed her illness on her taste for rich food—a ghostly echo of her lifelong desire for wealth.

Cassie was alone when she died on October 10, 1907. Her son and two of her sisters had been summoned to her deathbed, but they couldn't get to the penitentiary in time. She was fifty years old. Ironically, the prison doctor claimed she died of neurasthenia—a now-archaic concept that meant "nerve exhaustion." Her body was returned to her Canadian hometown, where her sisters welcomed back their strange, runaway sibling for the last time. They seemed to feel protective of their little Betty, who'd been gone for so long. They wouldn't let the public see her, even though plenty of people wanted to catch a glimpse of those famous eyes, now closed for good.

✳

FOR YEARS AFTER CASSIE'S CAPTURE, FEMALE SCAMMERS—AND even some male ones—were referred to as "Cassies" or "Cassie Chadwicks." Headlines crowed about a "Chinese Cassie Chadwick," a "Roumanian Cassie Chadwick," a "Russian Cassie Chadwick," an "Italian Cassie Chadwick," a "German Cassie Chadwick," an "apt pupil of Mrs. Chadwick," and so on. Just as future investor-philanthropists found themselves compared to Andrew Carnegie, these minor scammers were all held up against the great specter of Cassie Chadwick. But none of them managed to become quite as famous. For a while, in America, she was the original scammer—and everyone who came after her was, inevitably, a little less interesting.

When attempting to understand Cassie, the media grappled with the contrast between her ordinary background and her extraordinary career. "How could a woman of no particular brilliancy, of no particular learning, and of an age when, whatever personal attraction she may have had in her youth had been nullified by time . . . shred financiers and hard-fisted business men out of hundreds of thousands of dollars without giving them anything in return?" mused one journalist. Cassie had done the impossible: conjured money out of thin air. "To secure her creditors she has never had any tangible property of dependable value," another journalist wrote. "Her securities have, in nearly every instance, been mythical." And mythical they remained. Most of her victims never got their money back. Even her husband eventually went bankrupt.

Her astonishing ability, it seemed, was something you could only truly comprehend in person. If you only read about her in the finance section, or saw her not-terribly-attractive portrait printed on a front page somewhere, you might wonder what all the fuss was about. You had to be in the room with Cassie, to stare into her magnetic eyes and feel the full force of her impossible nerve, in order to understand how she got away with it all. Many who *had* been in the room with Cassie were branded with her influence forever—like poor Charles T. Beckwith, who insisted even on his deathbed that Cassie *was* Andrew Carnegie's daughter, despite the fact that she had ruined his bank and wrecked his health. Or like Kit, the Canadian journalist who had visited Cassie in prison. "One could see that an immense store of vital force lies sleeping in the brain and soul of this woman," she wrote. "The woman would have been a great human creature had she been highly trained, highly educated." And then, in the very next sentence, Kit seemed to change her mind about Cassie—perhaps remembering those eyes. *Would have been* great? No, Kit concluded. "She was great, even in an evil way, as it was."

WANG TI

1981–

CHINA, 2008. TWO OLYMPIC GYMNASTS ARE GETTING MARRIED on the island of Hainan, and the festivities are precisely calibrated to show off their youth, their wealth, and their lithe, sculpted bodies. The bride arrives at the ceremony in a hot air balloon and flings a cable to the ground. The groom climbs up, using nothing more than his own strength, which he's honed on the rings and the vault and the parallel bars. Back on earth, during the ceremony, the two of them joke about the lovely measurements of her breasts, waist, and hips, and she asks him, flirtatiously, if he'll buy her a BMW Mini Cooper when they're married. Money. Beauty. *Brands.* Later, she changes into a dress made out of real gold fiber that's worth almost four and a half million dollars. Even later, they'll retreat to their suite, which costs more than four thousand dollars a night.

But first, there's champagne, and fireworks. The whole thing is a fantasy, and the guests are all *somebody*: important, rich, gorgeous, or all of the above. Except for one of them. She's a working-class girl born hundreds of miles away from there. But nobody knows that. They think she's just like them. And if they have their suspicions, they keep their mouths shut. Better not to know. Pass the champagne.

✳

WANG TI WAS AN ORDINARY GIRL FROM DALIAN, A PORT CITY AT THE southern end of China's Liaoning Province. Her father was a handyman. Her mother was a bank clerk.

There were plenty of people just like her in her hometown. There were people just like her all around the world, in fact. Ordinary people, born to ordinary families. But then there were the others—the lucky ones. The athletes who won medals for their country and were rewarded with fame and golden dresses and hot air balloons. The actresses with their perfect faces who brought home a hundred times more money than their ordinary country-women. In China, perhaps the luckiest of all were the group of people known as the "princelings": the hyperprivileged sons and daughters of China's old Communist guard. They were the cream of the crop, the "red nobility," and they were so shockingly rich and so infinitely powerful that they could do no wrong—or at least, no wrong that couldn't be covered up by their fathers' connections. They were so far above people like Wang Ti that they might as well have been living in the stratosphere.

As a young woman, Wang Ti married a professional soccer player named Wang Sheng—and this meant that her lifestyle was now more glamorous than the one she'd been born into. Wang Sheng, who played for the team Dalian Shide, made good money, especially when you factored in his generous yearly bonus, and as his wife, Wang Ti got to benefit from it. It didn't take her long to start looking the part of a soccer player's wife. She bought herself a fancy car and a designer handbag. The two of them moved into an expensive house. She found that she was good at it: the dressing up, the flaunting of it all. The team wives called themselves the "Mrs. Group," and even though everyone had money, Wang Ti stood out as the most fashionable one.

She and her husband had a baby girl together, but by 2008, their marriage was growing strained. Wang Sheng wasn't playing much; he had transferred to another soccer team that was now bogged down with legal troubles. And perhaps their problems went deeper. Maybe Wang Ti wanted far, far more than he could give her. Their relationship deteriorated until eventually Wang Ti moved out and left her hometown altogether. She bolted to China's capital, a city that promised danger and romance and excitement—and as many brands as money could buy.

✳

BEIJING WAS A BIFURCATED CITY. ON ONE HAND, IT WAS SO CHOKED with smog from traffic, coal-fired power plants, and urban sprawl that it could be dangerous to step outside your front door. ("Beijing is not a livable city," its mayor declared in 2015.) On the other hand, it was a glittering metropolis irresistible to any ambitious young woman, a dreamland where money could buy you anything—even clean air. (By 2014, the city's most elite private schools were building huge domes over their buildings to protect students' lungs.) When Wang Ti moved there, the smog was so bad that sometimes the sun itself was blotted out. But who needed the sun when Beijing had just hosted the most glorious, luminous thing of all: the 2008 Summer Olympics?

For a woman who loved athletes, Olympics-mad Beijing must have been paradise. The festivities had been the most expensive Summer Olympics of all time, costing $6.8 billion. The opening ceremony alone was an orgy of futuristic excess: a gymnast ran through the air, suspended by wires, to light the Olympic cauldron, while weather modification technology literally held back the rain. Once the competition started, China continued to dazzle the world, taking home the most gold medals of any country. And after the whole spectacle was over, many of the country's athletes remained in Beijing to recover—and revel.

Wang Ti had rented a house in a prestigious area of the city, and now she was ready to start socializing. Though she wasn't getting along with her husband, she was still benefiting from his pro-athlete status, and in October, she attended a star-studded wedding in his place. There, she found the wedding guests very much to her liking. She was surrounded by Olympians— victorious and raucous and good-looking—and at the reception, she found herself sitting next to a particularly eligible one.

Her seatmate was a sexy gymnast named Xiao Qin, flushed with success from winning two gold medals for his country. He was so good at the pommel horse that people called him "Pony God." His recent wins were especially sweet, since he'd been expected to win gold at the 2004 Olympics, but lost his chance when he stumbled during the qualification round. In Beijing, after finally winning, he crowed, "I get to take a vacation!"

Wang Ti looked at Xiao Qin—now on vacation—and liked what she saw. Staring at him was like staring into the sun on a smogless day, if the sun had sculpted biceps and dreamily high cheekbones. Xiao Qin looked at Wang Ti and liked what he saw, too. Who wouldn't want to sit across from a pretty girl at a wedding, flushed with success (and maybe a glass or two of champagne), feeling the heat of her gaze upon him? These were halcyon days for him; he was beloved by his country, and women everywhere thought he was gorgeous. He asked Wang Ti for her number.

Three days later, Wang Ti was at karaoke with her friends when Xiao Qin showed up. They chatted, they flirted. He tried to hold her hand under the table. "We had both drunk a bit," she said later, "and I found him handsome, so I let him." Wang Ti told him that she was having marital problems, and Xiao Qin listened sympathetically. She found herself dazzled by the way the Pony God moved through the world. She was especially impressed at the end of the night, when he called an armored car to come and pick him up. They began seeing more and more of each other. At one point, he took her to a BMW dealership, and asked her which color of car she preferred. *Red*, she said. He replied, "That red one is going to be yours."

Clearly, this man was nothing like the dreary soccer player she'd left back in Dalian. This was a man worth knowing. So she went home and gave herself a makeover.

✳

Now that Wang Ti had an Olympian in her sights, it became vital that she look wealthy and important. She needed brands . . .

and a really good backstory. The brands were easy enough. Her time with the Mrs. Group had taught her the importance of appearing glamorous, and so now, every time she saw Xiao Qin, she made sure that she was carrying an expensive handbag, wearing a pricey watch, and driving a sleek Audi TT. Cars were a huge status symbol across the country—China was a place where most citizens never dreamed of owning an automobile until the early 1980s—and Audis in particular were so popular that there was a saying on the streets: "Men love Audi like women love Dior." Wang Ti knew the power of both. They covered a multitude of sins and prevented a multitude of questions.

The backstory, though, was more of a problem. Wang Ti was paying for the cars and the handbags with money sent by her estranged husband, who had no idea that she was back on the dating market. Though his checks helped her sustain a certain level of glitz, they were a rather embarrassing source of wealth. *This old thing? I bought it because my husband and I aren't getting along.* To really mingle with Xiao Qin and his celebrity friends, she couldn't be an estranged soccer player's wife from Dalian. She needed to be someone truly special.

Cleverly, carefully, she began to whisper to her new friends that she had a secret. A secret involving her parentage. She was the daughter of the politician Li Changchun, she said, who was a member of the Politburo Standing Committee, China's most powerful political leadership group. Her mother was Lu Xin, vice governor of Liaoning Province—and Li Changchun's secret lover. This pedigree made her someone very special indeed: *a princeling.*

China's princelings had a reputation for being influential, arrogant, spoiled, and untouchable. Their fathers fought in the revolution; they drove fancy cars, dated models, and hid their wealth in enigmatic offshore companies. It was like being a Kennedy, or a Trump—the world simply opened up for you. When one of China's princelings crashed his Ferrari, killing himself and horribly injuring the two half-naked models who'd been riding along with him, his father masterminded a cover-up of the whole incident, silencing the media and sending large payouts to the girls' families. That was the power of being a princeling, even after death: one wave of Daddy's wand, and your slate was wiped clean.

And now here was Wang Ti, claiming to be one of them. It was a risky move, but the bit about the affair made for a clever safety net. Now no one could fact-check her story without seriously embarrassing two high-ranking politicians. What were they going to do, waltz up to Li Changchun and ask him whether or not he had a love child? "A very delicate matter," one of her friends later called it.

The brands and the backstory worked, and it wasn't long before Wang Ti and the Pony God were sleeping together—and then moving in together. News of their relationship traveled quickly through the city's athletic circles, and the new couple began rubbing elbows with the who's who of Beijing Olympians. They went to dinner with the diving team. They became bosom friends with gymnasts Yang Yun and Yang Wei, who were engaged and taking flashy engagement photos for *Cosmopolitan China*. Wang Ti hit it off with Yang Yun instantly, and before long she was helping the young gymnast plan her wedding, at which Yang Yun planned to arrive in a hot air balloon. As a sign of their friendship, Wang Ti bought her new pal a BMW. It was a flamboyant gesture. She was solidifying her place in Yang Yun's constellation of important friends.

Even though her new friends were wealthier than she was, Wang Ti felt superior to all of them. It was like being in the Mrs. Group all over again—before long, she found herself at the top. "I thought these athletes dressed tastelessly," she said later. "Some of their clothes were even fakes." In contrast, her athlete friends thought Wang Ti was the last word in sophistication and importance. "She was not stunning, and her clothes were not spectacular, but you could tell they were very expensive," said one of them, later. "When we met she was always on the phone, talking about business or huge land deals. I though she must have some very high-level position, far away from my normal life." Sometimes she showed up in a Bentley convertible, which never failed to impress. One of her new acquaintances remembered that she always had the latest mobile phone.

The convertible and the phone calls created a smokescreen of wealth that Wang Ti's new friends never bothered to peer behind. After all, who didn't want to be friends with a princeling? Why go out of your way to look for cracks in the narrative? In their rarefied world, there was no point in prying too deeply into anyone's financial affairs. It was enough to know that they were all young, and rich, and beautiful. And so they nodded at her story, and believed her.

✳

As their relationship progressed, Wang Ti discovered that the Pony God had irritatingly expensive taste. He liked cars, so Wang Ti bought him an Audi and a Mercedes-Benz C200. He liked to shop with cash, so Wang Ti kept two huge bags of it in her apartment at all times. In fact, Xiao Qin was thoroughly spoiled, and if he didn't get what he wanted, he'd throw a fit. If Wang Ti refused to buy him something, he'd whine that his *other* girlfriend would buy it for him. "When you buy me things, it shows that you're a better girlfriend," he'd say, "and my family will be more likely to approve of our relationship."

His appetite for fancy things created a bigger problem for Wang Ti: she was spending so much money that her husband, back in Dalian, wanted to know where it was all going. She told him that she'd been buying gifts for her friends, but of course she couldn't tell him that she was also buying gifts for her shiny new live-in boyfriend. Soon enough, Wang Ti realized that she was going to have to find a new source of income—and fast, before Xiao Qin demanded another car.

In the meantime, she was surrounded by outlandish affluence wherever she looked. When her friend Yang Yun finally married her gymnast fiancé, the wedding was so extravagant that it drew criticism in the press. Outside of the wedding, people were starving, but inside, there was cake, champagne, fireworks, a dress made of real gold. For Wang Ti, attending that wedding—as a close friend of the bride, no less!—must have been like stepping into fairyland. The air her friends breathed was, quite literally, better than the air of most of their countrymen. Now that she knew what it felt like to be so close to the pulsing heart of Chinese wealth, how could she give it all up?

And so one day, Wang Ti casually told her newlywed friend that she knew of a little apartment available in a *very* good neighborhood, and she'd be happy to arrange a sale, for a fraction of what the place was actually worth. Yang Yun knew a good investment opportunity when she saw one—or so she thought—so she gave Wang Ti a hefty chunk of cash in exchange for the key. The apartment wasn't available right away, but Wang Ti assured her friend that there was always a bit of a lag when it came to selling properties like this one. There was paperwork to complete, a holdup with the property transfer—boring details, nothing to worry about. Thankfully, Yang Yun wasn't bothered by the wait. In fact, the deal was so good that she went ahead and bought a second property from Wang Ti, and then a third.

This was Wang Ti's new moneymaking scheme, and it was terrifyingly simple. She'd tell her friends that her princeling connections enabled her to get high-end cars and real estate at cut-rate prices, and then she'd "sell" them the cars and the properties—which she didn't own, but was merely renting. Her friends would pay Wang Ti, while Wang Ti continued to pay rent to the real owners behind the scenes.

Sure, there were weird moments—like when one of her victims noticed that one of Wang Ti's "properties" was registered under someone else's name—but Wang Ti knew how to win people back into her confidence. She would assuage them by name-dropping government officials, flaunting her Louis Vuitton, and reminding them that she was dating the Pony God. For nervous new homeowners, the sight of Xiao Qin's handsome face was worth a thousand lawyer-approved property transfers. Her brands were her armor, and he was the best brand of all.

✳

THESE WERE RITZY YET ANXIOUS DAYS FOR WANG TI. AS THE MONEY came pouring in from her famous friends, she continued to buy her equally famous boyfriend whatever he wanted, even helping him pay off his massive credit card debts. She was desperate to keep him happy. When he decided that he wanted to open a luxury car dealership, she dutifully funded that dream. But the constant lies were wearing on her. Some days, she found it hard to tell what was real anymore. Did she own this condo, or didn't she? Was she with the Pony God, or the soccer player? Was she the daughter of a handyman—or the bastard princeling child of one of her country's most powerful politicians?

As she lied, and shopped, and rented more and more real estate, Wang Ti wasn't working alone. She'd taken on an accomplice named Zhu Shuangshuang: an agent with a star-studded Rolodex that was oozing with potential victims. Zhu Shuangshuang had actually purchased a place from Wang Ti in late 2009, and then, after apparently becoming aware of the scam, chose *not* to go to the police and instead began to introduce many of her famous clients to the fake princeling. Every time Wang Ti made a "sale," Shuangshuang got a cut of the profits. Their victims ballooned beyond athletes to include celebrities like the actress Wang Likun.

And then suddenly there was another source of urgency in Wang Ti's life: she became pregnant. Xiao Qin was the father. (At least, she claimed to be pregnant. The baby would later drop off the record completely.) Technically, she was still married to her husband—they would finally divorce in 2011—but with this pregnancy, she was moving more and more into her new life. And Xiao Qin, despite his talk of other girlfriends, was planning to marry her. She couldn't reveal her true background now. It was far too late for that.

By the middle of 2009, Yang Yun had grown tired of Wang Ti's endless delay tactics. The young gymnast wanted to move into her fabulous new apartment, and when the fabulous new apartment failed to materialize, she asked for her money back. Wang Ti managed to delay her for a while longer by having her move into yet another apartment, claiming that this one belonged to her mother—but by March of 2010, Yang Yun was officially fed up. She decided to move out, and when she couldn't reach Wang Ti, she called the property manager—who in turn called the *real* owner of the house. The owner showed up and introduced himself. Yang Yun had never seen this man before, but she could be sure of one thing: he wasn't Wang Ti.

When Yang Yun told other people about the strange encounter, her friend's con began to unravel fast. On May 20, several of Wang Ti's victims confronted her at her home, demanding that she repay them. They held her hostage for 24 hours, refusing to let her eat or drink, while she pleaded with them to have mercy on her, saying that she was seven months pregnant. After they let her go, she managed to pay one of them back by selling her car, her designer bags, and even some of her parents' assets—but by then, more of her victims were realizing that she'd scammed them, and demanding *their* money back. Wang Ti found herself staring into an endless spiral of debt and angry celebrities. She begged them to go ahead and call the police on her, but they refused. They didn't want the law involved. They wanted their money, and they wanted it now.

The problem was that their money was simply *gone.* She'd spent almost eight million yuan on clothes, cars, and gifts, while Xiao Qin had spent twelve million, mostly on his car dealership, which never materialized. There was no possible way to pay her victims back. The situation was so dire that Wang Ti considered killing herself—but instead, she continued to con, "selling" more rented real estate in order to pay back her friends, and creating new victims in the process. The con was no longer something she was doing in order to buy new clothes; it was an exhausting meta-con that she performed, wearily, to assuage her furious victims. It was a snake eating its own tail.

When the police finally showed up at her door, it was a relief.

✳

SEVEN YEARS LATER, A MESSY-HAIRED RUSSIAN SCAMMER NAMED Anna Sorokin was arrested in California. She'd been pretending to be a German heiress named Anna Delvey, buzzing around New York City in designer clothes, eating at the best restaurants, and talking about how she was going to open up an art foundation. Her whole persona was a lie, predicated on little more than her wardrobe (Gucci, Yves Saint Laurent), her generous gifts ($100 tips for the staff, expensive meals for friends), and her air of confidence. She was a working-class nobody who wanted to be an upper-class somebody. In the middle of smoggy Manhattan, she wanted to breathe rarefied air.

The similarities between her and Wang Ti were striking. Their humble backgrounds, their flashy personas, their use of designer brands as both costume and armor. But when US media covered the Sorokin case—which they did, exhaustively, with hyperbolic headlines like "Will We Ever Be Over Anna Delvey?"—it was often positioned as a classic tale of the American Dream gone wrong. Article after article used Delvey to argue that scamming was a distinctly American phenomenon, a by-product of the country's obsession with exceptionalism and individuality. "At some point between the Great Recession, which began in 2008, and the terrible election of 2016, scamming seems to have become the dominant logic of American life," ran an article in the *New Yorker*. The *New York Times Magazine* referred to "old-fashioned grift" as "American ingenuity" in one article, and to grifters as having a "distinctly American ethos" in another.

The United States certainly has a rich history of grift, but there was something solipsistic about the American media's insistence on claiming scamming as their own. What was the difference between Wang Ti strapping on her Louis Vuitton and Anna Sorokin buckling up her Gucci? Both of them were clever, ambitious women who lied their way into places where they otherwise would have never been admitted. Both knew the power of an expensive handbag—but their real power went far deeper than a familiarity with name brands. Each woman had a sinister awareness of the foibles of the very rich: the greed, the superficiality, the refusal to question the narrative of someone who claims to be *somebody*. And of course, both got arrested for it. (If anything, Wang Ti was the better scammer: she made thirty times the money Sorokin did, and her sentence turned out to be much harsher.)

Sure, it was possible to read both women as metaphors for their country—Anna Sorokin as the American Dream gone criminal, Wang Ti as the product of China's obsession with foreign cars and local princelings—but at the end of the day, both women were proxies not for a country-specific desire, but for human desire in general. They were unflattering mirrors for all of us. They reflected our need to climb the social ladder, our longing to be adored by important people, our desperation to be seen as *somebody*. While Wang Ti and Anna Sorokin were lying about their wealth and strapping on their designer armor, they were breaking the law—but they were also obeying a deep, universal drive that knows no borders.

✳

WANG TI'S ARREST HAPPENED IN DALIAN, HER OLD HOMETOWN. One of her victims finally went to the police, and in March of 2011, the police came for her. (Her accomplice Zhu Shuangshuang was arrested a month later.) When Wang Ti's trial began, the numbers on display were stunning: she was accused of swindling sixty million yuan—about eight and a half million dollars—out of twenty-seven victims, most of them extremely famous.

At first, Wang Ti put on a cheerful front, waving at reporters

in the courtroom, as Zhu Shuangshuang wept in despair behind her. But when it came time for her to testify, Wang Ti began
weeping, too. She'd been doing some much-needed self-reflection
over the past year, she said, and she'd come to the conclusion that
there *was* no conclusion. She couldn't explain her own behavior.
Though her cons had started from something concrete—the desire to impress her new boyfriend—they'd grown into something
beyond her control. The whole thing had been a swirl of glitter
and lies—an exhausting, endless swirl.

"I'm so ashamed," she said. "I couldn't think of a good explanation for what I've done. All these years I've been living in this
fantasy world that I created by myself. When you tell a lie over
and over again, it becomes the truth. At the end, I didn't know
what was the truth and what was a lie." Wang Ti had managed to
turn her fantasy world into a reality, but at the end of the day, she
found it terribly lacking. "All these years, I had to lie to people
every single day," she said. "It was exhausting. Since I've been
taken into custody, my greatest joy is that I can speak the truth. I
don't have to lie anymore."

When the prosecutor pressed her to explain why her con
worked, Wang Ti found herself at a loss for words. Even though
she was the mastermind, she couldn't quite describe how she'd
been able to get away with it. She seemed mystified by the gullibility of human nature, by our vulnerability to status, by our desperate desire to get away from the smog. "Why did these famous
people believe you?" asked the prosecutor, and Wang Ti looked
down before answering, "I don't know."

As it turned out, her victims weren't the only Chinese athletes getting scammed. In fact, scammed athletes had become something of a countrywide phenomenon. People speculated that these young men and women were particularly vulnerable to swindles because their training had isolated them from the rest of society from a very young age. (Xiao Qin, for example, began training at age five.) Many of them never learned how the world works off the field. Their success left them wealthy, but naive. When one of Wang Ti's victims talked to the press right after her trial concluded, he mentioned that the money he lost had been particularly special to him. "I earned all that money from winning in the Olympics," he said, sadly. "It's hard to earn money."

On November 20, 2013, Wang Ti was sentenced to life in prison. All of her personal property was confiscated. Zhu Shuangshuang was sentenced to eight years for both her role in the fraud and for a terrible car accident she'd caused in early 2010, in which two people died. Each woman eventually got time off for good behavior. Zhu Shuangshuang was released in 2018, while Wang Ti is currently scheduled to get out of prison on November 11, 2035.

Xiao Qin had been asked to appear in court to testify—but he never showed up. In fact, the Pony God disappeared from the public eye completely. He was rejected by his fashionable friends. He'd been attending a local university, but he dropped out. Four years after the trial, a photo of him surfaced online, and people mocked him for gaining weight. "A Chubby Man Living a Miserable Life," screamed one headline. Today, he relies on parttime jobs to make a living. The brands have been sold, the glitter rubbed off, and the fantasy is no more.

THE SEERS

MISCELLANIA

TWO BEDSHEETS
ONE YELLOW ROOM
NUMEROUS SPELLS
$1,884,630 WORTH OF GOLD COINS
ONE GOLD WIG
MANY MESSAGES FROM THE DEAD
ONE FORMULA PURPORTING TO BE THE RECIPE FOR CLEOPATRA'S BUBBLE BATH
ONE OATH STOLEN FROM A SECRET SOCIETY
ONE BENGAL TIGER
THREE TERRIFYING PREMONITIONS
ONE YAHOO.COM EMAIL ADDRESS
ONE CREEPY REFERENCE TO AN ORCHID
ONE ADVERTISEMENT BEGINNING "IS LIFE A PROBLEM?"

THE SPIRITUALISTS

ONE SPRING NIGHT IN 1848, TWO BORED GIRLS DECIDED TO play a prank on their mother. Kate and Maggie Fox, aged eleven and fourteen, were silly and creative, but they lived in a tiny town in upstate New York and had only their imaginations to entertain themselves. So that night, they began dropping an apple on the floor and dragging it around by a string. They found that when they did this, the fruit produced a strange sound. A sort of fleshy *clunk*. A bump in the night. The type of unidentifiable noise that creeped their mother out. "Mother was a silly woman," Maggie said decades later. "She was a fanatic. I call her that because she was honest. She believed in these things."

It was thrilling to see their mother grow more and more confused about what was causing that mysterious sound, and so the sisters developed new tricks: rapping on their bedposts, then cracking their joints so loudly it sounded like the noises were coming from the walls. It helped that they were pale and frail looking, exactly the sort of ethereal young things who seemed like they'd attract otherworldly company. With each new noise, their mother became more and more convinced that she was in the presence of . . . *something else.*

Maggie and Kate persuaded her that they knew how to communicate with this shadowy presence: they would ask questions, and the spirit would rap a certain number of times for yes or no. Other times, they'd spell out sentences by reciting the alphabet and waiting for the spirit to rap at certain letters. Neighbors poured into their house to listen and were shocked when the spirit seemed to know who they were; they were even more shocked when the spirit explained who *he* was. *I am the spirit of a murdered peddler*—said the spirit, who claimed to be named Charles—*killed years ago by a local man and buried in this very basement!* A few brave men went down to the basement to look for evidence and came back horrified after their shovels turned up bone fragments and strands of hair. Just like that, they believed.

Forty years later, the Fox sisters cracked. They'd accidentally launched a religion that now had millions of followers, and though they pretended to be communicating with the dead, it was the living who wouldn't let them rest in peace. "We were but innocent little children," said Maggie. "What did we know? Ah, we grew to know too much!" Their benefactors had been sending them cases of champagne for decades, and decades of free champagne had turned them into alcoholics. They were sick of the séance rooms, sick of the "mysterious" noises, sick of pretending they had access to another world. The irony was that now, when they tried to explain their tricks to people, no one would listen to them. Their con had been too good, right from the start. In those early days, neighbors searched the house high and low to discover where the noises were coming from. They found nothing, not even an apple.

THE DEAD

HUMANS HAVE TRIED TO COMMUNICATE WITH THE DEAD FOR CENTU-ries, but when it came to Modern Spiritualism—as the Fox sisters' accidental religion was now called—1848 was the perfect year for a resurgence in the popularity of the attempt. It was a year of expansion, consumption, and crackling invention, when Americans were moving further from organized religion and closer to ideas of science, progress, and materialism. 1848 was the year of the California Gold Rush. The year America won the Mexican-American War and gained control of the entire Southwest. Many Americans were no longer content to sit in hard pews and pray—they wanted to rush into the future themselves, constructing their own gods out of steel and wire.

But that was only half of the story, because all the steel in the world was never quite able to staunch humanity's desperate longing to believe in *something.* Those who abandoned God found themselves looking for God in strange new places—or, if they weren't looking for God exactly, they were searching for something hazier. A feeling of hope. A sense of comfort. What America needed to assuage these people was a new product: something soothing, mystical, and vaguely applicable to a large group.

It was the perfect year for the dead to rise.

In upstate New York, word spread quickly about how two

local girls had started talking to the dead. Their older sister, Leah, realized that there was serious money to be made in this spirit-communication business, and she transformed her little sisters from hobbyists to professionals almost overnight. The girls began charging people to attend séances, and soon moved to New York City to reach a wider audience. As they started raking in the cash, other people started miraculously discovering that they too could communicate with the dead. Before long, these Spiritualist mediums were popping up all across the country, and then across the globe. It was a veritable spirit rush.

Within four short years, there were 2,000 "writing mediums" in the United States alone—that is, mediums who wrote down messages from the spirits—plus a host of mediums who specialized in things like spirit painting, spirit photography, and spirit music. Others could make furniture hover in the air or produce pale figures who would loom from a corner of the parlor. Mediums explained that each new technique was a "gift" from the spirits, and as the "gifts" got more and more elaborate, audiences grew more and more enthralled. It was all well and good when the dead came forward to say that they missed you, but it was even more exciting when they made a table levitate, or inexplicably began strumming the banjo.

There were plenty of men who were Spiritualist mediums, but from the start, the movement seemed designed for women. It was invented by two young girls, after all, and it was based in emotion and intuition, a far cry from the male-dominated world of science. Mediums were supposed to be passive channels for the spirits, which fit with the era's idea of women as empty vessels.

On a purely aesthetic level, Modern Spiritualism felt soft and feminine: believers gathered in candlelit séance rooms, held hands, wept when they received messages from their loved ones. The performances could be quite erotic, too, at least according to the standards of the time. In a world where young men were urged to court women with "your linen clean and neat, your collar on and buttoned, and your necktie in place," this was a chance to break away from all that stuffiness for one night. When else did you get the chance to sit in a hot, dark room and press your leg against your neighbor's, while disembodied voices flew about and mysterious substances spurted everywhere and, if you were lucky, a cold finger might caress your neck? With thrills like that, who cared if your dead uncle was watching from the corner?

Because of all this, Spiritualism turned out to be not just a form of comfort for grieving souls, but a fantastic way for confident young women to make their dreams come true.

"A WOMAN RESPONSIBLE FOR WRECKED HOMES AND RUINED LIVES"

AT THE END OF THE 1800S, A DAIRY FARM IN RHODE ISLAND BEGAN to reverberate with the telltale rapping noises that meant one thing and one thing only: a spirit was on the premises. The only person on the farm who was able to communicate with the spirit was a plucky little servant named Mary Ann Scannell, an Irish girl with a penchant for fancy dresses and attractive men. Before long, she was holding séances and summoning up spirits who always seemed oddly invested in improving her life. At one séance, the spirit told an audience member to give Mary Ann a new dress. At another, the spirit insisted that Mary Ann was supposed to marry the local priest's hot nephew. (Mary Ann was infamously boy-crazy. As her boss, one Mrs. Kenyon, remembered, "She used to write letters to herself proposing marriage . . . she kept up a regular correspondence with a young man she said lived in Brooklyn. I'm afraid he wasn't real.")

The hot nephew escaped Mary Ann's clutches, and so she moved on to other séance rooms, determined to use the spirits to get what she wanted. As her fame grew, she would plant her friends in the audience and then shock everyone else by revealing intimate details about their lives. Additionally, like many of her fellow Spiritualist mediums, Mary Ann researched the rest of her audience beforehand to find out who was widowed, who was recently married, who'd just lost their mother, and so on. Spiritualists had a word for this sort of data collection: *medicine.*

Now, the best way to make money as a lady medium was to fully embrace whatever feminine cliché your audience wanted. The séance room was no place for a woman in a sharp business suit with a balls-to-the-wall attitude. Oh no! Some mediums adopted a frail, sickly aesthetic, as though talking to ghosts drained the life from their delicate bodies. Others emphasized their sensitivity and emotional intelligence: Kate Fox spent months holding one-on-one meetings with a banker who was grieving his dead wife. And Mary Ann seemed to go for an aesthetic of cheerful materialism—or at least, she didn't bother to hide her materialism. As a young servant girl watching Spiritualism spread across the country, she must have realized that she could use her self-proclaimed "psychic gifts" to make a comfortable life for herself, and she shamelessly used her work as a medium to line her pocketbook. For example, she told everyone that she had an Indigenous American "spirit guide" named Little Bright Eyes who—despite being a spirit!—was able to talk on the phone, drive a horse named Charley, eat candy . . . and cash checks. The thinking seemed to be that if you wrote Little Bright Eyes a check, Mary Ann would be happy to, ah, deliver it to her.

As Mary Ann's "medicine" helped her make more and more money, she carved out time for her other hobby: chasing down men. Sometimes those men were already married. (A furious group of local Spiritualists declared that Mary Ann was "a woman responsible for wrecked homes and ruined lives throughout the section of New England in which she formerly lived.") Sometimes they were delectably single. By the early 1900s, Mary Ann was living in New York and working as the pastor of the First Spiritualist Church of Brooklyn, when she crossed paths with a tycoon named Edward Ward Vanderbilt—one of *those* Vanderbilts, the ones who made their fortunes on the railroad. Edward was a widower, so Mary Ann started sending him messages from his dead wife. (Oddly enough, all the letters were written in Mary Ann's handwriting and postmarked from wherever Mary Ann was staying at the time.) Then she introduced him to Little Bright Eyes, who began urging him to shower Mary Ann with gifts: $5,000 in cash, $1,000 in jewelry, and two houses. Eventually, both Little Bright Eyes and Edward's dead wife were insisting, from beyond the grave, that Edward should marry the jolly young medium. (It was beautiful to see the two spirits so united in their common goal!) Edward dutifully wed Mary Ann in secret, even changing his will so that Mary Ann was the sole recipient of his Vanderbilt fortune.

Alas, real life soon intruded on Mary Ann's ghostly fantasy. When Edward's adult children found out about the marriage, they were livid. His daughter dragged Mary Ann to court and tried to get her father declared insane and the marriage annulled. Though the trial played out in Mary Ann's favor, it destroyed her reputation, and she was never accepted in high society. She never had a chance to inherit all that Vanderbilt wealth, either—she died in 1919, seven years before Edward did.

Still, she had come a long way from scouring milk buckets on the dairy farm. After her death, her followers released a fawning biography titled *Mary S. Vanderbilt: A Twentieth Century Seer*, which declared, in capital letters, "IN THE GREAT STRUGGLE BETWEEN LIGHT AND DARKNESS, MARY S. VANDERBILT STOOD AS A LIGHTHOUSE." She hadn't *really* been a lighthouse between light and darkness. Her light tended to shine on her own pocketbook. But the fact that she had a biography at all—with the last name "Vanderbilt" on the cover, no less—was a telling monument to the way she bent the spirits to her mortal aims.

"THE GENITAL PASSAGE WAS NOT USED AS A HIDING-PLACE"

THOUGH THOUSANDS AND THOUSANDS OF PEOPLE BELIEVED THAT these new Spiritualist women were telling the truth, there were others out there determined to expose them as frauds. The exposures began in 1852 and continued on for decades, and they were often just as dramatic as the séances themselves. In 1853, a cabinetmaker admitted that he'd been making special hollow-legged tables for mediums for years, which enabled them to pull off one of their most iconic tricks: the levitating table. Sometimes religious furor drove the exposures, like the times when irate groups of Irish Catholics burst into séance rooms to chase the mediums around. In 1887, a skeptical banker held a séance in his home for the sole purpose of exposing a wild medium named Elsie Reynolds. When a ghost appeared in the darkness and began dancing around the room, the banker turned on the light—and everyone saw that the "ghost" was Elsie herself, wearing a bedsheet. In fact, the whole exposure business grew so intense that mediums started hiring bodyguards, called "sluggers," whose main job was to stand in the darkness and prevent people from discovering their tricks.

In 1894, an exciting new development oozed into the world of Spiritualism: "ectoplasm," a pale, gooey substance that would often emerge from the medium's body. Ectoplasm was blatantly sexual, at least in dim lighting. It looked, frankly, like semen. If a member of the audience jabbed at the ectoplasm with a curious finger, the medium might cry out or quiver in response. The realities of ectoplasm were less alluring: some mediums produced it by vomiting up cheesecloth or chewed-up paper, while one medium hid the "ectoplasm" in his own rectum. But if you were a true believer, watching ectoplasm emerge from your favorite medium could be desperately erotic.

One of the most famous ectoplasm-producing mediums was Eva Carrière, a French medium known for her shocking performances. Eva had a female assistant—and possible lover—named Juliette Bisson, who would help her put on quite the homoerotic show for roomfuls of quivering men. Before each séance, Juliette would inform visitors that every nook and cranny of Eva's body—*every* nook and cranny—had been examined to ensure that she wasn't hiding any props. Then, in the darkness, Eva would strip naked. The audience would sit there and chant, *"Donnez, donnez"* ("Give, give") as Eva trembled and breathed rapidly—until finally, she produced the much-awaited ectoplasm, which might ooze out of her mouth, or drip from her breasts, or emerge from her genitals like a snake rising from a snake charmer's basket.

There are even photos of Eva, nude, wrapped up in her trance. In 1913, a psychical researcher and photographer named Baron von Schrenck-Notzing published them in a book called *Der Kampf um die Materialisations-Phänomene*, and the book hides its soft-core heart beneath a veneer of scientific inquiry. Juliette Bisson loved to give von Schrenck-Notzing intimate details about Eva's body, as though the particulars of Eva's menstrual cycles would help him discover whether or not dead people could talk to the living. In one letter, she describes a time when she watched a batch of ectoplasm—"resembling an orchid"—disappear into Eva's vagina. Eva was also happy to ramp up the eroticism of the "investigation," and once asked von Schrenck-Notzing if he would give her a gynecological examination to make sure she wasn't faking anything. He did just that, writing, "I introduced the middle finger of my right hand pretty deep into the vagina. . . . It is, therefore, certain that the genital passage was not used as a hiding-place." In the photographs of Eva's séances, it's fairly obvious that she's using gauze and papier-mâché to conjure up her ectoplasm and her ghosts, but for men like von Schrenck-Notzing, it was far more titillating to just lean back in the darkness and believe.

Yes, to a true believer, all the exposures in the world didn't matter. And so, with audiences who were willing to forgive them almost anything, these mediums had real power. They made good money, they married rich, and sometimes they even ventured into politics. Spiritualists tended to be quite progressive, and mediums often gave lectures on abolishing slavery, forming labor unions, and establishing the rights of women and children—claiming that as usual, the spirits were speaking through them, so if you disagreed with their politics you should take it up with the dead. It was a clever bit of diplomatic slipperiness. Sure, the ectoplasm was gross, and the bedsheets were silly, but in many of these séance rooms, a fascinating revolution was taking place.

"STRICTLY GENUINE, HONEST AND HIGHLY QUALIFIED MEDIUMS"

HATTIE WILSON WAS A YOUNG BLACK WOMAN WHO KNEW AN ENTRE-preneurial opportunity when she saw one. By the late 1850s, she'd reinvented herself in a powerful way by working her way up from indentured servant to hair-care mogul. Her products promised that they could "restore the hair where it had fallen off, remove dandruff, restore the hair to its original color, cure entirely the most painful headaches—and in some instances most serious humors," and she filled newspapers along the East Coast with advertisements for "Mrs. Wilson's Hair Regenerator" and "Mrs. Wilson's Hair Dressing."

But hair care wasn't enough for ambitious Hattie. In 1859, she self-published a 131-page novel (the self-publishing alone would have been an enormous undertaking in those days). The book was semiautobiographical, and she titled it *Our Nig; or, Sketches from the Life of a Free Black, in a Two-Story White House, North. Showing that Slavery's Shadows Fall Even There.* Unfortunately, the book didn't sell well, as white Northerners didn't like the whole "slavery's shadows fall even there" part. Hattie's real name wasn't on the cover, and so most readers assumed that the book was written by a white author, probably a man. For over a century, no one knew or cared that Hattie was the real author, until scholar Henry Louis Gates Jr. uncovered her name in 1982. Today, the book is recognized as a monumental achievement: the first novel published by a Black woman in America.

But back then, with her book failing to sell, Hattie needed to find another source of income. Ideally, she would find an industry that welcomed women with open arms, a progressive industry where a Black woman could carve out a niche for herself. So, in the shell-shocked years after the Civil War, Hattie took a look around the country, noticed that there was a booming market for Spiritualist mediums, and decided to take a seat at the table. (From a morbidly entrepreneurial perspective, the post–Civil War era was a great time to be a medium. The war had claimed about 620,000 men, and so there wasn't a town in America where someone wasn't longing to speak to their dead son or father or brother or husband one last time.)

From 1867 until the 1880s, Hattie performed and lectured as a medium, claiming that she'd discovered her gifts by communing with her dead father, and carving out quite the name for herself in Spiritualist circles. Her name appeared frequently in Spiritualist publications, and she appeared onstage right next to white male Spiritualists. It seems clear, from the few remaining historical documents that mention her, that Hattie Wilson was acknowledged and embraced by the Spiritualist movement. One writer included her in a list of "strictly genuine, honest and highly qualified mediums" who were skilled at "form materialization": one of the toughest tricks of the medium trade, where a medium would make an entire spirit appear and interact with the audience. In early 1875, Hattie threw a wild New Year's party complete with dinner, dancing, and a mystical performance by Hattie herself. An attending journalist declared that Hattie's "enterprise and generosity was the subject of commendation among those who were fortunate enough to participate in the enjoyment." Several years later, she even opened up a Spiritualist school for children, though it was short-lived. She was holding "circles" in her home until 1898, two years before her death.

But Black Spiritualist mediums like Hattie were never quite immortalized—positively or negatively—the way white mediums were. Yes, the Spiritualist movement could be quite progressive, but there were still divisions within its walls. The National Spiritualist Association of Churches was formed in 1893, but soon segregated internally, and by 1922, Black Spiritualists were forming the National Colored Spiritualist Association of Churches. The two movements proceeded alongside parallel but separate tracks, and Black mediums often slipped through the cracks of history after their careers ended. This means that we know very little about Hattie Wilson's work as a medium today. We just know that she was good at it.

Still, it's remarkable to think of Hattie speaking to rooms full of white men, commanding their attention by making entire spirit bodies appear out of thin air. She was almost certainly playing tricks on her audience—after all, Modern Spiritualism itself was born from a trick—but from certain angles, this sort of deceit didn't seem terribly sinister. Was it any worse than today's vaguely spiritual industries, like crystal shops and tarot card readings? Did it really matter that the table legs were hollow and the ectoplasm was chewed-up cheesecloth, as long as people found real solace in the séance room? Wasn't it kind of great that the movement allowed entrepreneurial women to improve their own lives?

Yes, sometimes the tricks were harmless. Positive, even. But then there were the other times.

"IN THE MOST HEARTLESS MANNER"

Ann O'Delia Diss Debar arrived on this earth with little fanfare and vanished without a trace. But during the years when she *was* in the news, she was *always* in the news. Frankly, she was hard to miss. She was very short, very stout, and had a penchant for extravagant costumes, so whether she was going by Vera P. Ava or Swami Viva Ananda or Madame Laura Horos, you could see her coming from a mile away in her white togas and golden wigs. And you could see exactly where she'd been, too. The illusionist Harry Houdini, who was highly skeptical of the Spiritualists, wrote that Ann "left behind her a trail of sorrow, depleted pocketbooks, and impaired morals that has seldom been equaled."

She was always claiming to be someone she was not. Despite the fact that she was a poor, white, Kentucky-born nobody, she said she was the daughter of King Louis of Bavaria and the famous dancer Lola Montez. As an adult, she scurried around America, double-crossing anyone she could get her hands on. She pretended to be European royalty, lied to a series of husbands, spent time in a hospital (where she tried to kill a doctor), got thrown into an asylum, pulled someone's hair in Philadelphia, gained a reputation as a "beer guzzler" in Kansas City, pretended to be dead in Dayton—and that was just the tip of the Diss Debar iceberg. Suffice it to say that she was often racing out of one city or another, chased by hordes of angry locals, lawmen, or lovers.

Despite antics like these, it wasn't until Ann was nearing forty that she made the papers. In New York City, she presented herself as a Spiritualist medium to a famous lawyer named Luther R. Marsh who was mourning the deaths of both his wife and his lover. Ann won his trust by delivering messages from his two beloved dead women, and then impressed him by creating "spirit paintings": oil paintings that she'd buy from a dealer, coat in white chalk, and then "paint" with the help of ancient "spirits" by secretly rubbing a sponge soaked in cleaning fluid over the chalk.

Her tricks worked wonders on Marsh's susceptible mind, and gradually, she convinced him that the spirits *really* wanted him to give her a mansion. He obliged, transferring the deed of his house to Ann, but local detectives grew suspicious of her behavior. In April of 1888, she was arrested for conspiracy to defraud and sentenced to six months in prison.

Those six months did little to crush her swindling spirit. Once freed, she popped up in Boston in a gold wig claiming to be a world traveler named Eleanor Morgan. Then she made her way to Chicago, pretending to be a wealthy humanitarian named Vera P. Ava. She was thrown out of Italy after scamming an entire colony of Spiritualist American expats there. By 1899, she had materialized in New Orleans with a newer, younger husband named Frank Dutton "Theodore" Jackson, and the two of them flounced around town declaring that they were founding the "Order of the Crystal Sea" in Florida, where members would "conquer death by a diet of fruit and nuts." As part of this order, Ann and Theodore promised that they would make a pilgrimage to India, where they would—wait for it—invent a magnetic battery so powerful that it would force God Himself to appear.

The Order of the Crystal Sea never quite got off the ground. Instead, Ann and Theodore were given thirty days in jail for fortune-telling and then kicked out of town. But they traveled to India anyway, where Ann got her photo taken with a Bengal tiger, and then to South Africa, where Ann pretended to be a doctor named Madame Swami Viva Ananda. By early 1901, the couple had settled in London, ready to set down some deep, nefarious roots.

Up until this point, Ann's antics had seemed a bit silly. The gold wigs, the fruit-and-nut diet, the God-summoning battery? It was hard to get truly outraged about any of it. As one contemporary journalist pointed out, Ann didn't *seem* evil. In fact, she seemed "merely a jocose"—that is, a hilarious—"spectacle." But in London, all that changed. In London, Ann went hunting.

She began to place ads in the papers designed to lure naive country girls into the city to meet her. The ads read, "Foreign gentleman of 35, educated, attractive, of independent means, desires to meet lady of means with a view to matrimony." When young women responded, Ann would convince them to travel to London, and they'd show up overwhelmed by the big city and by the sight of Ann herself, who was now calling herself "Madame Laura Horos"—or "Swami" for short.

Ann would explain to each girl that the "foreign gentleman of 35" was Theodore, that he was "Christ returned to earth and the only perfect man in the world," and that she was his mother. She'd explain that she and her "son" were forming something called the Theocratic Unity and Purity League, and that there were all sorts of benefits to joining, including marriage to Theodore and the "uplifting of mankind" in general. Oh! And one more thing: if the young lady wanted to hand over all of her money, the Swami would make sure to invest it *properly*.

When girls agreed to join the league, Ann would indoctrinate them with the following oath: "In the presence of the Lord of the universe and of the Hall of Neophytes of the order of the Golden Dawn in the Outer, regularly assembled under warrant of the Great High Chiefs of the Second Order, I do hereby and herein most solemnly pledge to myself to keep secret this order." (Ann didn't write this oath—she stole it from a secret society called the Hermetic Order of the Golden Dawn.) She would blindfold the girls and lead them through a series of strange rituals, and then came the most horrifying part: at some point, as part of the ceremony, Theodore would rape them, and Ann would watch.

"Mother" and "son" presented the rape as a key component of the indoctrination. It was necessary, Ann argued, so that the girls would be open to "any such revelation of the truth as would ensure salvation." Theodore would corner the girls at other times, too, convincing them to let him touch them by talking about how he was definitely going to marry them. He would give them strange drinks that made them feel drowsy, or lay hands on them in a way that made them feel hypnotized. The girls were scared, confused, and all alone. Even though Ann had multiple girls living in her home at the same time, all undergoing the same "rituals" and each one convinced that *she* was Theodore's fiancée, none of them confided in any other. One of them testified that the experience made her feel "quite powerless."

When someone finally went to the police and Ann and Theodore were arrested in the fall of 1901, the two of them put on quite the performance in the courtroom. And in response, the courtroom often laughed. Ann looked ridiculous; she insisted on being her own lawyer, like so many narcissists before and after her, and she pranced around the courtroom in a "soiled, draggled white silk toga." Theodore claimed that he couldn't be a rapist because he'd had an operation that "made it impossible for me to be other than a celibate." Both of them yelled in the courtroom: Theodore called the onlookers "reptiles" and Ann shrieked at one of the witnesses, "Beast!"

Still, their antics—and the ensuing laughter—weren't enough to hide the dark heart of their crimes. Several of their victims testified, and the details were so bad that newspapers refused to print them, writing instead of how the girls "spoke in a scarcely audible voice of acts of depravity by the male prisoner so revolting that they cannot even be indicated." It became clear, through the testimony, that Ann was just as guilty as her husband, having procured, watched, and even instructed the girls. As one paper concluded: "His wife seems to have aided him in the most heartless manner."

For their crimes, Ann got seven years of imprisonment with hard labor, while Theodore got fifteen. Ann was released on parole in 1907 for good behavior, and straightaway returned to America to resume scamming. In Detroit, she started a cult as "Mother Elinor, Queen of the House of Israel," then fled with about $10,000 in cash and jewelry from her faithful followers. She returned to the East Coast and founded yet another cult called the New Revelation, which printed all of its materials on purple paper, with purple ink. In those days, she was calling herself "A-diva Veed-ya," but everyone recognized her as Ann. Who else would give a press conference sitting on a pure white throne? Who else would declare that she would live forever because she didn't eat meat? Who else would begin her speech, "Dearly beloved, I need no introduction"?

Eventually, Ann's cult-leader energy ran out, and the dangerous medium faded from the papers, like a spirit creeping out of the séance room and discarding its bedsheet. By 1913, the *Washington Post* was declaring, "The present whereabouts of Ann O'Delia Jackson, who is now more than sixty years old, is unknown to the police. She is likely to be heard of at any time, in any part of the world, with a new list of dupes." There were any number of imaginable endings for this most sinister and audacious of Spiritualists. She could have moved to yet another continent to start yet another cult. She could have been in prison. She could have been hard at work on that magnetic battery that was going to summon God. Or perhaps she'd retired by then, and was sitting around eating fruits and nuts. Yes, it was tempting to laugh at her. Her career had been a long series of silly illusions, outrageous costumes, and pseudoreligious babble. But in the end, all of that was a smokescreen for her real darkness—a smokescreen that she used, ultimately, to get away.

THE DEAD, REVISITED

BY THE TIME THEY REACHED THEIR FIFTIES, THE FOX SISTERS WERE sick of Spiritualism. They'd been the high priestesses of the movement, but life had not been kind to either of them. They were widows and alcoholics. They were furious with their older sister, Leah, for turning them into celebrities. And they were plagued with guilt over the fact that they had fooled so many grieving people. Before each séance, Maggie would mutter, "You are driving me into hell."

In the fall of 1888—a few months after Ann's big spirit-painting trial—Maggie appeared at the New York Academy of Music to give a speech. She was going to do the unthinkable: she was going to reveal all the dirty details of her forty-year-old con job. Kate sat in the audience, nodding along as her sister spoke. "After I expose it I hope Spiritualism will be given a death blow," Maggie declared from the stage. "I was the first in the field and I have a right to expose it."

She told the audience about the apple, about her gullible mother. She said that after the success of the apple trick, she and Kate realized that they could produce an even spookier sound by discreetly cracking their toes. "Like most perplexing things when made clear, it is astonishing how easily it is done," she said. "The rappings are simply the result of a perfect control of the muscles of the leg below the knee, which govern the tendons of the foot and allow action of the toe and ankle bones that is not commonly known. Such perfect control is only possible when a child is taken at an early age and carefully and continually taught to practice the muscles which grow stiff in later years." And then she lifted up her skirts and began cracking her toes onstage.

If Modern Spiritualism had been birthed with an apple, it should have died right there. It was like a pastor revealing that he'd been an atheist all along, or a president admitting he didn't care about the Constitution. Here was the movement's founder, a woman who convinced millions of people around the globe that the dead were talking, declaring that the whole religion was based on nothing more than a bit of dim lighting and a set of strangely flexible toes. Even worse, Maggie went on to say that she'd *tried* to believe—and hadn't been able to. "I have explored the unknown as far as human will can," she told a journalist, agonized. "I have sat alone on a gravestone, that the spirits of those who slept underneath might come to me. I have tried to obtain some sign. Not a thing! No, no, the dead shall not return, nor shall any that go down into hell. So says the Catholic Bible, and so say I. The spirits will not come back."

But Spiritualism didn't die that night. Some Spiritualists insisted that Maggie's confession had been caused by the influence of other, more negative spirits. Others said she was just a washed-up medium trying to pivot into a career of anti-Spiritualist lectures. A year after her great reveal, Maggie took it all back. And just when the movement began truly flagging in the early 1900s, World War I rocked the globe, claiming millions of lives and spewing forth a whole new generation of people who yearned to hear from their dead.

In fact, despite decades of exposures and bad press, the movement lives on to this day—albeit in humbler numbers. The National Spiritualist Association of Churches has about 2,500 members, and some young people, looking for answers and drawn to its comforting aesthetic, are starting to experiment with Spiritualism once again. Perhaps another war, another global tragedy, will bring the movement roaring back, and all the clever women along with it. The dead may never return, as Maggie Fox declared, but the movement itself had come alive thanks to the power of the grieving human heart—which had always beat so faithfully beneath the fraud.

FU FUTTAM

born: Dorothy Matthews

1905-1985

I F YOU HAD AN EVENING OFF IN NEW YORK CITY AT THE END OF 1933, you might find yourself chomping on a 3 Musketeers bar (recently invented), sipping a martini (newly legal), and flipping through the newspaper, looking for something to take your mind off of the Great Depression.

You'd flip past ads for furnished rooms in Brooklyn ("Steam-heat, hot water, $2, $4, $4.50. Apply after 4"), job postings ("BARBER wants one or two attractive young women, pleasant personality,"), and agonizing public notices ("Not responsible for any debts incurred by Lelia Wheat [wife]. Left me fourteen months ago.—Clarence Wheat [husband]"). Hmm. None of it applied to you. None of it quite did the trick.

And then, under the "SPIRITUALIST" section, you'd see her:

Fu Futtam, scientific East Indian Yogi. Helps thousands; business, love, cross condition. Are you in trouble? Unsuccessful? Unhappy? Come to me when others fail; free

reading with a purchase of East Indian Oil of Success or
Holy Oil of Moses. Fu Futtam magical spiritual book, all
stores.

This mysterious woman was advertising her services—and
her Oils—in almost every issue of the *New York Amsterdam News*,
one of the oldest and largest African American papers in the country. Clearly, this woman knew how to market herself. And her
timing was perfect. *Are you in trouble?* Who wasn't, these days?
The stock market had crashed four years ago and now about one-
fourth of America's workers were unemployed. *Unsuccessful?*
Right there in New York, one-third of the manufacturing plants
were closed, and 1.6 million people were on government relief.
Unhappy? Central Park was full of shanties. Breadlines swelled.
Come to me when others fail. Normally, you knew better than to
buy into all that wishy-washy occult stuff. And maybe tonight it
was just the martini talking. But by God, it felt like the woman
was speaking right to you.

✴

THE ENIGMATIC FU FUTTAM, WHOSE NAME WAS TUCKED INTO THE
back pages of so many 1930s newspapers, walked the fine line between scammer and entrepreneur with a skill that was amazing to
see. She avoided the law almost entirely, unlike many of her swindling sisters. Most of her clients seemed happy with her services;
if they were unhappy, they usually weren't unhappy enough to go
to the police. She was a PR genius. A businesswoman par excel-
lence. Sure, you couldn't take what she said at face value. Her Oils

did not necessarily bring Success, nor did they have anything to do with Moses. She wasn't East Indian. But was that a crime—or just good advertising?

Fu's real name was Dorothy Matthews, and she had come to America to make her fortune just like so many other vaguely devious entrepreneurs across the centuries. Young Fu was born in Kingston, Jamaica, on September 9, 1905. Her mother was Black, and her paternal grandfather was Japanese. This Asian heritage would become a cornerstone of her business, though journalists often grew confused over where exactly she'd come from, and Fu herself didn't help at all. Some claimed that she was Chinese; Fu liked that "East Indian Yogi" appellation, which she used as a savvy marketing tool. In the 1930s occult business, everyone was pretending that they had Asian or Middle Eastern heritage, and it was particularly trendy to claim a connection to India or Egypt. It was a way of seeming more exotic, which in the occult world made you seem more legitimate. Who wanted to take advice from a regular old Betty or Shirley when you could visit the storefront of "DE Larz, The Girl from India"? Who wanted their future told by Dorothy Matthews, when you could get it from "Fu Futtam"?

Fu's world was a fairly expansive one. She traveled to Panama and Japan and all fifty states (or so she said), she had a "moderately rich uncle" who sent her money now and then, and by fifteen, she had emigrated to the United States for good. But her inner life was plagued with magic and fear. She claimed that she had always been susceptible to "seeing visions and dreaming dreams," and at seventeen, she saw into the future for one brief, horrifying moment. She was engaged to be married—in fact, she was putting on her wedding dress—when she felt overwhelmed by a sense of heat, and an apparition of her fiancé appeared in front of her. Fifteen minutes later, she learned that he'd been killed in a car crash.

As a young woman, Fu settled down in Harlem to build her empire, and Harlem turned out to be the perfect place for her. In the 1920s and '30s, the neighborhood was a fever dream of churches and cults and occult storefronts, each one promising passersby a better life. For struggling Harlemites, these storefront seers and their colored candles—purple for self-mastery, pink for celestial happiness—were a welcome relief from the Great Depression. The scene was hugely exploitative, preying on people who were despairing and broke, but at the very least, it offered some temporary comfort to its followers. ("Like drug addicts accustomed to their special stimulant, the devotees must have their occult medicine," wrote Claude McKay, the Harlem Renaissance writer, who then admitted that he himself enjoyed going to séances.) And being one of these "modern 'miracle workers,'" as one journalist called them, was a path to genuine economic freedom for many Black women. Whether or not you were really "The Girl from India," or a "scientific East Indian Yogi," simply *saying* that you were could help you earn a decent paycheck in difficult times. The same journalist wrote that the occult scene was "one of the few businesses in Harlem which has actually flourished during this latest period of economic stress."

By the mid-1930s, Fu was one of the most successful occultists in the city—*the* most successful, according to McKay. She'd made a fortune writing a series of "dream books," which helped readers interpret dreams, pick lucky numbers for gambling, and cast spells. One journalist noted that dream books were "as universally read in Harlem as the Bible," and Fu's were sold anywhere you could grab a newspaper. She was so successful that she even had copycats: *Madame Fu Futtam's Magical Spiritual Dream Book* was the real deal, but the cheaply made *Madam Fu-Fu's Lucky Number Dream Book* was not. Cleverly, Fu's books sometimes referenced *other* products that she sold, the way a cookie recipe printed on a bag of flour might demand that you bake with the company's brand of sugar, too. Her spell for getting rid of a lover was a complicated one that involved walking until your feet began to sweat, filling your left shoe with wine, sprinkling that wine in your doorway, and then flinging open the door while gasping, "So my pledge was sealed, so my covenant is broken." But that wasn't all! This whole ritual *must* be done, wrote Fu, "while burning Mme. Fu Futtam's special blessed candles."

While Fu rose to prominence as a Spiritualist medium, author, and saleswoman, most people couldn't help noticing her extremely good looks. A "voluptuous dream book publisher," one journalist called her. "A young and comely spiritualist with more curves than a winding mountain grade," wrote another. A third described her as "crystal gazing Mme. Fu Futtam of the sumptuous curves and the ball-bearing hips."

Ball-bearing hips? There was a reason, sort of, for all this editorial focus on her figure. See, by 1937, Fu was appearing in sections of the paper other than the classifieds. She'd gotten herself tangled up in an extremely dramatic love triangle, featuring two of Harlem's most famous and controversial figures. The man? Sufi Abdul Hamid, a labor agitator nicknamed "Black Hitler" who had a penchant for turbans and colorful capes. The woman? Stephanie St. Clair, a glamorous, arrogant, fur-coat-wearing lady mobster with the nickname "Madam Queen." Sufi and Stephanie were married, but now Sufi and Fu had gone and fallen in love—and Stephanie was loading her gun.

✳

STEPHANIE AND SUFI WERE MADE FOR EACH OTHER, AT LEAST ON paper. Both were larger-than-life community organizers. Both were famous for their fashion. And both were *always* getting into trouble.

Stephanie was about ten years older than Fu, and just like her rival, she'd been born elsewhere—the French-owned archipelago of Guadeloupe—but settled in Harlem as a young woman. It didn't take her long to rise to the top of the neighborhood's organized crime scene. In stylish dresses and flowing fur coats, she led a local gang called the 40 Thieves and began to take over the numbers racket, which was a form of illegal gambling that involved picking numbers that would appear in the next day's horse races. People turned to the numbers for the same reason they turned to dream books and pink candles: they promised a quick, cheap shot at a better life. And Stephanie turned to the numbers racket for the same reason that Fu turned to the occult business: it promised money, and lots of it. By the 1970s, word on the street was that sixty percent of Harlem's economic life was bankrolled by the numbers racket, and that as much as $1 billion was being poured into the racket citywide.

Back in the 1930s, Stephanie was going head-to-head with

New York's white mobsters, who were salivating for a slice of her very lucrative pie. She loved the conflict, taunting her competitors in the papers and killing their men when they killed hers. But she was fighting a losing battle, and eventually, the Mafia took over her turf. "It cost me a total of 820 days in jail and three-quarters of a million dollars," she said, when describing her defeat. She was out of the game—but at least she was rich. Rumor had it that she retired from the racket as a millionaire.

After retiring, Stephanie had time to turn her thoughts to love. No ordinary man would do for a woman nicknamed "Madam Queen," of course. She needed someone extraordinary—and she found him. "The story of Sufi Abdul Hamid and Mme. Stephanie St. Clair—one of the most colorful stories emanating from Harlem—may be told in a few words," wrote one journalist. "They met and loved; they married and fought; she shot him and went to jail; he bought a plane and crashed to his untimely death."

Her lover, Sufi, was born Eugene Brown in either Massachusetts or Pennsylvania—though he liked to say that he was born beneath a pyramid in Egypt. Sufi was a strange, controversial figure: a do-gooder and a con man, a liar with a big heart, an entrepreneur who could never quite decide what his angle was. For a while, he marketed himself as a bishop, mystic, and "Oriental philosopher," but by 1930 he was in Chicago, heading up a Black labor movement with the slogan "Buy Where You Can Work." Then he converted to Islam—or *said* he'd converted to Islam—changed his name to "Sufi Abdul Hamid," and moved to Harlem to continue his labor work.

The Great Depression was hitting Harlem hard in those days.

Unemployed white workers from all over the city were coming into Harlem to find work, displacing the Black workers there. In response to this infiltration, Sufi organized several successful job boycotts against white-owned Harlem stores who refused to hire Black employees. But this turned into a public relations nightmare for him when people realized that many of these white storeowners were Jewish. Sufi was shocked—or at least, he *claimed* to be shocked—when journalists began calling him "Black Hitler," and he was even more appalled when two Nazis paid him a casual visit, wondering if he wanted to, ah, work together. "I couldn't imagine collaborating with the Nazis any more than with the Ku Klux Klan," he told Claude McKay. But this was Sufi, king of controversy, and though McKay believed him, the rumors of his anti-Semitism persisted. Harlem's Black leaders decried anti-Semitism in general and Sufi in particular, calling him a "hothead" and a "harbinger of hatred."

The turban-wearing agitator crossed paths with the fur-wearing mobstress on June 19, 1936, and they fell in love fast. One night, Sufi left Stephanie's apartment and then came right back, whispering through her door that he was so in love with her that he couldn't possibly go home. Stephanie flung open the door and brought him into her yellow room (every room in her apartment was painted a different color), and the two of them stayed there, curtains drawn, until the sun came up. When Sufi proposed, she told him that she needed three days to think about it. On the third day, she said yes.

The two were wed secretly, with only the necessary witnesses, a pastor, and a notary public. They signed a strange contract, which decreed that their marriage would last for 99 years and would include a trial period of one year to test the "feasibility of the plan." Stephanie was unfazed by the unromantic nature of her wedding. It was all done "as they do on the continent," she said.

But a marriage like this, between two strong personalities who couldn't avoid drama if you paid them to avoid it, was doomed to fail. By the fall of 1937, their marriage was crumbling, and Stephanie was more than happy to tell journalists why. Sufi had been trying to get her involved in sketchy business propositions, she said. He was only interested in her money. He was staying out all night. He was a gambler. A player.

And he was seeing a younger woman.

✳

FU FUTTAM MET SUFI ABDUL HAMID SEVERAL YEARS EARLIER, IN Chicago, where Sufi had helped her with her burgeoning dream book business. Now, despite the fact that Sufi had a brand-new wife, he was finding Fu especially irresistible, what with those ball-bearing hips and all. Sure, he had a lot in common with Stephanie, but he also had a lot in common with Fu. Both were hustlers with a keen eye for branding, a sharp nose for reinvention, and a fondness for fake heritages: East Indian for Fu, Egyptian for Sufi.

When Stephanie got wind of their affair, she went raging to the papers, telling journalists that Fu Futtam was a vicious snake in the grass who had tried to *poison* her. One day—according to Stephanie—Fu showed up at her door without warning, asking Stephanie if she was feeling ill. When Stephanie asked, "Who sent you here?" Fu responded, creepily, "Oh, I always like to be nice to the sick." She nursed her enemy lovingly, bringing her wine, chicken, and "other delicacies," as Stephanie grew weaker and weaker, losing so much weight that she felt like a "walking skeleton." When Stephanie decided to move into a new apartment, Fu offered to help, but swindled her out of $80 instead. Then, Fu began enacting a sort of bizarre psychological warfare on her rival, hinting that Sufi had had a baby with a white woman, trying to borrow Stephanie's diamonds, and asking Stephanie for a loan to start a fertilizing business.

When a journalist asked Fu to respond to Stephanie's wild charges, Fu snapped, "The woman is insane." She wasn't trying to break up anyone's marriage, she said. She was all business. "Sufi and I are interested in esoteric work," she insisted, "and he has been helping me on philosophical passages in a book I've just finished. And now, I have had to stop Sufi from coming here, I don't even let him come into my apartment any more."

Fu could protest all she wanted, but Stephanie didn't believe her. And she certainly didn't trust Sufi. "He was just 'conning' my confidence," Stephanie raged to journalists. "Then he turned to his 'con' woman against me. He bit the hand that fed him." And so, on January 18, 1938, Stephanie loaded her gun and jumped out at Sufi when he was walking into his lawyer's office. *Bang, bang, bang.* One bullet singed his mustache and chipped his teeth, another blazed a hole through his clothes, and the third grazed his forehead—at least, that's how Sufi described it, though he was admittedly prone to exaggeration. Stephanie was arrested, and although she claimed self-defense, she was sentenced to two to ten years in prison.

Her sentencing was awfully convenient for Fu and Sufi. About a month after Stephanie was found guilty, the two of them were married. "The pair should really knock the spirits for a loop," wrote one journalist. "May tranquility be upon them."

✷

FU HARDLY TOOK ANY TIME OFF FOR HER WEDDING. WITHIN A WEEK, she was back to work, distributing a customized lucky numbers book titled *W.Y.N.S. Daily Names Vibrating Hunch Number Calculation* to one fortunate couple. Only the spirits could say what exactly that title meant, but clearly, despite the scandal of her recent marriage, Fu's vibrating hunch number calculations were still in high demand.

It's not surprising that Fu and Sufi didn't take much of a honeymoon. Both were incredibly hard workers, with an endless supply of schemes stuffed up their ornamental sleeves. Where Stephanie and Sufi had clashed, Fu and Sufi harmonized. "He was so kind, so true, so devoted, so lovely," Fu said of her new husband. "He was like a baby around the house. In the thirty years of my life, I have been around plenty of men. I never saw one like him." She urged him to abandon his risky work as a labor leader and return to "the more tranquil business of preacher of oriental mysticism." Her support worked wonders on him. "After eight years of strife and struggle, Sufi underwent a change of heart and seemed to have craved tranquility," one journalist noticed.

Sufi was indeed all about the tranquility those days—at least, tranquility as a marketing tool. He and Fu plunged into their latest scheme, a gathering spot called the Universal Temple of Tranquility, which they advertised in the papers as a place where "divine mystery and wisdom of the East are being revealed at last!" As with Fu's dream books and Stephanie's numbers racket, this temple was designed to appeal to Harlem's most hopeless residents. "IS LIFE A PROBLEM?" screamed the ad. "Have you tried with all your courage for success and attainment and failed? Let us help you in every way to achieve contentment and happiness." Word on the street was that Fu had invested a lot of her own money into the temple. Say what you will about Sufi, but he certainly wasn't afraid of strong, independent women.

The Temple flung open its doors on Easter Day of 1938 to an audience of over two hundred people. The lights grew dim, a gong clanged, and the curtains rose to reveal Sufi—who was calling himself "Bishop Amiru-Al-Mu-Mimin"—wearing a Roman Catholic-inspired outfit that consisted of "a black and gold biretta at a cocky angle and a chartreuse brocaded robe over which was a twenty-two karat solid gold vestment." His followers were awed; the journalists in the audience were unimpressed. In a cloud of incense, he began to chant: "O, arach lo cha, gyah gyah, oon she foorah. Allah she foorah, she susa, she susa, shu sheelee." This language, he said, was Chinese. "How would I know Chinese if I had not been reincarnated?" he crowed, clearly satisfied with his performance. Journalists mocked him for this, but the temple's opening was a resounding success. Sufi and Fu seemed poised to become Harlem's new power couple, with all the gods and ghosts of the city on their side.

But Sufi was starting to become haunted by premonitions of his own death. One Sunday, as he was meditating, he stopped and told Fu, "Next Sunday my picture will be on the front page of every newspaper in the country." Later that day, he lit a special candle that he used for his own mysterious purposes. Fu stood there, watching the flame. It was burning just fine, she said, and then "suddenly, without any apparent cause, it went out." At least, that's the story she told later, when it made sense for her brand to tell stories like that.

✹

SINCE SUFI WAS SUFI, THE KING OF GOING THE EXTRA AND UNNECESsary mile (a twenty-two karat solid gold vestment!), no one was surprised when he bought a plane and told everyone he was planning to take a flight straight to Egypt, the "land of his birth." This had been a dream of his for a long time. On July 31, 1938, he decided that it was time for a test flight.

Sufi strode into the plane, accompanied by his secretary and his pilot. Nearby, Fu and a handful of his followers watched. The plane rose into the air, bringing Sufi closer and closer to the sun. But something wasn't right. The plane began spinning like a Frisbee. Something was very, very wrong. The plane slipped sickeningly into a nosedive, headed straight for a nearby field—and crashed.

All three of the passengers were thrown out. The pilot died instantly. The secretary was rushed to a nearby hospital in critical condition. And Sufi tried to sit up, attempted to say something— and then fell back to the ground, dead. For the second time in her life, Fu's love story had ended in flames.

✳

SUFI WAS GONE AND FU WAS ALONE AGAIN. THANKFULLY, HER OLD knack for marketing hadn't left her. She stepped easily into the role that her more flamboyant partner had just left, giving interviews in a fetching red dress and weeping lavishly in front of journalists while informing them that she hadn't cried since the plane crash. As if to remind everyone that Sufi wasn't the only mystic in their marriage, she announced that he was going to rise from the dead in ninety days. She threw him two funerals—Sufi wasn't a one-funeral type of guy—that featured a mash-up of Muslim, Buddhist, and Southern Baptist traditions. Hundreds of Sufi's followers crowded into the room to pay their respects, and Fu stood in front of them, wearing an "inscrutable half-smile." One of her followers said, admiringly, "She was born smiling."

From one angle, Fu was handling the tragedy perfectly. Rumors flew that she would be the new leader of the Universal Temple of Tranquility, and journalists wrote that "Harlem was about to have its first black prophetess." From another angle, though, the tragedy proved what some had suspected all along: that her work was a scam. Certain disgruntled Harlemites whispered that it was awfully weird how Fu hadn't predicted or prevented her husband's death, given that she could see the future and all. An even more sinister rumor emerged: Fu *had* predicted his death but had chosen not to stop it—which was why she didn't accompany Sufi on the doomed flight. "Was it that she 'saw' what had been happening all the time and 'knew' what was going to happen, and kept clear of all tragedy?" wrote one journalist. "Harlemites want to know."

Ignoring her critics, Fu returned to what she did best: the work. She dove headfirst into running the Universal Temple of Tranquility, though she was never chosen to officially succeed Sufi. (That honor went to a man who called himself Bishop El-Amenu and who liked to cry, "Tranquility! It is the Light.") Sometimes, she taught free classes on "how contacts are made to hidden soul forces through concentration in order to compel willingness and obedience." Other times, she could be found in the Temple's meditation room, and followers started calling her their "Little Mother of Silent Devotion."

Perhaps realizing that Sufi's death was an opportunity for her to promote her skills as a seer, she told journalists that she often visited the field where Sufi died in order to commune with his spirit. The visits, at least, were real: her chauffeur confirmed that he frequently drove her to the field and left her there overnight. There, Fu claimed that she would sleep "on sheets of ice and snow," and on those sheets of ice and snow, she would have visions—which you could read all about in her forthcoming book. The book was going to be two volumes, titled, simply, *She*. "'She' represents the mother of Life," Fu told the press, enigmatically. "Before Eve was 'She' was."

Sufi's death had been tragic, but it had certainly boosted

Fu's profile, and her occult knowledge had never been more in demand. In 1939, a journalist came over to her apartment to get her opinion on a notorious murder case that was rocking the city. The case was an odd one: first, a young man was murdered in front of his girlfriend, then the girlfriend mysteriously died before being called in to testify. The journalist wanted to know what Fu thought about the strange death, spiritually speaking. Fu declared that the girlfriend had *wanted* to die, since her boyfriend was no longer on this earth.

"It is quite possible that the young man had only passed through the change of so-called death into the Great Unknown," Fu explained. "When the Supreme Absolute Intelligence lowered the elevator, his soul mate followed him. . . . The desire for death can be such a powerful subconscious factor that it can easily cause the death of a person whose system has been weakened by illness or who is unable to fight such a mental state."

Perhaps the interview was just another way of enhancing her brand. But maybe not. Fu was a clever businesswoman, but she was also human. Perhaps she ached with sympathy for the dead girl. Maybe, like so many of her clients, she was turning to the supernatural to explain away something painful. She'd lost a soul mate, too.

✳

SAY WHAT YOU WILL ABOUT THE EFFICACY OF HER EAST INDIAN OIL of Success—the truth was that Fu's work never seemed to hurt anyone. Until 1941, that is, when she was tossed into jail on a charge of grand larceny. For the past seven years, she'd been taking money from a woman named Mrs. Ida Liimatainen, who was convinced that evil spirits were following her around. Ida was willing to pay Fu whatever it took to stop the hordes of spirits from destroying her life; Fu was more than willing to accept payment for the delicate task. Unfortunately, Fu never did manage to cure poor Ida of her spirits, and one day, Ida woke up and realized that she'd been swindled. Ida went to the authorities. Fu was arrested. She wore a long veil in court to hide her famous face, but reporters recognized her anyway. But then her luck changed—or perhaps the spirits came to her aid. Fu's friends bailed her out, saying that she had recently started a "mission" and they were hoping she'd be able to continue it. And the charges against her were mysteriously dismissed.

Over the next two decades, Fu continued to hustle like never before. She reinvented her brand, pivoting from faux–East Indian to faux-Egyptian, perhaps as a nod to her late husband's obsession. She opened up a store called "Fu Futtam Egyptian Products," where she sold items like Egyptian Sweet Air Incense (a strange non-burning incense that filled the air with perfume when you opened it) and All Purpose Luxor Bath (a bubble bath that Fu claimed was the exact type used by Cleopatra). The store was a huge success. Who wouldn't want to bathe like Cleopatra? By 1949, she was advertising a new book, *Flight to Power*, in which she would reveal "formulas of the ages." In 1950, she had changed the name of her store to "Fu Futtam's Religious Store," which promised to "satisfy the most discriminating." By the end of 1952, she'd launched a new product, a numerology guide called "Fu Futtam's Mirror Guide Green Card." You could buy her merchandise at religious stores, drugstores, grocery stores, stationery stores, or newsstands—and you could also order them through the mail. There wasn't a corner of the occult market that Madame Fu Futtam didn't dominate.

She kept on advertising her dream books and psychic services in the papers all the way into the late 1960s, when she would have been just over sixty years old. In those days, if you were sitting there in your furnished room, smoking a joint, wearing your bellbottoms, and flipping through the classified section, your eyes might be drawn to brasher, bolder advertisements that screeched, "STOP!! READ THIS!!" and "GUARANTEED BLESSING IN 3 DAYS" from psychics like "Mme. Rosalie from the Virgin Islands" and "Mrs. Lukas, Indian healer advisor" and the "Miracle Lady of Jamaica." Fu Futtam's ads were in small font now, and shorter than they used to be. Chances were you'd flip right past them. Unless you knew who she was. Who she'd been.

Free reading $3 purchase. Helps love, money, cross. When others fail . . . Fu Futtam passed away as Dorothy Hamid in 1985, at almost eighty years old. Maybe by then she had retired to enjoy the fruits of her mystical labor. But knowing Fu, she probably kept working until the very end, selling hope to the hopeless and dreams to the dreamers, smiling that inscrutable smile.

ROSE MARKS

alias: Joyce Michael, Joyce Michaels

1951–

THERE WERE SO MANY SAD WOMEN IN MANHATTAN. THEY WERE educated and successful and desperate. They had MBAs and books on the *New York Times* Best Seller list and jobs in international finance; they had abusive husbands and drug-addled sons and mothers who were dying. Their daughters were depressed and their boyfriends were leaving them and their bodies were riddled with cancer. What could they do about any of it? These women had grown up believing that there was something more out there, something to cling to, and now, as they dragged their aching hearts through the city, something appeared in front of them, as if by magic: a little storefront, all lit up.

The sign on the front read, LAWS OF ATTRACTION GUIDED BY PSYCHIC JOYCE MICHAELS, WALK-INS WELCOME. Inside, the store was decorated with religious paintings and statues, and the psychics wore long dresses and sweaters that covered them up to the wrists. The room wasn't claustrophobic, exactly, but it was small. Intimate. It was across the street from the legendary Plaza Hotel, a stone's throw from Central Park, and mere blocks from the designer shops of Fifth Avenue—a beacon of calm spirituality in the middle of one of New York's ritziest neighborhoods. Most customers walked in, paid $50 or so for a palm reading or an analysis of their astrological chart, and left. But when one of these sad women walked through the door, the psychic on duty would perk up.

How can I help you? The sad woman would pour out her problems. The psychic would listen intently. *I may be able to help,* she'd say, *but first, I need a personal item to pray and meditate on.* The loan of the personal item was like a trust fall—would the sad woman do it? Did she have the nerve? *What about that bracelet, there on your wrist? Oh, it was given to you by your grandmother? Perfect.*

The next day, the bracelet would be returned unharmed, and the sad woman would sigh with relief. But the psychic would be waiting with bad news: *You've been cursed in a previous life.* Thus the abusive husband, the cancer, or the dying mother. Then, the good news: *I can help you. I'm here to do God's work, and the work is free.* And then the catch: *In the course of this work, there are . . . sacrifices that have to be made.*

Sacrifices? Yes, in the ancient days, the removal of a curse this serious would involve human sacrifice, but these days, they weren't going to slaughter anyone, of course, ha ha. No, these days, the sacrifice was simply money. After all, money is the root of all evil, and so it must be cleansed. But once the curse is lifted, the money will be returned unharmed—just like the bracelet. Everything will be wonderful. Everyone will be happy again. But first—there's an ATM across the street.

✳

On May 3, 1951, little Rose Eli was born into a world of spirit guides and second sight. Her ancestors were Roma, an ethnic group that migrated from India toward Europe about one thousand years ago, where they encountered persecution, slavery, and eventually, slaughter by the Nazis. (The Roma are often called "gypsies," a slur based on the false idea that they originated in Egypt.) The Eli family came over to the United States from Greece around the turn of the twentieth century. Like so many other immigrants, they performed an intricate dance between assimilation and sequestration, pursuing the American dream while trying to maintain their ancient rituals like dowries, arranged marriages, and fortune-telling.

Rose grew up outside Newark, New Jersey, and as was customary in her community, her family pulled her out of school after only a few weeks in the third grade, leaving her nearly illiterate. Instead, she was taught a different set of skills: how to clean, how to cook, how to care for a husband, how to be a good daughter-in-law, and how to tell fortunes. Right away, she started to work in the family trade. Rose's mother was a psychic, as was her grandmother. For hundreds of years, the women in her family had inherited these skills; Rose called them a "gift from God." The gift could be something of a curse, though. Rose had her first premonition at age nine, and it was terrifying: she accurately predicted her own grandmother's death.

When Rose was a teenager, her parents picked out her future husband. That marriage didn't work out, and neither did the next one, but eventually her parents suggested a man named Nicholas Marks, and Rose and Nicholas were wed. Together, they had three kids, and Rose worked as the breadwinner, plying her trade—her gift. The gift was her birthright. There was never a question that she would do anything else. Never a chance, either.

✳

BY THE TURN OF THE MILLENNIUM, BUSINESS WAS BOOMING FOR Rose. She'd adopted the alias Joyce Michael (sometimes spelling it Michaels) and had opened up a place in Manhattan called Joyce Michael Astrology, which was pulling in a lot of very lucrative clients. She and her husband had moved down to southern Florida, where she'd opened up a little empire of psychic storefronts. She filled these storefronts with family members, employing her sister, her three kids, their spouses, and even her granddaughter. Mostly, the women in the family worked, and the men oversaw the work and spent the money that the women earned. And oh, that *money*! What couldn't it buy? Expensive cars, flashy motorcycles, designer clothes. Diamonds. Extra bathrooms. Rose and her husband lived in a multimillion-dollar, glass-walled, seven-bedroom, nine-bathroom home on a palm tree–lined street right by the water in Fort Lauderdale, with a cream-colored 1977 Rolls Royce in the garage and hundreds of thousands of dollars' worth of jewelry in the many closets.

All this wealth was made possible because Rose was an extremely skilled fortune-teller. Despite her lack of formal education, she could read people like a book, and her raw intelligence served her well in the delicate business of cold reading and hot reading and palm reading. Later, when Rose was in so much trouble that she had to hire an attorney, that attorney, Fred Schwartz, found himself impressed with the natural workings of her mind. "When I met her, she could hardly read, and had a lot of trouble writing," he said. "But she's a very bright, charming woman. She can be mean on occasion, but she's able to . . . look at a problem, analyze it, and solve it. And that's what she did with people."

Sure, Rose had her own demons. She enjoyed gambling a bit too much, for example. The money poured in, and she gambled much of it right out again. But at work, she was killing the game. If her younger psychics got in over their heads—if their clients grew skittish and reluctant—Rose would take over, and suddenly those clients would be writing checks for five, ten, fifteen times as much money as before. Rose was the one who pulled the family strings. The one who called the psychic shots. The matriarch. "She had more vast knowledge . . . she ran, basically, the operation," said one of those clients, later. Another put it simply: "She was very good at what she did."

And nothing proved that Rose was good at what she did quite like her number one client, a sad woman who paid Rose one million dollars a year for the sheer privilege of being able to get her on the phone.

✳

ROSE'S MAIN CLIENT WAS THE ROMANCE NOVELIST JUDE DEVERAUX, a multimillionaire with dozens of books on the *New York Times* Best Seller list. At least, Deveraux had been a multimillionaire back in 1991, when she walked through the door of Joyce Michael

Astrology in Manhattan. To a stranger, her life would have looked incredible—fame! fortune!—but behind the scenes, it was in shambles. She was trapped in an emotionally abusive marriage. She desperately wanted a child but couldn't get pregnant. She was in love with someone else. She'd talked to therapists, lawyers, and friends, but couldn't figure out a way to get out of her marriage and into some better future life. She'd started to think that the only way to escape the whole mess would be to kill herself. "It was beyond depression," she said, later. "I had given up." And so when she saw the lights blinking in the window of Joyce Michael Astrology, she walked toward them.

Deveraux didn't really believe in psychics, but "Joyce Michael" turned out to be an incredible listener, which was soothing. And so she came back for a second appointment, and then a third. At that third visit, Rose promised Deveraux that she could give her the thing she wanted most in the world: a peaceful divorce. It wasn't long before Deveraux was seeing Rose four or five times a week.

To Deveraux, Rose seemed to have an authentic connection to the spirit world, or whatever you wanted to call it. She *knew* things. She predicted that Deveraux's husband would finally file for divorce, which he did. She said that the divorce papers would be delivered between 4 and 5 p.m., and wouldn't you know, she was right. Once, Rose called Deveraux in hysterics, screaming that Deveraux needed to leave her apartment right away because her husband was coming to murder her. Deveraux checked into a hotel and, when she returned to her apartment a few days later, the men who worked in the building told her that her husband had indeed stopped by and that they'd "never seen another human being as angry as he was in their life."

Slowly, Deveraux became a true believer. She had no idea that Rose had hired a private investigator to peer into the messy crystal ball that was her love life. She just knew that Rose was telling her things that were starting to come true. Before long, she asked Rose to work for her full-time, and Rose responded that her fee was one million dollars a year. (Later, Rose claimed that she had been joking.) For one million dollars a year, Deveraux would be able to call Rose for guidance at any hour of the day or night, and Rose would deliver her a smooth divorce, a new soul mate, and the baby that she so desperately wanted. Even better: once the "Work" was complete, Rose would return every penny of that annual fee—minus a modest $1,200 for her services. Deveraux found this a compelling deal. She agreed to pay up.

Yes, Rose was good. Good enough to demand a million dollars a year. Good enough to get it. But for all her skill, there were forces out there operating far beyond her control.

In the mid-2000s, Rose lost both of her parents, her husband, and her seven-year-old grandson in the space of about three years. Reeling with grief, she turned to pills, alcohol, gambling—anything that promised to numb the pain. She became a regular at the Seminole Hard Rock Casino in Hollywood, Florida, where she spent over $9.65 million in four years. She was spiraling into darkness. Her youngest son, Michael, noticed that his mother's personality had started to change. She was snappier than normal. Angry all the time. He believes that she turned into a "pathological gambler" during this period in her life—a disorder that's been recognized by the American Psychiatric Association's *Diagnostic and Statistical Manual of Mental Disorders.* (To put it roughly, a pathological gambler is addicted to gambling, dependent on it, irritable without it.) "I lost control over everything," Rose said, later. "I allowed my addictions to take over."

Through a haze of grief and booze, Rose continued to work, though she often stayed behind the scenes. Instead of greeting clients as they came through the door, she'd delegate, telling her family to direct their clients' cash through a complicated maze of bank accounts and pseudonyms. Some of her relatives whispered that she was gaining too much weight because she wouldn't "get out on the street and hustle clients." But why hustle when you're the matriarch? After decades in the business, Rose was still at the top. Now, though, she was wealthy and alone, devastated by tragedies that she'd been unable to predict.

✳

DETECTIVE CHARLIE STACK WAS NO STRANGER TO SHADY FINANCES. He was the only cop in the Fraud Investigations Unit of the Fort Lauderdale police department with an accounting degree, and hardly a day went by when someone didn't slap a money-related case down on his desk. On any given week, he was drowning in Ponzi schemes and mortgage fraud, and so when his sergeant tossed a new case onto his desk in April 2007 and he saw that it was about fortune-telling, he was tempted to roll his eyes—at first.

Stack, the Irish-Catholic son of a New York City cop, seemed like an intimidating guy when you first met him. He coached kickboxing. He was a former national champion in karate. He'd gone undercover with drug kingpins and Russian mobsters, and one public defender called him "maybe the toughest S.O.B. I've ever met in my life." But if there was one thing that got him emotional, it was the plight of the victims he encountered, especially the women. Chalk it up to the fact that he grew up with five sisters, or that his mother had emigrated over from Ireland and he'd seen firsthand just how hard she worked. Either way, when he took a closer look at the case that had just been tossed onto his desk, he saw that beneath the racket about spirits and premonitions, there were real people who were getting seriously hurt.

The case involved a storefront called Joyce Michael Astrology and a woman who was missing several thousand dollars. Her complaint had originated in New York but trickled down to Florida because, according to bank records, that's where her money had ended up. When Stack traced her money further, he noticed a suspicious pattern. There was a spiderweb of accounts involved, and all of them fed into larger accounts for people called "Rose Marks" and "Joyce Michael." The smaller accounts, belonging to people like "Nancy Marks" (Rose's daughter-in-law), were receiving deposits of thousands of dollars, but the accounts for "Rose" and "Joyce" took in painfully large sums: two hundred and fifty thousand dollars here, three hundred thousand there. Stack couldn't believe it. "I'm going, *This is for fortune-telling?*" he said.

His colleagues found the case rather silly. After all, no one had died. No one was heavily armed or slinging cocaine or raving about revenge. The case involved a bunch of sobbing women who believed in a whole lot of woo-woo nonsense and who had willingly handed over their money to these fortune-tellers. As police liked to say in cases like this: Nobody put a gun to their heads. But Stack felt compelled to pursue the situation further. So he marched over to his friends in the US Attorney's Office and the Secret Service and told them that this case could be big. Really big.

Thus began four and a half years of investigation into the matriarchy of Rose Marks, as Stack surveilled her family from Manhattan down to Florida, taking thousands of photos, recording their phone calls, and even sifting through their garbage—where he found things like empty Cartier boxes, the castoffs of their glamorous lifestyle. He watched the Marks women pour out of Rose's mansion in high heels and short skirts. He saw them drive off in their expensive cars: a black Mercedes-Benz, a bloodred Pontiac Trans Am, a blue Bentley convertible. He saw the men jump onto their high-priced motorcycles: Harley-Davidson, Ducati, Yamaha. "They all had nicknames, just like mob figures," he said. "When you watched them out at night, they *acted* like they were mobsters. They partied hard, they spent money hard, they lived large." It wasn't unusual for Rose, who went by "Pinkey," to blow through $100,000 in a single month.

The Cartier watches and Ducati motorcycles were paid for by clients so damaged that it made Stack's blood boil. As he began to interview them, they'd weep with shame, humiliated that they'd given decades of their lives and drained their savings for . . . nothing at all. There was the British solicitor whose husband refused to have children with her, announced that he was leaving her, got diagnosed with pancreatic cancer, and then died—leaving a secret vial of his frozen sperm to a younger woman. There was the Japanese woman whose brain was crawling with tumors, and who had spent so much money on psychic services, hoping to be cured, that she was about to lose her home. There was the schizophrenic Turkish man mourning the death of his father, convinced that the voices he was hearing were spirits. There was the American woman with an enlarged heart who hoped that the spirits would bring her ex-husband back to her. When she died, she was so isolated from her family that they had no idea she'd given all her money to a fortune-teller.

The victims varied, but the techniques for hooking them were largely the same. A grieving, credulous client would leave a personal item with Rose or one of her relatives and come back the next day to receive the bad news that they'd been cursed. Rose would tell them that money was the root of all evil, and then she'd ask for a very specific amount of money—five thousand, say, because "five is your number." She would explain that she was going to cleanse that money, but if the client demanded the money back before her Work was finished, the Work would be undone, and Rose would have to start over from scratch. Above all, she'd say: *Don't discuss this with anybody.*

As the days turned into weeks and months, Rose would grow more intense. The Work would never end, never. She'd call clients in the middle of the night, forcing them to act fast: *Run to the bank! This is a spiritual emergency.* She'd be kind, re-winning their trust, and then suddenly she'd be cruel. She'd say, "Calm down, calm down, you're getting hysterical." She'd tell them that if they didn't continue the Work, their lives would be utterly destroyed. She'd demand more and more, instructing her victims to sell their houses, to share the proceeds from the sale of their yachts. She and her family members would ask their victims for extremely specific things, like gift cards from Saks and Neiman Marcus, or lingerie and maternity clothes, or Gucci shoes, or a watch to "turn back time." Dazed, her victims would acquiesce to the demands, no matter how bizarre. *Calm down, calm down.* Even when her predictions backfired—like when one client's supposed soul mate ended up in bed with another woman—Rose wouldn't let them escape. If her client asked for their money back, she'd tell them that she'd been forced to "sacrifice" it, or that only "Michael the Archangel" knew where it was. If they *really* protested, they'd wake up one day to find Rose's lawyer at their door, holding a paltry check . . . and an agreement for them to sign that said they had never been the victim of any fraud at the Marks family's hands.

It was the sort of situation that sounded outrageous until you found yourself inside it, twisting and turning in Rose's web. She wove a skillful web—but now it was being investigated. To prove that the Marks women could not, in fact, tell the future, Charlie Stack asked some of their victims to feed them false stories. The psychics were never able to tell the truth from the lies.

✳

On January 15, 2008, Charlie Stack knocked on Jude Deveraux's door. It was a motel door, actually. The romance novelist was living there now, transient and lost. She was dreaming of suicide again. Seventeen years ago, when she met Rose, she may have been miserable, but at least she had her money, her properties, and her health. And now she had nothing at all.

Back in the 90s, when Deveraux and Rose began working on Deveraux's divorce, the novelist had ignored warning sign after warning sign. Even though Rose seemed to have a real gift, there were times when her skills faltered. The much-promised "peaceful divorce" never happened. Instead, Deveraux's husband took *everything* in the divorce—all her hard-earned houses, cars, and cash—and Deveraux got stuck with the bills. Rose had advised her to sign whatever paperwork came her way, saying that her husband would die in three years and so the settlement didn't matter. Seventeen years later, he was still very much alive. "He's now worth millions of dollars," Deveraux said later. "He's much richer than I am."

Still, Rose's one-million-dollars-a-year services were worth it, thought Deveraux. After all, Rose was powerful. *Really* powerful. She told Deveraux that the FBI came to her for advice— along with movie stars, former presidents, Prince Charles, and the Pope himself. Even the long arc of history bent to Rose's will. She informed Deveraux that she had controlled the 2000 Bush-Gore election recount and the dramatic 1987 saving of Baby Jessica from a Texas well. Oh, and the 1973 movie *The Exorcist* was actually based on one of her cases.

Awed by Rose's power, Deveraux continued to write checks. Sometimes the checks she gave Rose were blank. Between 1991, when she met Rose, and 2008, when she met Charlie Stack, Deveraux handed around $17 million to Rose, and in exchange, Rose took control of her entire life. She walked Deveraux through the process of in-vitro fertilization, picked out both the egg and sperm donor, accompanied Deveraux to her fertility appointments, and comforted her through eight devastating miscarriages. She told Deveraux to sell her New York apartment because she'd had a vision that Deveraux's future child would fall from the 21st-floor terrace and die. (Deveraux complied and gave Rose the money from the sale.) Perhaps the novelist would have grown skeptical sooner, had not Rose worked her greatest miracle: in 1997, when Deveraux was fifty years old, she finally had her son.

Her boy, Sam, was perfect. But as he grew up, Rose drew Deveraux further into her web, and the web became more and more bizarre. In 2001, Rose convinced the novelist that her next husband would be the then secretary of state, Colin Powell. To make this romance slightly more believable, Rose asked a friend in Arizona to write letters and emails from "Powell" to Deveraux, as Rose herself didn't know how to use a computer. The correspondence convinced Deveraux completely. In one email, "Powell" wrote, "I am sure that you can imagine how occupied I am with the potential war crisis in place. But . . . I plan on being in Colorado the second week of February for a private vacation and thought perhaps I could break away and meet you." Deveraux was so sure she was talking to the real Colin Powell that she even dared to gossip about Rose to him. In one email, she complained that a simple phone call to her psychic was now costing her hundreds of thousands of dollars. "I hesitate to call her anymore," she wrote.

As the years marched on, Deveraux found herself with less and less money. She was still writing and selling books, but Rose was draining her bank accounts as fast as she could fill them. And so she moved to rural North Carolina with her son, to live a simpler, cheaper life in the country. Sam was eight years old then, a playful kid who loved to fish and hunt. The two of them were happy there. But those old, dark forces that Rose was never able to control were still operating just out of sight, and on October 6, 2005, they descended on Deveraux with a vengeance.

That evening, Deveraux was making dinner. Sam was playing with a friend down the road. He'd driven there on his little motorized bike. As Deveraux cooked, she kept looking out her kitchen window, because she knew Sam would be back soon. It was getting dark.

At his friend's house, Sam knew he wasn't supposed to be out after dark. And so when he saw that night was falling, he got back on his bike and drove as fast as he could back to the warm house where his mother waited for him with dinner. But there were no lights on those country roads. And the darkness was falling fast.

The truck driver, going sixty miles an hour, never saw him.

When Sam died, Deveraux collapsed—and Rose was right there to catch her. Rose arranged the funeral, the burial, and the sale of the North Carolina house, since Deveraux couldn't bear to live there anymore. (As for the money from the sale? Rose kept it.) She even rented an apartment in Florida for Deveraux, where the author spent the next two and a half years weeping in the fetal position.

These gestures seemed like the work of a kind, caring friend. But behind the scenes, Rose was spinning her web tighter and tighter. After all, Rose said, the Work could not stop for death.

In fact, the Work was more vital than ever—said Rose—because there was a chance that Sam's soul would be thrown into hell itself unless Rose intervened. Deveraux sat there, listening blearily to talk of flames and damnation and "some really serious black magic people" who had been hired by her ex-husband to curse Sam forever . . . and wrote checks when Rose told her to write checks.

The narrative grew stranger and stranger. Rose told Deveraux that she had *always known* Sam would die, which is why she'd stashed away one of the embryos from Deveraux's IVF procedure eight years earlier. According to Rose, she had given this embryo to a virgin named Cynthia Miller, and the virgin had given birth to Sam's biological brother. Before long, Deveraux would die and be reincarnated into the body of the virgin, and would then become the bride of none other than the actor Brad Pitt. Yes, Brad Pitt was having marital problems with Angelina Jolie, Rose said, and to prove it, "he" began writing Deveraux from the email address legend0999@yahoo.com.

Later, Deveraux would admit that her willingness to believe was, frankly, unbelievable. But at the time, she was in such a fog of despair that Rose's stories didn't look like fraud to her. They looked like a lifeline. She changed her will, leaving everything to "Cynthia Miller," her future reincarnated self. She left her door unlocked—just like Rose told her to—so that once she died, Rose could come in and go through her belongings. And one day, she met Rose on the beach to see a vision of her future. There, Rose pointed into the distance, where a woman and a little boy were walking across the sand, and told Deveraux that she was looking at the empty, soulless bodies of "Cynthia Miller" and her own biological son. Deveraux watched the two figures walk across the sand—and she hoped.

And so when Charlie Stack knocked on her motel door and told her that he was investigating Rose Marks, aka Joyce Michael, for fraud, Deveraux didn't believe him. She didn't believe anything he said until he told her one small, brutal piece of information: "Cynthia Miller," the supposed virgin who had given immaculate birth to Sam's brother, was no mystical, otherworldly vision of the future. She was Rose's daughter-in-law.

"It was like someone hit me with a hammer," Deveraux said. "I realized it was all a scam."

✳

THREE AND A HALF YEARS LATER, CHARLIE STACK'S INVESTIGATION was finally finished. On Tuesday, August 16, 2011, Rose Marks and her family were arrested and charged with sixty-one counts of wire fraud, mail fraud, conspiracy to commit mail fraud and wire fraud, and money laundering. (Fortune-telling itself isn't illegal, and neither is belief in spirits, so the case against the Marks family always centered around money.) "I've reported about lot of fraud cases in South Florida, but this one is twisted enough to make me say: Wow!" wrote a reporter for the *South Florida Business Journal*.

Deveraux had proven vital to the investigation. After her come-to-Jesus moment in the motel room, she'd flipped on Rose—and gone undercover. Stack instructed her to stay in touch with Rose and play along with her mind games; in the meantime, he was recording their phone calls. In one of the calls, which would eventually be played at Rose's trial, Deveraux tried to ask for her money back. All those millions and millions of dollars, given to Rose for cleansing and safekeeping—where were they now?

Rose was ready with her answer. "I don't have any money to give you," she declared.

"What happened to it all?" asked Deveraux.

"It all went. It all burned in the fire."

"What fire?"

"The fire, the 9/11 fire. It all burned. It's gone."

Much of it *was* gone—not because of the 9/11 attacks on the World Trade Center, but because Rose and her family members had spent it. In the long indictment against the Marks family, money was by far the primary theme, though in between charges of a $27,000 personal check here and a $373,750 wire transfer there, the family was accused of other, stranger things, like taking the wedding veil of a victim's mother, or demanding that someone bring them a bedsheet in order for the Work to continue. (The indictment also asked the family to forfeit "approximately $1,884,630 worth of gold coins"—the family would often demand these coins from their victims, perhaps because gold seemed more spiritual than a check from Bank of America.)

Eventually, all eight of Rose's family members pled guilty. They were ordered to pay back millions of dollars in restitution to their victims and given fairly slim sentences: a few years in prison, a bit of probation, several months of house arrest. Only Rose refused to admit that she'd done anything wrong. And so, in August 2013, she went to trial.

Many of her former clients took the stand, including Deveraux. They told the courtroom everything: how sad they'd been, how much they'd dared to hope, how much they'd lost. At points, both the judge and Rose's defense lawyer expressed skepticism at their stories, wondering how anyone in the world could be so gullible. Many of these victims were wealthy, educated people—what in the world were they thinking, selling their houses because a fortune-teller said that Michael the Archangel wanted them to? At one point, when the federal prosecutor tried to argue that Rose's schemes were "sophisticated," the judge snapped, "It's ridiculous. It's absurd. How is it sophisticated? It's a completely ridiculous story that some people actually believed or were convinced to believe was possible or true."

The stories *were*, in their way, ridiculous. (One of the victims admitted that she'd been conned into buying her fortune-teller a vacuum cleaner because the "spirits" wanted a new one.) But on the witness stand, the victims didn't always try to justify their behavior—they just tried to explain how powerless they'd felt. "Whatever Joyce Michael told me to do, I did," said one of them. Another said, "I was doing things I wouldn't normally do. I don't take crap from anybody. I don't let anybody boss me around. It was just the strangest feeling . . . it was as if someone just spun me around."

Despite all the talk of hellfire and gold coins and vacuum cleaners, Rose's trial was really about the rather prosaic question of fraud. The question was simple: Did Rose promise to return her clients' money and then refuse to return it? After nearly a month of testimony, it was pretty obvious to the jury that the answer was yes. They found her guilty on all counts.

✸

TODAY, ROSE IS SERVING HER TEN-YEAR SENTENCE IN A FEDERAL prison in Illinois. She regrets her behavior, and yet she believes that she's innocent, according to her sons. Her clients were her friends. Her *friends*. That's precisely what she called them at her sentencing, as she sobbed out her apology, occasionally struggling to breathe. "We grew old together and shared very intimate details of our lives with one another," she cried. "Those once-in-a-lifetime friendships I have lost forever and I will regret that for the rest of my life."

Did Rose know that she was doing something wrong? Or did she honestly believe she was helping her friends? Her youngest son, Michael, thinks that something changed when she lost her husband, parents, and grandson. "I think that she probably started making promises to her clients," he says. "I think that the gambling addiction had a lot to do with the decisions that she made toward the end. Charging more money, asking for more money." That being said, he doesn't believe his mother committed a crime. He thinks she provided a service—a solace, even. And anyway, he says, she's not all that unique. "There's nothing that she did that any other fortune-tellers don't do," he says. "I think it just got under a microscope because of the investigation that was going on."

The tragedy at the heart of Rose Marks's life was that whether or not she believed in her own promises, it *almost* didn't matter. She'd been raised to tell fortunes. She'd been working since she was eight or nine years old. She never had a chance at another way of life. In 2016, her family sent a letter to the judge who had sentenced her, begging him to withdraw his judgment. "Her offenses have been very much a part of our culture," the letter ran. "This was her understanding but that is done now and will remain so understandably." As soon as Rose was born a girl, her fate was laid out for her. No one put a gun to her head. And yet. "I think it's tragic," says Michael. "She's a very intelligent woman. She could have been the president."

At the age of 65, Rose earned her GED in prison. Her family praised this accomplishment in that same letter to the judge: "May not seem like much but for the Romani community it's a major achievement considering she's never gone to school and hardly knew how to read or write." After getting her GED, she realized how important dictionaries were, which inspired her to write her own. Using her old nickname, she self-published *Pinkey's Dictionary* on Amazon; it promises to teach readers "over 1,000 words translated from English to Gypsy!" The cover is pink and features a shower of gold coins. Her family's request to the judge as well as all her petitions for early release have been denied.

Jude Deveraux and Charlie Stack have become good friends. He even introduced her to the art of boxing, which helped her re-enter the real world—and start writing again. These days, she's writing murder mysteries, and spends almost half of every year on a world cruise, where she writes "like a fiend," according to her website. "When something rotten happens to me, I can often settle my mind by figuring out how to put the incident into a novel," she declares in her FAQ section. "Now that I'm writing murder mysteries, I have a list of people I want to kill."

And as Rose serves her time in prison, people all over the world continue to squeeze what they can out of those who dare to believe. In the spring of 2019, the *New York Times* published a piece called "Psychic Mediums Are the New Wellness Coaches," and then another titled "Venture Capital Is Putting Its Money Into Astrology," which identified the "mystical services market" as worth $2.1 billion. The world of belief is a tangled web. Some who offer belief are prosecuted, others are praised. Some believers go to the cops; others stay faithful until the end. Everyone wants to believe in something. Everyone longs for solid ground. This longing makes humans tender and hopeful and open—and able, of course, to be tricked.

While Silicon Valley tries to extract money from crystals, Michael Marks says that, in the storefronts where Rose used to run her empire, new fortune-telling shops have opened up. "It's kind of like . . . the mafia," he says. "You eliminate one family, all you're doing is creating an open territory for another family to take over." And somewhere, a sad woman is looking at a little window, all lit up, and wondering if she should walk through the door.

THE FABULISTS

1. THE ANASTASIAS
2. ROXIE ANN RICE
3. THE TRAGEDIENNES
4. BONNY LEE BAKLEY

MISCELLANIA

TWO BAD RUSSIAN ACCENTS
ONE DECENT GHANAIAN ACCENT
TWO EXPLOSIVE GERMAN HEADLINES
ONE SELF-PUBLISHED BOOK
TWO SELF-PUBLISHED SONGS
ONE PILE OF POTATOES
COPIOUS FAKE HUSBANDS AND BOYFRIENDS
ONE NFL PLAYER'S CREDIT CARD
SEVEN FAKE PREGNANCIES, POSSIBLY EIGHT
FOUR REAL PREGNANCIES
ONE *DR. PHIL* APPEARANCE
ONE NUDIST COLONY
TWO REAL SCARS USED IN FAKE STORIES
ONE NIGHTMARE NANNY
ONE PASTA DISH NAMED AFTER A CELEBRITY

THE ANASTASIAS

1918-today

IT WAS A COLD FEBRUARY NIGHT IN 1920 WHEN A BERLIN POLICE-man saw the young woman jump off the bridge. He dragged her out of the river, wrapped her in a blanket, and tried to get her to explain herself. She wouldn't talk to him. He took her to a local hospital. She wouldn't talk to the doctors or nurses, either. So they nicknamed her *Fräulein Unbekannt*: "Miss Unknown."

Miss Unknown intrigued everyone who saw her. She was clearly traumatized by something. Her teeth were rotting, and her skin was riddled with scars. There was one on her foot that looked like it could have been made by a bayonet. At the same time, she seemed mysteriously well-bred. *Who was she? What had she seen?* Since she wouldn't speak to anyone at the hospital, they sent her along to an asylum, where she stayed silent for nearly two more years.

In the fall of 1921, Miss Unknown wandered into the asylum's library, where she spotted an issue of the magazine *Berliner Il-lustrirte Zeitung*. On its cover, there was a haunting photograph of several young women, all presumed to be dead. They were the daughters of the last Russian Tsar, the lost Romanov princesses, and most people suspected that they had been gunned down by revolutionary bullets over three years earlier. But others held on to an improbable hope. Beneath the photograph ran the headline: "Lebt eine Zarentochter?"

Does a Tsar's Daughter Live?

Miss Unknown turned red and began to shake.

✳

IF YOU READ ABOUT THE FOUR DOOMED ROMANOV PRINCESSES IN A fairy tale, it would seem obvious that Anastasia was the one destined for adventure. She was the youngest daughter of Russia's last imperial family, born to the weak-willed Tsar Nicholas II and his wife, Alexandra Feodorovna, loathed by her people. Anastasia's older sisters Olga, Tatiana, and Maria were dreamy and pretty; her little brother, Alexei, was sickly and pampered; but Anastasia was the fun-loving one. The rascal. While her sisters drifted around in white dresses, flirting with the guards, she was scrambling up trees and throwing snowballs with rocks hidden inside of them. "The originator of all mischief," one lady-in-waiting called her. "In naughtiness she was a true genius," remembered a playmate.

For sixteen years, Anastasia lived a charmed, monotonous life—and then came the revolution. The Romanov family had ruled over Russia for three centuries, but people were growing restless with the indecisive ways of this last Tsar. In March of 1917, striking workers and furious soldiers forced Anastasia's father to give up his throne, and the entire family was arrested. By the fall, Vladimir Lenin's Bolsheviks had seized power from the scattered provisional government that sprang up after Nicholas's abdication, and by the following spring, the imperial family was transferred to the city of Yekaterinburg—a hostile, Tsar-hating place—and locked up in a mansion called Ipatiev House. There, the entire family waited submissively for someone to determine their fate, while Lenin's revolutionaries argued about what in the world they should *do* with the damned royals.

By midnight on July 16, 1918, the revolutionaries had decided. A guard woke the imperial family up and told them to go down into the cellar.

For decades, no one knew what happened next. Some people were pretty sure the entire family had been slaughtered, but then again, no one had caught so much as a glimpse of a Romanov body. And so the rumors started. Maybe the entire family went free. Maybe some of them died, but others survived. Maybe, just maybe, a princess had escaped. The lack of information and wealth of rumors created a "fertile soil," as one historian put it, for imposters to rise up.

At first, there were only a couple of these imposters, hawking their dramatic tales of survival and asking sympathetic Russians for money. And then there were tens of them, and then *hundreds*, each fake prince or princess claiming that the entire family had died except for them, the chosen ones. (There were rumors that the Romanovs had a lot of money hidden in banks across Europe—reason enough for an impoverished con artist to try on their identity for a month or two.) One Anastasia appeared as early as the fall of 1918, mere months after the mysterious activity in the Ipatiev House cellar. She managed to snag an audience with the wife of a Romanov prince, but the wife didn't believe her tale. A few months later, a woman in a Siberian convent declared that *she* was the Empress Alexandra and the two children at her side were Alexei and Anastasia. The Bolsheviks eventually exposed her. But the imposters just kept coming.

There were fake Tatianas, and Olgas, and Marias, and every now and then a really bold con man would claim to be the Tsar himself (a risky move, since the Tsar's face was so recognizable), but the most memorable imposters always turned out to be the Anastasias—the shadow selves of the youngest, most rambunctious princess. As sloppy as their stories were, most of them found an audience. After all, their timing was impeccable. They were performing for a world that was desperate for happy endings. This was a world reeling from the First World War, a world that sensed revolution around every corner, a world where the *Titanic* could sink, and dynasties could fall, and there was no reason to believe in fairy tales anymore—unless a princess could rise from the grave. And so a strange hope spread across the globe. *Does a Tsar's daughter live?* Maybe, people thought. After all, if anyone could have survived whatever happened in that cellar, it would have been a girl like Anastasia.

✳

MISS UNKNOWN, WANDERING THROUGH THE HALLS OF THE ASYLUM with her copy of *Berliner Illustrirte Zeitung*, was really a young Polish woman named Franziska Schanzkowska, but nobody in the

Berlin asylum knew that. And so, when she solemnly informed them that she was Anastasia Romanov, riddled with scars and silenced by the trauma she'd been through, people sat up and took note.

Franziska had always felt that she was destined for greatness. She had noble ancestors, but by the time she herself was born, the last scraps of wealth had been stripped off her family tree. There was no gold for Franziska. No adoring recognition. There was only farmwork—which she hated. Instead of working in the fields, she was always running away and curling up with a book somewhere. She was also extremely close to her father in a way that seemed a little odd. They were so intimate, and her relationship with her mother was so obviously strained, that some historians have speculated she may have been a victim of incest. If true, that would at least partially explain her desire to escape from her real life. Or maybe she just had a princess fantasy, like so many other little girls. "She was always talking about how she wanted to be someone grand, someone important," said one of her friends.

But her adult life was anything but grand. In fact, misery seemed to follow Franziska like a dark cloud. After her father died, she moved to Berlin and found a dangerous job: polishing live grenades at a munitions factory. Her health was already poor, and one day at work she fainted—and dropped the grenade she was holding. It rolled toward the line foreman and exploded, blowing the man into a million pieces. Franziska had a nervous breakdown and ended up hospitalized. After she was released, she found a new job working in an asparagus field, where she was brutally attacked by a male coworker. Her attacker battered her face and body so badly that he left scars—scars that some people later thought were the work of a Bolshevik bayonet.

Wounded, traumatized, guilt ridden, grieving: this was Franziska's life when she leaped off that Berlin bridge in 1920. Upon being rescued, she refused to tell her story—maybe she *couldn't*—and so she passed the next two years in total silence. And then she saw that magazine, with the ghostly, romantic photograph on the cover, and that alluring question, which was almost a challenge:

Does a Tsar's Daughter Live?

Franziska pored over the magazine for a while, then asked a nurse if she noticed any resemblance between Anastasia and herself. The nurse finally admitted that she did look a little bit like the lost princess. At that, Franziska began to talk, flushed and trembling. *I* am *Anastasia*, she explained. Her entire family had been murdered in the cellar of Ipatiev House, but she'd merely fainted—and woken later in the back of a cart. She'd been saved by a Polish soldier who smuggled her into Romania and then raped her during one of her long periods of unconsciousness. She got pregnant. In Romania, she went into labor, gave up her child, and eventually made her way to Berlin, intending to kill herself there rather than live with the shame of being a disgraced princess. And that—said Franziska—was the real story of Anastasia Romanov.

As word of Miss Unknown's new identity spread through the city, the local Russian émigrés decided to see this woman for themselves. *Could it be?* At the asylum, they found a strange woman who hid behind her bedsheet when she was overwhelmed. If they were being honest, they had to admit that she looked nothing like their lost princess. *And yet.* She was about the same age (how odd!) and had Anastasia's distinct gray-blue eyes (what were the chances?) and somehow, impossibly, she even suffered from the same malformation of the big toe (called *hallux valgus*) that Anastasia had. They couldn't possibly write her off just yet. The *what if* was too compelling.

So they'd try to jog Franziska's memory by telling her stories about the imperial family, stories that Franziska would cleverly file away for the future. She was a quick study, dropping impressive "insider" facts into conversation that she'd picked up from newspapers, photographs, or previous visitors. If all else failed, she'd fall silent, which was one of her simplest, greatest tricks. Her silence gave her a convincingly royal air, and plenty of people who met her were sure that whoever she was, she *had* to be aristocracy. "My reason cannot grasp it," said one of Anastasia's aunts after meeting her, "but my heart tells me that the Little One is Anastasia."

Others were positive that she was nothing but a base imposter. "I saw immediately that she could not be one of my nieces," wrote another aunt, Princess Irene of Prussia. "I could see nothing of the tsarina in her," wrote Crown Princess Cecilie of the German imperial family in 1925 (but then, decades later, she changed her mind: "I am convinced she is the tsar's youngest daughter"). Anastasia's former music teacher took a quick look at Franziska and declared, "There is not the slightest resemblance with my dear little pupil."

Franziska changed her name several times, but eventually began calling herself "Anna Anderson"—which is how she's remembered today—and her Anastasia act was so bad that it would have been laughable if everyone's emotions weren't running so painfully high. First of all, she didn't speak Russian. (Her excuse: the language of her parents' killers was simply too traumatizing for her to speak.) She didn't look like Anastasia: her lips were thicker, her nose was longer, and her profile was completely different. She didn't understand how Russian Orthodox church services worked. And when people asked her what *really* happened in the Ipatiev House cellar, she was shockingly inconsistent: sometimes she said she hid behind Olga, other times she said she hid behind Tatiana; sometimes she claimed that she had fainted, but other times she said she was beaten into unconsciousness, or even shot in the neck.

Still, to a true believer, her failings and inconsistencies could always be explained away through the lens of trauma. (Of *course* she didn't remember which dead sister she hid behind during the gunfire. Would you?) She became something of a mirror: when you looked at her, you saw whatever you wanted to see. For example, sometimes she could be found studying photographs of the Romanovs in total silence. To skeptics, this looked like a con woman doing her homework. But to believers, this looked like a princess communing with the ghosts of her past.

In 1927, seven years after Franziska jumped in the river, a Berlin newspaper uncovered her real identity and published a dramatic exposé with the headline "Unmasked!" The article declared once and for all that this woman with the mysterious scars was not, in fact, the Grand Duchess Anastasia Romanov of Russia, but was merely a Polish farmer's daughter. The exposé should have ruined Franziska's burgeoning career. But it didn't. The people who believed that she was Anastasia simply ignored the facts and went on believing.

They believed her even when she began acting out. After being released from the asylum, Franziska began moving from place to place, always dependent on the charity of her Russian supporters. They fed her. They housed her. They bought her fancy dresses. In return, she was a nightmarish houseguest: rude, sulky, and prone to explosions of imperial anger. Sometimes she raved that she would "pave the streets with the skulls of her enemies." But her anger only convinced them further. After all, who is entitled to rant and rave and make extreme demands—if not a princess?

✳

ACROSS THE OCEAN, ANOTHER WOMAN WAS STOMPING AROUND IN A royal rage. For twenty-five years, a Ukrainian woman named Eugenia Smith had been living on charity in Chicago. "Charity" was perhaps the wrong word. She was living in style, fawned over as an honored houseguest, because her hosts were positive that they were feeding, housing, and protecting the last Romanov princess herself.

Eugenia arrived in the United States in 1922 and had been dropping subtle hints that she was Anastasia ever since. For years, she took odd jobs in Chicago while occasionally working on a tell-all memoir and accepting help from any wealthy Chicagoans who felt bad about how the Romanov family had, um, disappeared. Just like Franziska, she was a terrible guest. "She was difficult to live with, she was unhappy, and she found fault with my friends," said one of Eugenia's hostesses, "but she seemed so lost that I wanted to help her."

As Franziska grew more and more famous for being "Anastasia"—to the point where Ingrid Bergman actually played her in the 1956 film *Anastasia*—Eugenia languished in American obscurity. But by 1963, Eugenia had had enough. *She* was the real Anastasia, she declared. It was time that the world started talking about *her*.

And so, at sixty-four years old, Eugenia traveled to New York City, clutching a box with a large manuscript inside, and showed up at the doorstep of the publisher Robert Speller and Sons. She had a book full of Russian bombshells, she said, and she wanted to see it in print. The publishers read it. At first, Eugenia claimed that she was merely a friend of the real Anastasia, but Speller and Sons suspected that Eugenia knew more than she was letting on, because her manuscript was packed to the gills with insider information. "It read real," said Robert Speller Sr. "It didn't sound objective so much as it was subjective. It read like, 'This is something I experienced.'" The Spellers pressed her, and finally Eugenia admitted it: she was no friend of the family, she was Anastasia herself.

Before long, *Life* magazine was knocking on Eugenia's door with plans to write about her and publish an excerpt of her memoir, and the article, titled "The Case for a New Anastasia," was published on October 18, 1963. The article noted that Eugenia had passed thirty hours of lie detector tests without so much as breaking a sweat, and quoted a respected psychiatrist who declared that "the findings of these interviews have indicated to me the possibility of Mrs. Eugenia Smith being the Grand Duchess

Anastasia of Russia." (Across the Atlantic, Franziska read the article and exploded with anger.)

Granted, the article wasn't all positive—not even close. As had happened with Franziska, people who had known the real Anastasia came to see Eugenia for themselves, and many of them left unimpressed. Anastasia's cousin declared that "the whole face is wrong" and "the Russian accent is not at all right." Anthropologists compared photos of Anastasia with those of Eugenia and found that Anastasia's face was more symmetrical than Eugenia's, and that their noses were very different. Their handwriting was also visibly dissimilar, and in fact, Eugenia had a lot of trouble writing in Russian. For example, when writing the Russian word for "greetings," she messed up two of the letters and ended up with the word "inoculate." One would almost think that she wasn't Russian at all.

Ignoring the skeptics, Eugenia dove headfirst into her new life as an official Anastasia contender. She moved to Newport, Rhode Island, where she filled her apartment with Russian Orthodox iconography and portraits of her "parents," Nicholas and Alexandra. She spent hours making borscht. She even met up with one of the Alexei imposters and announced that he was indeed her long-lost younger brother—a surprising twist, since her memoir claimed that Alexei had been killed.

But the princess fantasy was stronger than any of Eugenia's inconsistencies. The people who longed to believe her simply chose to believe her and would not be shaken. Strangely, the person most emotionally affected by Eugenia's story may have been Eugenia herself. On the forty-fifth anniversary of the Romanov family's disappearance, Eugenia attended a Russian Orthodox memorial service. She wore gloves and a flowered hat. She clutched a candle. During the service, she stared straight ahead of her, looking for all the world like she was remembering some unspeakable loss. Her eyes were filled with tears.

✳

FOR MOST OF THE TWENTIETH CENTURY, THE ENTIRE WORLD BElieved that the bodies of the Romanovs would never be found—if there actually *were* bodies, if they actually *had* died. After the Romanovs walked down to the Ipatiev House cellar, they more or less vanished into thin air. Lenin's government pretended that they had no idea what had happened to those pesky old royals. Had they died? Survived? Escaped? Been buried six feet under? Who could say? In 1924, a criminal investigator named Nikolai Sokolov went searching for their bodies, but found nothing more than a bit of ash, a bone or two, and a severed finger. He concluded that the Romanovs *had* died, but that their bodies had been chopped up, doused in acid, and burned completely. It was the only plausible explanation for both the lack of living Romanovs and the lack of Romanov bodies, he thought. Most people accepted his conclusion.

But a few remained skeptical. Would a regular bonfire be able to destroy not just all those bodies, but all those sets of *teeth*? Decades later, in 1979, a geologist named Alexander Avdonin and a filmmaker named Geli Ryabov decided that they were going to dig for the Romanov bodies themselves. They met up with the son of Yakov Yurovsky—the man who had last been in charge of

guarding the Romanovs—who handed them something definitive and damning: a copy of Yurovsky's report to the government
about what, exactly, had happened in that cellar. Using the information in the report, the geologist and filmmaker located what
they thought was the site of the Romanovs' burial. They dug. They
knelt down and felt around in the dirt with their hands. They
touched something cold. "We felt the parts of no fewer than nine
bodies," said Ryabov. "We pulled up some skulls and the hipbone
of Nicholas II."

Ryabov and Avdonin didn't tell anyone what their hands had
just touched. Given the tense political climate in Russia at the
time, the two felt that their news was just too explosive. So they
reburied the bones, and didn't breathe a word of their discovery until 1989. By the summer of 1991, Russia's president, Boris
Yeltsin, ordered a commission to officially dig up the bodies.
The commission could tell from the state of the bones that the
violence done to the Romanovs had been enormous. Their bones
were disfigured by bullet holes, their skulls had been smashed in
by rifle butts; some of the skeletons were crushed "as though a
truck drove over them." The main archaeologist said that she had
never seen remains that were "so badly damaged—so violated. I
was ill."

Still, something wasn't right. Eleven people should have died
that night (seven Romanovs, three servants, and their family doctor), but there were only nine bodies in the mass grave. Four male,
five female. Young Alexei was clearly missing, as was one of the
princesses, but scientists couldn't agree about who it was. Russian
scientists thought Maria was missing; American scientists were

sure the missing girl was Anastasia. By 1993, DNA testing had confirmed that these were indeed the bones of the Romanovs, but the last two bodies were still nowhere to be found. Hope glimmered in the air. Maybe one of the imposters was actually telling the truth.

✳

THE FINAL ACT OF FRANZISKA SCHANZKOWSKA WAS BIZARRE. FOR decades, she'd lived with other people, but when she finally started living on her own, she became a hoarder. She boarded up her windows and surrounded her yard with barbed wire. She brought in wolfhounds to guard her solitude. She adopted more than sixty cats. She ate very little, preferring to put her food on the floor so that her cats could eat it, which meant that her house was filled with rotting food. When her beloved pets died, she buried them in shallow graves, or tried to cremate them in her own fireplace. Her place smelled so horrible that the neighbors complained.

In 1968, she moved to America and married an eccentric man named Dr. John Manahan. The two of them bought a home in Charlottesville, Virginia, that was soon overflowing with cats, the corpses of cats, rotting dog food, stacks of newspapers, bags of garbage, strange "traps" that Franziska liked to set for potential intruders, and random piles of objects—like an inexplicable mountain of potatoes. She became a local curiosity, a joke. People called her "Annie Apple," and a Charlottesville restaurant advertised its wine by saying that once you had a couple of glasses, you'd start to believe that you were Anastasia Romanov, too.

Sometimes Franziska seemed burdened by her own charade,

hinting to visitors that she was living a double life. Other times, she seemed to revel in her duplicity. Once, she chirped to a dinner guest, "Maybe I am not me. Maybe not. All I care about is let's eat this ice cream!" As she aged, her stories of life in Russia grew weirder: at one point, she claimed that her entire family had hired doubles, and that the doubles were the ones who'd been executed. Sometimes she'd declare that no one had been murdered at all.

As her life drew to a close, perhaps she began to forget that she *wasn't* Anastasia. Prince Nicholas Romanov, one of the tsar's cousins, told the *Washington Post*, "I am certain at the end of her life she believed in her own story, and in a confused way she forgot her own life." The many doctors who examined her agreed that she was "sane, if highly strung," and today, some of her biographers think she may have had a "borderline personality struggling with what today might be classified as post-traumatic stress disorder," but that it was "unlikely that she was actually clinically insane." As always, she was an enigma. But she never stopped claiming to be a princess. She died on February 12, 1984. Her tombstone reads "Anastasia."

DNA, that great equalizer, eventually came for her and her rival. In 1994, scientists tested strands of Franziska's hair and a scrap of her intestine, which proved conclusively that she was not Anastasia Romanov. The next year, Eugenia was asked if she wanted to donate a vial of her blood to be tested. She refused to give scientists a single drop. She lived to the ripe old age of 95, still quietly insisting that *she* was the real princess, and passed away in 1997 (the same year that Disney's animated *Anastasia* came out, a movie that also maintains that Anastasia lived). An article on the Romanovs in the *Chicago Tribune* mentioned Eugenia off-handedly, saying that her tale was "believed by virtually no one." In her obituary, a Russian history expert called her tale "absolute nonsense." By then, it had been almost eighty years since anyone had seen the real Anastasia Romanov. It should have been the end of the little princess's story. But it wasn't.

✳

THE LONG, TORTUOUS QUESTION OF THE ROMANOVS' FATE WAS FI-nally answered in 2009. The final two bodies had been discovered in a second gravesite not far from the first, and DNA confirmed that these were the bones of Alexei and the last of his sisters. It was official: no one had survived the Ipatiev House cellar. None of the women wandering the globe, claiming to be Anastasia, was telling the truth. Anastasia had never lived past seventeen years old.

Here's how her story really ended. Around 1 a.m. on July 17, 1918, Yakov Yurovsky—the cold-blooded, black-mustached head guard of Ipatiev House—woke up the imperial family and told them to dress and come down into the cellar. There was trouble brewing in town, he said. They'd be safer downstairs. The family obeyed, sleepily. Once in the cellar, Yurovsky lined them up against the back wall, explaining that they were going to take a photograph. Just then, eleven other men filed into the room. All of them were armed.

As the family and their servants waited obediently for the photograph, Yurovsky took out a piece of paper. He read it fast: "In view of the fact that your relatives are continuing their attack on Soviet Russia, the Ural Executive Committee has decided to execute you."

"What? What?" said Nicholas, and then Yurovsky shot him in the chest.

The last Tsar of Russia fell to the floor. His wife began to cross herself. She was shot point-blank in the head. The servants and the family doctor were also killed immediately. The executioners fired steadily at the children. Smoke filled the room. Screaming. Shouting. Somehow, the children weren't dying. In fact, the bullets seemed to be bouncing off their clothes. The executioners started to panic. They didn't know it yet, but the children had sewn jewelry into their clothing, and those hidden gems were now acting as armor. Finally, the executioners swarmed around Alexei, stabbing him with bayonets and then shooting him in the head. The princesses clung to each other, screaming. The men turned toward them.

They shot Olga in the head. They shot Tatiana in the jaw. Maria and Anastasia proved harder to kill. The men shot them, and stabbed them, and shot and stabbed them again and again, until finally the two girls lay silent. Suddenly, one of the servants— Anna Demidova, Alexandra's lady-in-waiting—sprang up, saying, "Thank God! God has saved me!" One of the men leaped toward her and bayoneted her until she fell back again. The floor was slippery with blood.

But it still wasn't over. As the men carried the bodies outside toward a waiting truck, Maria and Anastasia sat up, sobbing and choking. Somehow, they were still alive. Their diamonds had protected them too well. One of the guards began crushing their faces with the butt of his rifle. Others, watching this, started to vomit, and ran away. The men carried all eleven of the bodies to a mineshaft and threw them down, and then came back later to move them to an even more secret location. Yurovsky sent one of his men down into the mineshaft to fish around in the chest-deep water until he found the corpses. By then, the bodies were so bloated that Yurovsky couldn't tell the servants from the royals.

This was how Anastasia's story ended—drawn out, horribly, by the very jewels that marked her as a princess.

✳

THE STORY, WHICH HAD TAKEN ALMOST A HUNDRED YEARS TO FINish, was too terrible. Too detailed. Too relentless. It was the opposite of a happy ending. And so there was only one thing left to do: throw out the facts, and cling to the fairy tale. The Anastasias continued to rise up. In 2011, a self-published book appeared on Amazon, titled *The Real Anastasia Romanov: Her Life in the United States After the 1917 Revolution as Told By Her Grand Daughter.* In 2012, an article on Inquirer.net claimed that "Filipino's grandmama could be Russia's Anastasia." In 2014, the *Daily Mail* reported that an "explosive new book" by a "respected Russian historian" had just proven, in retrospect, that Franziska had actually been Anastasia all along. And in 2018, an "amateur genealogist" with a "nagging feeling [he] was onto something" republished Eugenia Smith's memoirs, certain that *she* was the real one. He told one reporter, "Eugenia was also a prolific artist, and there are photographs of Anastasia painting as a teenager in Russia. Was that just coincidence?"

It was a very human reaction to tragedy. "People look for exceptional events to change the past," said Prince Nicholas Romanov, the tsar's cousin. "But history is brutally effective in its solutions, and brutally simple." Who wanted to hear about brutal simplicity, though? Who wanted to hear about bayonets and bloated bodies when you could believe that Anastasia woke up in the back of a truck, saved? Who wanted to debate nose shapes and Russian accents when you could simply convince yourself that your favorite Anastasia was telling the truth? What these Anastasias offered was a form of redemption. The world was cruel, and death was pitiless. Sometimes it came for seventeen-year-old girls. Far better to ignore all the evidence and believe that history was kind, and men had mercy, and princesses lived.

ROXIE ANN RICE

alias: Mrs. Kenneth Houston, Dr. Andiza Juzang, Roxie Ann Christian, Roxie Houston, Lara Borga, Roxanne A. Harris

1955-

THE WOMAN ON THE PHONE SOUNDED AWFULLY INTRIGUING. She had an *accent*. She was name-dropping *celebrities*. But it was December 7, 1974, which meant that it was almost game day, and Rick Forzano of the Detroit Lions *really* didn't have time to talk to journalists. He had a football team to coach. A football team of talented, devastatingly handsome young men—not that Rick Forzano was thinking in those terms. He was just thinking about the next day's game, thinking that he was already running late for the team meal and that he didn't have a whole lot of time to sit around and chat.

But the woman on the phone kept holding his attention. She told him that she worked for the Ghanaian embassy to the United States. Ghana! That's where the accent was from. She explained that she wanted to send over one of her representatives from Ghana to interview Forzano all about the wonderful world of American football. And she just so happened to mention that her boss was none other than Shirley Temple, the child star with the adorable curls, who was all grown up and working as the US Ambassador to Ghana. It was that name—*Shirley Temple*—that did it. Forzano had been obsessed with the actress since he himself was a child. Suddenly his packed schedule didn't seem all that important. He agreed to do the interview that evening, after the team meal, as long as the representative from Ghana brought along a couple of autographed Shirley Temple photos that he could give to his kids.

Several hours later, the representative from Ghana arrived at his door and introduced herself as Dr. Andiza Juzang. At almost six feet tall, she cut an imposing figure in her Ghanaian dress and headwrap (not that Forzano would have been able to tell the difference between a Ghanaian headwrap and an American one—he didn't actually know where the country of Ghana was located). She told Forzano all about her prosperous background: she had studied at the University of Oxford, and her father owned both a plantation and a diamond mine. He also had six wives, she said.

As the two of them talked, Forzano felt glad that he'd made time for the interview. Dr. Juzang was all charm, teasing him about how he wasn't big enough to be a football coach. "You don't look like a coach," she'd say. "You ain't got no whistle!" When she asked to get some pictures of the players—those talented, devastatingly handsome players—Forzano obliged. By the time the interview was over, the two of them were getting along so well that she was inviting him to visit her in Ghana. The request was, admittedly, quite tempting. He could stay at her father's plantation, she said, and as a special gesture of traditional Ghanaian hospitality, he would be allowed to sleep with a different one of her father's six wives every night.

The next day, Forzano's team beat the Cincinnati Bengals by a nerve-racking four points, and Forzano couldn't help feeling like the fantastic interview with Dr. Juzang had, in a way, contributed to their success. Glowing, he filled a box with football parapher-nalia and shipped it to the address that Dr. Juzang had left him, 5,439 miles away in Ghana. He even sat down and wrote a letter to Shirley Temple herself, complimenting her on the "fine repre-sentative" that she'd sent over.

Dr. Juzang never wrote him back. Forzano didn't understand it. Wasn't he supposed to visit her in Ghana? What a disappoint-ment. The whole encounter had been so pleasant. It didn't make sense, he thought, that such a nice woman would just disappear like that.

✹

ON PAPER, THE LIFE OF ROXIE ANN RICE WAS BORING. DEPRESSING, even. She was a teen mom and a college dropout. She lived with her mother in St. Louis. Her father was dead, and her brother was suicidal. Life stretched out ahead of her—same old, same old, same old.

Roxie was born on March 11, 1955, to a hardworking mother of six and a drug-addled dad. She grew into a great student who tested as "gifted" in middle school and was put on an academic fast-track in high school, but she dropped out of high school af-ter a year and joined a Department of Labor program called Job Corps that offered her free education and vocational training.

Maybe she just wanted an excuse to get out of her hometown. Job Corps transferred her to Albuquerque, New Mexico, where she earned the equivalent of a high school diploma and discovered that she had another, more secretive talent: she was a pretty good scammer.

She started with a couple of basic swindles. She faked her references and tricked a local woman into hiring her as a house-keeper. Then, she stole the woman's credit card and checkbook and got out of town. By the fall of 1972, she was attending South-ern University in Baton Rouge, Louisiana—but that, too, was a short-lived experiment. She got pregnant, dropped out after her first semester, and moved back in with her mom. The same year, her father was killed in a drug-related gun battle.

When the fall of 1974 rolled around, Roxie was working a rather boring job at the General American Life Insurance Com-pany in St. Louis. Her mom had remarried and was working mul-tiple jobs to support the family. Earlier that year, Roxie's brother, Roderick, tried to jump from a gigantic bridge that stretched across the Mississippi River. Life wasn't easy for any of the Rice family. If Roxie opened up a magazine, it might have seemed like everyone in the world was out dancing, drinking, and having fun—except for her.

1970s America was firmly in the post–civil rights era, and Black Americans were breaking records right and left: Newark and Los Angeles and Atlanta and Detroit got their first Black may-ors, the Pulitzer Prize for Drama went to a Black playwright for the first time ever, the Congressional Black Caucus was established, the first Black woman posed on the cover of a major fashion publication, the first Black politician campaigned for a presidential nomination, Black History Month and the National Black Feminist Organization were founded, a Black baseball player broke Babe Ruth's home-run record, and magazines like *Essence* and *Black Enterprise* launched. The era wasn't perfect—far from it— but if you were a Black teenager prone to dreaming, 1970s America was a time when you could open up a magazine like *Essence* and see that there were more and more people who looked like you achieving *their* dreams.

And Roxie was always prone to dreaming.

✳

THE WOMAN ON THE PHONE SOUNDED AWFULLY INTRIGUING. SHE said that her name was "Dale," and she was calling with a dramatic story about an orphan from Ghana. It was a terrible story, really, full of loss, slaughter, blood, and loneliness. On the other end of the line, Fred Christian listened, captivated. He wanted to help. He'd do anything that Dale asked him to do.

Christian was a struggling car salesman from St. Louis who could spot a liar from a mile away. He wasn't used to getting phone calls about orphans from Ghana. But this woman—this "Dale"— was so convincing. She told him that they'd met before, at a party in Los Angeles. Christian *had* been at a party in Los Angeles, and though he didn't remember meeting anyone named Dale, she described the party so well that he felt sure that she must have been there, too.

Dale explained that she was calling him because she was worried about her friend, a sweet girl from Ghana who had come to the United States to finish medical school. Unfortunately, her friend was now an orphan and a widow, because back in Ghana, both of her parents and her husband had just been slaughtered in the bloody Mau Mau Uprising. (The Mau Mau Uprising actually happened in Kenya, two decades earlier, but Fred Christian didn't know this.) Now, said Dale, this precious orphan girl was entirely alone in the world. Could Christian take her under his wing? Show her around the city? Help her get back on her feet, etc.? Dale also mentioned, casually, that the girl stood to inherit seventy thousand dollars when she turned twenty-one.

Intrigued, Fred Christian agreed to help.

When Christian met up with the grieving Ghanaian orphan—who introduced herself as Dr. Andiza Juzang—he was instantly charmed by her. He wasn't *attracted* to her, but she was a fantastic conversationalist. So he took her out to dinner. "She's one of the nicest persons I ever met," he said, later. "She was zero physically, but she had a personality like velvet." The two of them quickly became friends. Sometimes, he'd pick her up at one of the hospitals where she worked; once he even saw the girl at the front desk page her, and she came down shortly afterward, chatting easily with her fellow doctors. Dr. Juzang was living in a motel nearby, but when she complained about the noise, Christian decided to let her move in with him for a while.

Despite her velvety personality, there was something about Dr. Juzang that Christian found hard to explain—something almost otherworldly. "Don't quote me as saying the girl's a Martian," he said, "but I know she was privy to what I was thinking. She knew too much—things I never told her." Sometimes Christian would assume that he was alone in the apartment, only to realize with a shock that Dr. Juzang had been sitting there for hours, staring out of a window. He told himself that she was just fascinated by the St. Louis skyline, since she was from Ghana and all. Other times, she would run up his telephone bill by making hundreds of dollars' worth of long-distance calls, and yet when he left cash lying around the apartment, she never touched it. Speaking of phone calls, Christian couldn't help but notice that Dale never called him when Dr. Juzang was around, and though Dale made plans to meet up with him at least five times, she always backed out at the last minute.

Still, none of this was enough to really worry Christian, and so when Dr. Juzang asked to be introduced to his younger brother, Adrian, he complied. If Christian had been entertained by Dr. Juzang, Adrian was completely enamored. "My brother was charmed, you might even say possessed, by that woman," said Christian. Two weeks after meeting each other, Dr. Juzang and Adrian had decided to get married.

Their wedding was on a Saturday. By Monday, Dr. Juzang was gone.

The Christian brothers couldn't believe it. Fred Christian was a car salesman—he was practically trained in the art of identifying fake stories. "If a dude crossed the lot, I can tell when he was going to tell at least three lies," he said, shaking his head. Adrian, abandoned after three days of marriage, was even more shocked. "I'm not bragging, but I thought I was pretty slick," he said. "I was taken in. I knew a totally different person."

It was only after Dr. Juzang vanished that the brothers

acknowledged how strange she'd actually been. "She is a professional liar," Adrian said. "I caught her in a lot of lies and when you keep talking, you trip up sooner or later." Even though Christian was stunned, he couldn't help being impressed by Dr. Juzang's act. "The girl is astute. Her mind is very sharp," he said. He remembered that her "Ghanaian" accent never faltered, not even early in the morning.

✳

ON DECEMBER 7, 1974, ROXIE ANN RICE WALTZED INTO A LOCAL motel and told the owner that she was married to a professional football player.

It had been a busy fall for Roxie. She'd been making up stories—lots and lots of them. One could almost say the stories were her real work, since she quit her job at the General American Life Insurance Company a mere thirty-six days after she started. She'd pretended to be Dale, using her silkiest phone voice to convince Fred Christian that they knew each other from Los Angeles. She'd pretended to be Dr. Andiza Juzang, the grieving orphan and widow from Ghana who was about to inherit seventy thousand dollars. She'd hung out at the local hospital long enough for Fred Christian to believe that she worked there. Hell, she'd even gotten married to Adrian Christian—*married!* And now she was about to hop on a plane to Detroit and interview Rick Forzano of the Detroit Lions while pretending to be a representative from Ghana and the Oxford-educated child of a diamond mine owner. She was going to make him adore her, just like she'd made Fred and Adrian Christian adore her. If her velvety personality didn't charm him, an invitation to sleep with her fictional dad's six wives should do the trick. And then, when she was done interviewing Rick Forzano, she could ask to meet some of his football players—those talented, devastatingly handsome players she loved so much.

But hours before she got on the plane to Detroit, she was planting the seed for another scam, another story. At the Royalty Motel in St. Louis, she walked up to the front desk and informed the owner, Hugh Robnett, that she worked for the National Football League. Her job was to travel around the country, she said, choosing the motels where football players would stay during their away games. She explained to Robnett that once a year, representatives from every professional sports team in the country met up to pick their favorite motels, and if Robnett wanted to slip her a $600 negotiation fee, she would be happy to put in a good word for his Royalty Motel. And why should he trust her? Because she was none other than Roxie Houston, the loving wife of NFL superstar Ken Houston. Look! She even had Ken Houston's credit card.

Ken Houston was a defensive back for Washington, a lean six-foot-three athlete whose face was all over trading cards. His sideburns were lush. His smile quirked up a bit at one side. He was talented, devastatingly handsome—total husband material. He already had a wife, but Hugh Robnett had no idea what she looked like, so when Roxie told him that *she* was Mrs. Kenneth Houston, he believed her. He wasn't ready to give Roxie the $600 she wanted, but he was interested enough to listen to her tale.

After chatting with Robnett as "Mrs. Kenneth Houston," Roxie headed to Detroit to meet up with Rick Forzano as "Dr. Andiza

Juzang." A month later, she reappeared at the Royalty Motel, pressuring Robnett to give her that $600 fee and paying for her room with Ken Houston's credit card. By that point, something about her story wasn't sitting quite right with Robnett, and so he began doing a little digging before handing over $600 to this professional football player's wife who looked an awful lot like a teenager. It didn't take him long to find out that Ken Houston's real wife was named Gustie and was currently in Texas. He called the police, who tracked Roxie to the airport—and arrested her there.

With Roxie booked into jail, a sergeant placed a phone call to a rather surprised Ken Houston, who confirmed that his credit card had been missing since November. Astonishingly, Houston told the sergeant that he actually knew who Roxie was. She'd stayed at his house in DC, he said. But he didn't know her as Roxie Ann Rice; he knew her as Dr. Andiza Juzang, of Ghana. They'd met about a month earlier, when a representative from *Ebony* magazine called him and told him that the magazine was planning to do a story on him—but first, would he mind picking up her friend Dr. Andiza Juzang from the airport? Houston obliged, and "Dr. Juzang" stayed with him and his wife for two days, during which they spoke pleasantly of her life in Ghana and her goals in America. On the third day, she disappeared with his calculator and his credit card.

The police thought it was strange that this nineteen-year-old girl from St. Louis had actually managed to talk her way into being Ken Houston's houseguest. But other than that weird little detail, Roxie's crime seemed fairly straightforward. She had used a stolen credit card at the Royalty Motel. The charge against her was boring: "Attempt Stealing Over $50.00 by Deceit." Just another teenage thief trying to make a quick buck. Nothing terribly serious. Nobody terribly special.

And then Roxie started telling a different story.

✸

BACK IN SEPTEMBER, I MADE A FRIEND, SAID ROXIE.

Her new story was explosive, almost unbelievable. But the police had to believe her—or at least, they had to fact-check her—because if Roxie was telling the truth, then everyone in American sports was in big trouble. And so they listened as she wove her tale. *Once upon a time . . .*

Roxie told them that back in September, while she was still working at the General American Life Insurance Company, she met a Cuban woman named Pat Cleveland on her lunch break. As the two of them chatted, Roxie felt comfortable enough to tell Cleveland all about her troubles. Her son was sick, money was tight, and she was worried.

Cleveland perked up. *You need money? There's someone you've got to meet.*

That someone was Tony, a fifty-something white guy who ran a complicated cross-country drug ring that dealt in the most dangerous, elusive drug of all: marijuana. Cleveland and Tony had been looking to hire a third person, someone who was a quick learner, good with accents, excellent at impersonation. Someone just like Roxie. They explained that they sold drugs to professional athletes all across the country, and they needed her to deliver the drugs. But she couldn't deliver them as "Roxie Ann

Rice," of course. She needed a new identity. So they taught her
all about the history of Ghana, and trained her in the nuances of
the country's accent. They showed her how to bind up her hair in
a traditional Ghanaian fashion. They gave her a white smock and
a stethoscope. And they slipped her an ID that read *Dr. Andiza
Juzang.*

With her hair in a headwrap and a new accent dripping from
her tongue, Roxie plunged into a life of wealth, intrigue—and
talented, devastatingly handsome men. She never knew exactly
where she was going; all she had to do was show up at the airport,
and Cleveland and Tony would take care of the rest. One day,
she'd fly to Miami and hop into a limousine that carried her to a
beachside mansion full of Great Danes, airline stewardesses, and
football players. Another day, she'd be on her way to Los Angeles.
She flew to Dallas, Chicago, Cincinnati, Cleveland, Denver, San
Diego, Houston, Washington, New Orleans, and Kansas City.
She carried a briefcase stuffed with drugs and decorated with
NFL stickers, which she'd swap out for an empty briefcase at des-
ignated drop-off points. Sometimes she and Pat Cleveland would
attend football games, and as they watched the field, mysterious
people would sidle up to them and hand over wads of money,
which Roxie would tuck inside her pockets. (She always wore
clothes with big pockets, just in case.) She spoke with coaches and
people who worked in the NFL's front offices; she met the players
themselves; she even *stayed* with some of them. It was glamorous
work—rubbing elbows with the most physically perfect men in
America—but it could be terrifying, too. Tony was a cruel boss. If

he wasn't happy with her work, he'd threaten her, saying that if she got greedy, he'd hurt her son.

The end, said Roxie.

The St. Louis police couldn't believe their ears. There was no way this story was true—right? They wrote it down anyway in a thirty-nine-page memo and fumed when someone in the station leaked the entire memo to the press. The press, naturally, loved what they were hearing. She wore a *what* and delivered drugs to *who?* By January 22, newspapers all over the country were publishing amused stories about Roxie's fantastical tale. Many of them mocked her height, her weight, and her colorful turbans, noting that she wasn't exactly an inconspicuous figure. How in the world had this costumed teenager managed to infiltrate the highest athletic offices in the country? The whole thing was too bizarre to take seriously—right? Silly Roxie.

The very next day, the laughter died in everybody's throats. A bit of digging revealed that Roxie actually *had* been in many of the cities she said she was in. And people in the NFL *did* remember meeting her, like Jess Peters, the director of promotions and advertising for the Kansas City Chiefs, or Solomon Freelon, a player for the Houston Oilers. (Roxie told Freelon that she was studying the link between water pollution and cancer. "[Drugs] never entered my mind," said Freelon, "because she seemed too interested in water poisoning.") There were records of her receiving press privileges for teams like the Chiefs, the Detroit Lions, and the Minnesota Vikings. Every little detail that emerged made Roxie seem more credible.

In Detroit, Coach Rick Forzano recalled their interview with embarrassed clarity. "I was taken in by her," he told the press. "I don't even know where Ghana is."

✳

FOR A COUPLE OF WEEKS, THE PRESS, THE POLICE, AND THE NFL scrambled to make sense of Roxie's tale. The Drug Enforcement Administration got involved, as did the American Basketball Association, since Roxie had hinted that she and Pat Cleveland had plans to start distributing drugs at basketball games. From jail, Roxie began denying the entire story, but it was too late to take it all back now. The St. Louis administrator of the DEA told the press that her account contained "enough substance to warrant a full-scale investigation." After all, if even a fraction of Roxie's tales were true, the NFL might never recover from the disgrace. They had just weathered an embarrassing drug scandal during which the San Diego Chargers were fined $40,000 for their "widespread use of drugs," and Roxie's story was far worse. According to her, drugs were everywhere in the NFL, being carried in right through the front door in stickered briefcases. People *had* to take her story seriously. The stakes were too high.

For nineteen years, Roxie Ann Rice had been a nobody, but now her name was in headlines all across the nation. "Hollywood material," one headline called her. Journalists dug up the story of her whirlwind marriage to Adrian Christian—a marriage she had apparently abandoned for good—and now he and his brother Fred were talking to the press, spilling all the details of her strange con. (To the brothers, every moment of Roxie's stay with them seemed weird in retrospect. Fred Christian told the press that once she told him that she broke a lamp, but he later found that the lamp wasn't broken, but had instead been taken apart . . . and there was a sticky substance on some of the pieces. *Could it have been glue?* This ominous mystery, if it was indeed something ominous, was never resolved.) Journalists even tracked down her mother, who told the press, "She's an intelligent girl, but she hasn't used it to her ability." The attention must have been overwhelming for Roxie, and maybe even a bit frightening. In jail, she made what police called a "weak effort" to kill herself by cutting herself once on the left wrist. She was taken to the hospital and treated for "sociopathic hysteria, slight depression, and suicidal gestures."

Despite the media frenzy, Roxie was still only charged with credit card fraud. Her trial was set for March 3 and she was let out on bail, while everyone in the sports world waited with bated breath to see whether or not she was telling the truth. From jail, she called Fred Christian three times. He begged her to tell him why she'd conned him, and she would only respond, "Don't worry, they told me to do it."

But there was no *they* there. On February 7, a special agent from the Drug Enforcement Administration announced to the world that Roxie's story was just that: a story. The DEA's investigation hadn't turned up a scrap of evidence that supported her claim of countrywide drug trafficking. Roxie herself was little more than "a very good con woman," the special agent said, and the NFL players she tricked were "very gullible" but "completely innocent." There was no trace of the cryptic Pat Cleveland or the evil Tony. They had been fictional characters, grown straight from the rich soil of Roxie's mind. "As far as we can tell," said the agent, "she was doing this on her own."

Roxie's story was a con within a con, a hall of mirrors with no apparent point. She'd lied about the drug trafficking, but not about meeting the NFL players, though she'd lied *to* the NFL players in order to meet them in the first place. She adopted accents, swiped credit cards, conned Fred and Adrian Christian, pretended to be someone else on the phone. Then she claimed that someone else *told* her to adopt accents, swipe credit cards, con Fred and Adrian Christian, pretend to be someone else on the phone. When you examined her story in retrospect, it was obviously fake. "Tony" didn't have a last name. The "Ghanaian" details were often wildly incorrect (see: the Mau Mau Uprising). And, as Fred Christian told the press, "Nobody goes to that much trouble to sell marijuana." But there was just enough truth in her tales to keep people guessing.

All of her anecdotes had a fairy-tale quality to them: the diamond mine, the six wives, the slaughtered parents, the dead Ghanaian husband, the beachside mansion in Miami full of Great Danes. "Malice in Wonderland," one paper called her. But why had she constructed this wonderland in the first place? If she was working alone—if no one was forcing her to do anything—then what was she doing it all for?

✳

THE CLUE WAS FOUND IN AN UNEXPECTED PLACE. WHEN THE DEA special agent announced that Roxie wasn't actually a cross-country drug mule, he drew his audience's attention to an unusual source: a single issue of *Ebony* magazine.

Roxie had started visiting NFL coaches and players in November of 1974. That same month, *Ebony* magazine published an issue with Marvin Gaye on the cover. On page 143, prancing toward the reader in a swirling purple dress, was a model named Pat Cleveland: one of the decade's biggest supermodels, and one of the first African American models to be signed by a major agency. And starting on page 166, there was something even more delicious: a roundup of the best Black football players of the year. Their photos filled page after page of the magazine, as they grinned at the camera or stared off into the distance or sprinted down the field. Ken Houston appeared on those pages. So did Solomon Freelon. So did every single team to which Roxie would later claim a connection. Page after page of talented, devastatingly handsome men. The effect would have been mesmerizing for a teenage girl prone to dreaming.

In fact, the entire magazine oozed with images of a better life, a life far from St. Louis. There were ads for whiskey, for airline travel, for "Lustrasilk scalp cream" and "clingy lingerie that ties in back" and "exquisite ring bargains" from World Wide Diamond Co. Roxie must have come across the magazine that fall, while she was stuck at her boring job, worried about money, burdened by her family's problems. The magazine was designed to make girls like her dream—and perhaps shell out a little money for clingy lingerie that ties in back. But maybe Roxie was sick of dreaming. Maybe she wanted to turn her dreams into something real. So she picked up the phone.

✳

As soon as the world realized that Roxie Ann Rice was not, in fact, going to bring the entirety of American sports crashing to the ground with her tales of marijuana delivery, they forgot about her. She was back to being plain old Roxie, the teenage thief. Her name dropped from the headlines. Her trial for credit card fraud took place on March 26. She pled guilty, received a $50 fine, and was handed a year of probation. "It was a definite comedown," wrote one journalist.

So Roxie returned to her life of ordinary cons. In October, she was arrested for writing a bad check. In November, she was extradited to New Mexico to answer for those forgery and fraud charges she'd racked up so many years earlier, when she was with the Job Corps and stole her employer's checkbook. In January 1976, she was given two 1–5 year sentences, to be served concurrently.

By the fall of 1978, Roxie was released from prison and put on probation, but she apparently skipped out on her probation, because she ended up in Buffalo, New York. There, she broke out one of her old, familiar lies: she told everyone that she was a doctor. This time, though, she didn't just *tell* people she was a doctor, she actually *worked* as a doctor, racking up a total of $28,000 for her rather DIY medical services. She rented a house from an unsuspecting couple who were happy to have a doctor in the building. They asked her to examine their new baby, which she did. Later, when a dog bit the husband on the face, they begged Roxie to treat the bite. Apparently she handled both situations so professionally that no one became suspicious.

In Buffalo, she became pregnant again, and convinced a local hospital to let her give birth there at a discount, telling them she was a med student. Eventually, though, someone grew suspicious of the young doctor who was going around treating babies and dog bites, and the FBI started looking into her. In October of 1978, she was arrested and charged with "grand larceny by trick" and with violating a state law that specifically forbade people to pose as doctors. When asked about the weird little case, local authorities told the press that Roxie had a "gift for adopting a wide range of accents and professional roles."

Roxie wasn't the first or last con artist to impersonate a doctor. Some of these fake doctors, like Frank Abagnale or Ferdinand Waldo Demara, became renowned for their illicit medical antics. Hollywood made movies about their lives. They became beloved, in a way. But aside from a couple of disgruntled, dog-bitten residents of Buffalo, Roxie's doctor act flew under the radar. At the end of the day, the only people who seemed to appreciate her dubious skills were the men who'd tried to pin her down. "She's a smart girl," said the detective in Buffalo who arrested her. "A woman with a very vivid imagination," said the DEA agent who denounced her. "She's not a dummy," said a reporter who followed her back in St. Louis. "She's sharp and she's playing all the angles."

And Fred Christian—her ex-roommate and brother-in-law of three days—couldn't help but admire the strange power that Roxie had accrued with nothing more than her imagination. "This was better than *The Sting*," he said, referencing the 1973 movie about an elaborate swindle. "She did it better because she didn't have any props." To Christian, Roxie's hoax was an incredible thing, a mystery of wild proportions. "She's a nineteen-year-old poor black girl who got all these important people involved and fooled these people," he mused. "It's awful, awful strange."

It *was* strange. It was impressive, too, even if no one ever made a movie about it. Roxie pled guilty to a misdemeanor charge in Buffalo and was sentenced to forty days in jail. She got credit for time served and was released on November 20, 1978, after which she vanished from the headlines. She has yet to reappear. Maybe she was sent back to New Mexico to finish out her probation. Maybe she returned to St. Louis to live with her mom and raise her children. Or maybe she left Buffalo that autumn and struck out for some brand-new city. She had already treated a dog bite, swindled a car salesman, terrified the Drug Enforcement Administration, discussed water poisoning with football players, faked a connection to Shirley Temple, talked her way into the inner sanctums of the NFL, and fooled a nation—and she was only twenty-three. There were so many stories left for her to tell.

THE TRAGEDIENNES

RUKSANA

The headlines were outraged.

EVIL CONWOMAN

INSURANCE GHOUL

VILE FRAUDSTER

CALLOUS & HEARTLESS

DISGRACEFUL

On paper, the crimes of the forty-four-year-old woman in question seemed fairly inoffensive. She was an insurance fraudster: the most boring con job in the world. She'd stolen money from insurance companies—she hadn't kidnapped a baby or killed anyone. So why all the hate in the headlines?

Ruksana Ashraf was born in Pakistan in the 1970s and raised in Edinburgh, Scotland, by a family that seemed cursed with bad luck. Her father died, her sister was in a terrible car accident and lost her job, and her brother was jailed for being one of the biggest heroin kingpins in Scotland—which left Ruksana to care for their aging mother alone. And Ruksana had plenty of her own troubles. She drank too much; she gambled too much. She suffered through two bad relationships. She was unemployed and living off benefits, the UK's equivalent to welfare. And she had a secret life that no one else in her family knew about.

By 2012, Ruksana was living with her mother and her sister in a decrepit Victorian mansion that had been converted into apartments. There, she turned her room into a little cave full of paper and scissors and SIM cards and lists of addresses. She could often be found there, snipping and pasting, all alone. She was creating a web of names, addresses, email addresses, and bank accounts, and using them to take out a series of home insurance policies. Then, she would start claiming that her things—her beautiful things—had gone missing. She would buy a Louis Vuitton purse and return it the next day but keep the receipt. Then she'd file a claim saying that she'd lost her Louis Vuitton purse—but look! She still had the receipt! Then she'd doctor the original receipt and do it all over again.

Her background was perfect for the work: she had a degree in computing from Edinburgh Napier University and had subsequently worked at Scottish Widows, a company that dealt in life insurance and pensions. Now that she'd gone freelance, so to speak, she was able to keep numerous policies and claims bubbling along at the same time. She would doctor her receipts with scissors, glue, and photocopy machines; she'd switch out the SIM card in her phone so that she was able to call each insurer from a different number. To find addresses to use in her policies, she'd look for homes that had recently changed hands. (She knew that when a new homeowner receives mail with someone else's name on it, they're not suspicious.) And so, with her technique perfected, she continued to file claim after claim: for Gucci leather loafers, for Louis Vuitton Moon Shadow sandals, for iPads and iPhones, for bars of gold.

In this secret life, Ruksana was crafty—but not terribly creative. Her claims were all quite similar, and eventually one of her insurance companies started to grow suspicious. They notified the City of London's Insurance Fraud Enforcement Department (IFED), and IFED police tracked Ruksana down. But she refused to speak, and since there were still a number of inquiries that needed to be carried out before convicting her, the police released her.

This was a close call for the fraudster. She realized that she couldn't keep filing the same sorts of *help I lost my iPhone* claims over and over again. She needed something else. Something new and fresh. Something that would make insurance companies bow to her every demand.

And then tragedy struck the United Kingdom. On May 22, 2017, fans were filing out of an Ariana Grande concert at England's Manchester Arena, when a suicide bomber detonated a homemade explosive device full of nuts and bolts. The metal bits tore off limbs and ripped through hearts, killing twenty-two concertgoers and wounding more than one hundred others, many of whom were children. Twelve days later, three extremists drove a van onto London Bridge, right into a crowd of happy people, and then leaped out of the vehicle and began attacking people with knives, leaving eight dead and forty-eight wounded before police shot the assailants down. Eleven days after that, a huge fire scorched through Grenfell Tower, a public housing block in London without sprinklers or working fire alarms. Seventy-two people never made it out. The bodies of entire families were discovered in the hallways, clinging to each other.

Three horrible tragedies, in less than a month.

Ruksana's ears perked up.

ASHLEY

THE HEADLINES WERE ABSURD.

POSSIBLY MADE UP HUSBAND

FAKE PREGNANCY PART OF A CON

FABRICATED FIREFIGHTER

STUFFING A CUSHION UP HER BLOUSE

In 2018, California—a place always prone to burning—experienced its worst wildfire season yet. The rest of America watched, horror-struck, as flames engulfed the state. What could they do? They donated to the Wildfire Relief Fund and the California Fire Foundation. They bought T-shirts and bottled water off Amazon wish lists. They opened up their homes to evacuees. It didn't feel right to just sit there and do nothing. And so, when a pretty blond firefighter's wife named Ashley Bemis started raising money for her brave husband, people were thrilled to chip in.

On August 10, Ashley posted in her local Facebook group, saying that her husband, Shane Goodman, was fighting the Holy Fire—a brutal Southern Californian blaze that consumed 23,136 acres and forced thousands of people to evacuate their homes. Her post was frantic. "Shane works for Cal Fire and is out on the Holy Fire right now," she wrote. "I also have two other family members and many friends out on this fire and other fires burning here in California. I received a text today from Shane saying it's pretty much a living hell out here battling the unpredictable 'Holy Hell Fire.'" The post went on to say that any donations for Shane and his coworkers would be much appreciated, and that she would be happy to meet up with donors who wanted to drop off supplies. She even included a helpful list of all the things that her husband and his coworkers needed: bottled water, socks, underwear, facial wipes, Gold Bond powder, protein bars, T-shirts, air mattresses, earplugs, candy . . .

Within a week, Ashley had raised about eleven thousand dollars' worth of cash and supplies. The Holy Fire was still raging, and her handsome husband was still on the front lines of the inferno—and oh, as his Facebook profile picture showed, was he handsome!—but this overwhelming response from her community was as happy an ending as a terrified little wife could hope for.

Ashley's life, up until that point, had been a series of unhappy endings. Her number one goal in life was to have a family—a *good* family—but that dream had proven elusive again and again. Her parents divorced when she was young, and her dad left her with the impression that he "didn't want anything to do with" her and her mother. When her mother did find love again, it was a sordid, secretive love: she started having an affair with a married man. Ashley found their relationship infuriating. She believed that the man was just using her mother. So she told everyone who would listen that the man had raped her.

But no one listened, not really. And all the men in her life continued to disappoint her. For a while, Ashley's grandfather became more involved in her life as a surrogate father figure, but that relationship deteriorated when he "believed something that his second wife told him"—Ashley wouldn't specify what that *something* was—and cut Ashley out of his life. Her boyfriends were no better. They lied to her. They cheated on her. They left her feeling, she said, like a "very broken person." At a certain point, she believed it was better to retreat from real life altogether than to continue bothering with these terrible men. Better to construct a fantasy, where everything could go her way. And what was more fantastical than a raging inferno?

TANIA

THE HEADLINES WERE APOCALYPTIC.

ATTACKED

ACT OF WAR

A CREEPING HORROR

DEATH TOLL "HORRENDOUS"

CHOREOGRAPHY OF CARNAGE

AMERICA'S DARKEST DAY

On the perfect blue morning of September 11, 2001, two hijacked airplanes crashed into the twin towers of the World Trade Center. Men in business suits leaped out of windows. Smoke blanketed Manhattan. Inside the towers, people tried desperately to reach the ground. Most of them would die. The ones who lived would emerge from the smoke carrying a difficult burden: survivor's guilt.

Nobody knew survivor's guilt better than a woman named Tania Head. Earlier that morning, she had been wrapping up a meeting at Merrill Lynch on the 96th floor of the South Tower. Her husband, Dave, worked across the way on the 98th floor of the North Tower, and they'd parted on prickly terms—it was a couple's spat, nothing serious, but they hadn't officially made up yet. At 8:46 a.m., when the first plane hit the North Tower, Tania realized that they never would.

But there was no time to mourn Dave, not yet. "We have to get out of here! Now!" she cried to her coworkers, who were panicking all around her. She and her assistant Christine managed to scramble down to the 78th floor when the second plane came screaming toward them. Tania watched its wing slice through the huge glass window. She thought to herself, *We're all going to die here.* She flew through the air. And then she blacked out.

When she woke up, her skin was on fire, and Christine's body was slumped beside her—missing its head.

Suddenly a man with a red bandana over his nose and mouth was slapping her on the back, trying to put out her burning flesh. He told her to get up, that he'd help her get to the stairs. When she stood, she realized that her right arm was almost completely severed, connected to her body by a pathetic strand of tissue. And so she tucked the arm inside her jacket to keep it from falling off entirely, and picked her way across the fiery floor . . .

It was a horror story—possibly the most horrible survivor story out there. Every time Tania told that story, people shuddered and wept. But it took her a long time to actually tell it. Many of the survivors of 9/11 felt like they couldn't talk about what they'd seen; in fact, they felt like America had forgotten about them altogether. The country's sympathy had already been poured out on the first responders, the victims' family members, and the thousands of dead. Survivors like Tania—the ordinary people who had scrambled out of the towers in their button-down shirts—were less compelling figures. By the second anniversary of 9/11, some of them were even turned away from the remembrance ceremonies at Ground Zero. That *hurt*. It was hard for the survivors to make people understand that even though they had lived, many of them wanted to die, worn down by PTSD and suicidal thoughts. And so they went online to see if there was anyone else out there like them.

Tania had actually launched an online forum for 9/11 survivors to talk about their pain, but for a while, she lurked in the background of her own website, unwilling to share her story. When she finally got up the courage to speak, her fellow survivors listened in awe. Her tale was so awful, so detailed, so *vivid* that some of them felt almost guilty about their own trauma. How could *they* complain, they thought, if Tania could survive . . . *that*?

Before long, Tania emerged as a sort of unofficial spokeswoman for the survivors, a hero that the rest of them could unite around. She suggested merging her online group with another online group, the World Trade Center Survivors' Network, and gradually, under her guidance, a scattered community of troubled individuals turned into an entity with real power. Tania recruited members, organized trips to Ground Zero, even lobbied Washington. She was doing so much good for her community.

Okay, so she could be difficult sometimes. She suffered from frequent breakdowns and intense flashbacks during which she screamed things like, "I tried to save them!" She could be cruel to her friends. She often seemed confused about the past—calling Dave her "fiancé" in one breath and her "husband" in the next. But who could blame her, after what she'd been through that day? She had been right there, *right there* on the 78th floor when the second plane hit. She had seen the wings of the plane, driven by Marwan al-Shehhi himself, coming right at her. She had experienced the crash—as a fellow survivor said—"personally."

And so she was untouchable.

"MAYBE I CAN GET A PIECE OF THE ACTION"

WHEN TRAGEDY STRIKES, MOST PEOPLE TRY TO HELP. THEY OPEN up their pocketbooks and overwhelm charities with their donations. After the 2016 Pulse nightclub shooting in Orlando, people donated so much blood that the website of one blood bank crashed. At another blood bank, over six hundred people waited in line, longing to assuage even the smallest bit of suffering with their own bodies.

The CEO of the organization Charity Navigator, a man named Michael Thatcher, says that behavior like this represents the sort of exquisite communal empathy that practically *defines* us as human beings—but it's complicated. "We care for people that are less fortunate than ourselves, and that is a vulnerability," he says. "It's a beautiful vulnerability. It's also one that can be exploited."

Because for every tragedy, there is an equal and opposite reaction: the scammers rise up. These are the tragediennes, always waiting in the wings for the world to implode. They perk up their ears at the sound of crisis; they smell blood in the water from miles away. There is perhaps no other type of person so callously detached from the body collective. For the tragediennes, a bombing is a real coup, and a tsunami is a fantastic opportunity for personal advancement.

"There's a window of opportunity that happens when there's a crisis," Thatcher says. "Ill-intentioned individuals see that there's this opening when hearts are opening and so are wallets, and think, *Maybe I can get a piece of the action.*" These "ill-intentioned individuals" have risen up after the shooting at the First Baptist Church in Sutherland Springs, the massacre in Las Vegas, the Notre-Dame fire, the Boston Marathon bombing, the 2011 tsunami in Japan, the 2015 earthquake in Nepal, the coronavirus pandemic, and even—inexplicably—after the death of Robin Williams. So many scammers rose up after the Pulse shooting that the IRS had to issue a consumer alert warning people about them. As soon as the headlines are printed, the tragediennes appear, mascara already running down their cheeks. *My husband has been shot! My nephew was in the burning building! My sister's boyfriend's best friend was sucked into the hurricane! Won't someone, anyone, help me?*

In a crisis, there's no time to fact-check their statements. In fact, it feels inhumane to question them too much. Just in case, though, the tragediennes pack their stories full of details. *I was there when the plane came crashing into the 78th floor of the tower at precisely 9:03 a.m.!* As for any inconsistencies in their stories? They chalk those up to "trauma," understanding instinctively that aligning themselves with catastrophe makes them impervious to criticism.

And they are the ultimate improvisers, ready at the drop of a hat to come up with a tale of woe. "To pull this off, you have to have some smarts," says Thatcher. "You've got to be able to think fast and move." None of us knows when the next fire will roar up or the next skyscraper will come falling down, so the tragediennes stay light on their feet, always ready to profit from the flames.

RUKSANA

DETECTIVE CONSTABLE PETE GARTLAND STOOD OUTSIDE RUKSANA Ashraf's bedroom, calmly explaining to her that if she didn't emerge *right now*, he was going to have to kick her door down. In response, she shrieked that she was naked.

Detective Gartland had been looking into Ruksana Ashraf's crimes for two years now. And it had to be said: she wasn't exactly the most ingenious fraudster he'd ever encountered. He'd seen his share of slicker criminals and bigger backstories. Still, the detective found himself impressed by Ruksana's sheer *thoroughness.* "She'd really thought about how she was going to get ahold of the addresses, of people's names," he remembers. "She'd put a lot of effort into thinking about the mechanics of the fraud so that it was successful. All the effort she put behind it, to hide who she was, was quite well-done." Other tragediennes were flashier and more inventive, but Ruksana was the equivalent of a working actor—not a star, but she took home a steady paycheck anyway.

A little digging, though, revealed the cracks in her act: her insurance claims all ended up in the same bank accounts, and her fake email addresses tended to follow the same format. Plus, many of her claims used addresses that were hundreds of miles away from the bank accounts where the money would eventually end up. It would be like filing a claim for a pair of designer shoes that went missing from your home in New York, but cashing your reimbursement check in Vermont. The patterns were obvious, and they all pointed to Ruksana. So on July 5, 2017, Detective Gartland and Detective Sergeant Matt Hussey showed up at the apartment where Ruksana lived with her sister and mother, thinking that they were about to arrest a run-of-the-mill insurance fraudster.

Her sister let the detectives in, while Ruksana herself sprinted for her bedroom and locked the door. Inside, she began destroying evidence, all while calling out to the police that she *couldn't* open up the door because she didn't have a scrap of clothing on.

"We politely informed her we were going to kick the door in and she opened it up—dressed," says Detective Gartland. In the room, they discovered what Detective Gartland called a "cave" of fraud: all the evidence listed on their warrant, and then some. There were fake driver's licenses and passports, forged documents, fraudulent receipts, and paperwork for claims that she just hadn't gotten around to filing yet. "What was a reasonable-sized job suddenly became a lot larger," says Detective Gartland. "I suspect we saved the insurance industry several hundred thousand pounds, certainly tens of thousands."

But the most shocking discovery was that Ruksana's claims, which had always been so similar, had recently branched out into a different narrative. She had started to claim that she was a *survivor*. She said that she was at the Manchester Arena during the bombing. She claimed to have been at London Bridge during the terror attack. And she insisted that she had also been at Grenfell— visiting family inside the doomed building itself—during the fire. All three times, she'd supposedly "fled the scene," leaving behind a variety of expensive designer goods for which she was now seeking reimbursement.

These new claims of hers had been quickly reimbursed by insurance companies, because what were they going to do, ignore a woman who was so obviously grieving? The companies were also paranoid about the bad press that might ensue if word got out that "survivors" like Ruksana were being denied their insurance money. Ruksana must have known this, which is why she aligned herself with three major tragedies in such short order. She was name-dropping catastrophe for quicker service, the way you might whisper the name of a famous friend to the bouncer, hoping that he'll let you cut the line.

Of course, Ruksana hadn't been at any of the tragic scenes, but she wouldn't tell the detectives why she chose them. As it turned out, the real Ms. Ashraf was silent, enigmatic, and scornful. "She was a quite secretive individual," says Detective Hussey. "She kept what she was doing from the rest of the family." When they interviewed her, she refused to answer a single question, and when they drove her three hours from Edinburgh to an English police station, she didn't say a word the entire time. In court, she would barely talk to the judge, even when it came to simple requests—like, "What is your name?"

"She has a complete and utter disdain for anyone in authority," says Detective Gartland, "and that spills over to how she was in the claims. When we consider Grenfell and Manchester, she just doesn't *care*. She wants to do what Ruksana Ashraf wants to do, to line Ruksana Ashraf's pockets."

It was this disdain for anyone other than herself that doomed Ruksana in the press. When news of her arrest broke, the public was appalled. It wasn't the bit about the insurance companies that shocked them. It was the audacity of claiming that she'd been *there*, right there with the blood and the screaming and the flames. "Vile Edinburgh conwoman," ran an article in the *Scottish Sun*. "Scotland's sickest fraudster," shrieked the *Daily Record*. "Disgraceful," said the judge, when he handed down her sentence in December of 2018.

Her sentence was fairly light: three years. She'd pled guilty, and the judge chose to give her a light sentence because she was in poor health and under financial pressure to care for her elderly mother, which he considered mitigating circumstances. She had received £50,116 from insurance companies (almost $64,000). She'd filed claims for an additional £129,030 (about $164,000), but companies had turned those claims down. In total, she had taken out over seventy policies at three different insurance companies and filed fifty fake claims.

It wasn't a terribly impressive crime. Less than $100,000 lost. Only three years behind bars. But you wouldn't know that from the headlines. *Callous. Vile. Evil.* She was being cast out of the collective for benefitting from their tragedy. The irony was that she never seemed to want to be part of the collective, anyway. Their pain was not her pain. She answered only to herself.

ASHLEY

As the Holy Fire burned, Ashley Bemis's fundraising efforts were crackling along nicely. There was just one problem: her past.

Certain people in Ashley's community knew that she had a tendency to embellish the truth. So when they saw that she was posting on Facebook about how her "husband" needed donations to continue fighting the "Holy Hell Fire," they were immediately suspicious. One of these vigilantes happened to be an employee at Cal Fire—the alleged employer of Ashley's alleged husband—but when they ran the name "Shane Goodman" through a database at work, nothing popped up. And so they went to the police.

What the police discovered was that Ashley had a ten-year history of bizarre scams, all centering around marriage and motherhood. Despite the fact that she'd been posting online about "Shane Goodman" for years, a reverse image search revealed that Shane was actually an Australian actor named Jesse Spencer, who merely played a firefighter on the show *Chicago Fire*.

And that was just the tip of the iceberg. Much of Ashley's social media activity involved fake pregnancies and photos of babies that were not actually hers. She'd been faking pregnancies for years, in fact. In high school, when she told people that her mother's married boyfriend had raped her, she also claimed to be pregnant. As the months progressed, she padded her stomach, and even let her friends throw her a baby shower. After the shower, she sold and donated some of the gifts—but kept her favorites, hoping that one day she'd use them for a real baby.

The real baby never came. Instead, Ashley faked another pregnancy, and then another, and another. She would post dreamy maternity photos online, or silly videos in which she danced around the living room with a massively pregnant belly. The belly, which was surprisingly realistic, was just a folded blanket held in place by a maternity bellyband and finished off with a wad of tissue paper—a pert little fake belly button. (Later, when Ashley was caught, she seemed offended at the allegation that she had purchased a fake belly. She had *made it herself*, she insisted.) She would download ultrasound photos from the internet and show them to coworkers. The coworkers would throw her baby showers. She would attend them, smiling and grateful, taking all the gifts, and then after a while she would say that her baby had been stillborn, or had died young. Usually, she blamed a heart defect. Everyone would mourn with her. She would accept their grief. And then, before long, she'd be "pregnant" again.

In 2010, Ashley began nannying for a woman named Emily Strickland who had a baby boy named Blake. Unbeknownst to Strickland, Ashley liked to take Blake out and pretend that he was her own son. Sometimes she posted his photo on Facebook. Other times, she dressed him in girl's clothes and posted those photos on a different Facebook account, claiming he was her daughter, "Cheyenne."

Ashley also told Strickland that she was pregnant, and for a while, Strickland believed her. After all, Ashley's stomach was nicely rounded, and she always seemed to be taking phone calls from her doctor. But one day, Strickland saw Ashley walk to her car—and pull a pillow out from underneath her shirt.

Chilled, Strickland dug around on social media, and found out that Ashley had been posting photos of Blake online. She immediately fired Ashley, who took to social media to inform her friends that Blake had been killed in a head-on collision with a drunk driver *and* that she'd lost her most recent pregnancy, too. On another Facebook page, the one where she posted about "Cheyenne," Ashley told people that her daughter had died of a heart attack. "No words can explain the pain of losing a child!" she wrote. As usual, her Facebook friends responded with an outpouring of support.

All in all, Ashley faked seven pregnancies, including one twin pregnancy. Her narratives were always underscored by tragedy. She claimed that her twins were born early, and posted photos of two tiny babies in the NICU—photos that she'd stolen from a *Huffington Post* article. "Shane Goodman" often appeared in these narratives, but his personality was inconsistent: sometimes he was the perfect husband, sometimes he was an abusive cheater. Once, she claimed that he, too, had died.

And now, as the Holy Fire raged, Ashley's past was catching up to her. While police continued to investigate her, Ashley decided to explain herself to the world by going on the talk show *Dr. Phil.* On TV, she wore a blue dress and looked nervous and wild-eyed. She claimed that her Holy Fire fundraising had been sincere and that she never intended to keep the $11,000 worth of donations, but that she'd invented a firefighter husband in order to legitimize her claim. "I felt like if I was just a girl who wanted to help, no one would believe me," she said. "I felt like I needed to give it a *why*." When Dr. Phil asked her about all those fake pregnancies, Ashley started crying. "I think I wanted it to be real," she said. "Anyone that knows me knows that being a mom is what I want the most." She'd loved the attention, she said, the "feeling cared about." And in her own little fantasy world, *she* controlled the narratives. "The times I have taken a break from this life and done the real life, I get hurt," she said. "I get cheated on. I get lied to."

Real life was much harder, but real life won out. In December 2018, Ashley was arrested, and by March, she was pleading guilty to one count of grand theft, four counts of second-degree burglary, six counts of dissuading a witness from reporting the crime, and two dozen counts of fraud. She was sentenced to 177 days in jail.

By then, the Holy Fire was finished. Its last embers had finally burned out, but not before it destroyed eighteen buildings and devoured over twenty-three thousand acres of land. Like Ashley, it was ravenous for what it could not have.

TANIA

BY 2007, TANIA HAD BECOME THE UNDISPUTED QUEEN OF THE SUR-
vivors. As her best friend liked to say, she was the "World Trade
Center superstar." She'd transformed a little online survivor's
group into a respected advocacy organization, and she was its
president. She'd led the mayor of New York on a tour of Ground
Zero. She'd given countless quotes to journalists. And now the
New York Times wanted to profile her, because she was such an in-
spiration, such a *fighter*—a woman who encapsulated everything
beautiful and resilient about the American spirit.

The profile was obviously going to be a glowing one, so Tania's friends were confused when Tania refused to talk to the reporter. In fact, the more he tried to get in touch with her, the more
agitated she grew. When he tried to ask her simple fact-checking
questions—like, "What was your husband's last name?"—she
would break down crying. This was *harassment*, Tania fumed to
her fellow survivors. She was being *persecuted*! How dare this
reporter make her revisit her trauma, the trauma of being on
the 78th floor when the second plane hit at exactly 9:03 a.m.,
only minutes after the first plane hit the North Tower where her
husband-slash-fiancé Dave worked on the 98th floor, where he
had gone after she said goodbye to him earlier that morning after
they had a small fight?

The more evasive Tania grew, the more the reporter from
the *New York Times* kept digging. His article came out on September 27, 2007, with the headline "In a 9/11 Survival Tale, the

Pieces Just Don't Fit." Tania's friends read it and felt sick to their stomachs. Tania had never been employed by Merrill Lynch. She had never been married to a Dave who worked in the North Tower. There had been no couple's spat that morning. Tania never had an assistant named Christine whose head was ripped off. She was never saved by a man with a red bandana over his face. In fact, Tania Head had never been in the World Trade Center *at all*.

The real Tania Head was a survivor, but not of terrorism. She was born Alicia Esteve Head, the privileged daughter of a wealthy Barcelona family. As a kid, she was obsessed with American culture, even hanging a gigantic American flag on her bedroom wall. She was always making up stories about dating boys, and her friends knew she was lying, but accepted it as part of her personality. At eighteen, she was in a terrible car crash and thrown from the car—with her right arm completely severed from her body. (Doctors managed to reattach it; later, she would use the scars to bolster her 9/11 story.) Her father was a corrupt businessman, and when he and her oldest brother were thrown into prison for embezzlement, Tania began retreating more and more into her fantasy worlds. On September 11, 2001, she was most likely in Barcelona, attending business school. After graduation, she moved to New York City, where she crafted a tale that would shock the world.

The genius of Tania's con lay in the extremely sensitive nature of her story. If she didn't want to discuss something, or if she flew into a rage when a reporter asked her a simple question, or if she failed to get her facts straight, her friends assumed she was too traumatized to revisit it. (Besides, she got just enough of her facts straight to seem believable. There really *was* a man with a red bandana on the 78th floor of the South Tower. His name was Welles Crowther. He saved many people that day before he died in the flames. Creepily, Tania had dinner with his family at one point.) Her story generated sympathy and yet demanded distance. Like Blanche DuBois in *A Streetcar Named Desire*, like Ruksana, whose claims were approved so quickly by worried insurance companies, like Ashley, whose online fundraising was bolstered by tales of a husband in danger, Tania's story depended entirely on the kindness of strangers.

For the tragediennes, 9/11 always had a particular pull. It was so huge that there was plenty of room for fakers. With thousands dead, who had the time or the ability to fact-check and cross-reference every single story of woe? 9/11 scammers were so prolific that even Tania encountered one of them, a man who had the audacity—the *audacity*—to log onto *her* 9/11 survivor forum and lie about being a survivor. ("Who would want to fake being a World Trade Center survivor, right?" she wrote to a friend, outraged. "God knows how much I've been through and this guy is just here for the attention or whatever sick reason.") A psychiatrist named Jean Kim encountered so many fake 9/11 survivors that she wrote an op-ed for the *Washington Post* about it. "No other event has inspired so many false claims among my patients," she said.

The false claims didn't seem to be about money, per se. Tania herself never cashed a single victim compensation check from the government or swiped a dollar from the organization she ran. Instead, as Kim wrote, "People of all stripes and socioeconomic classes seemed to sense the power lurking behind that type of attention, that kind of historic relevancy." *The power.* To claim a connection to global tragedy was to embody a certain eerie authority, and for the tragediennes, that authority was terribly alluring. The real survivors of tragedy wouldn't have wished their fate on anyone—but of course the tragediennes never cared about the real survivors.

After her big unveiling, Tania was kicked out of her own survivor organization. Then she vanished. Her friends, the real survivors, writhed in anguish and betrayal. But Tania never apologized, and she was never prosecuted. After all, there was no law against telling stories, and hers had been a good story, based—like so many good stories are—in just a bit of truth. The real Tania was already familiar with trauma, but her private griefs wouldn't make the world sit up and take notice. And so she rewrote her role, placing herself in the center of the biggest tragedy she could find, the flames falling on her like a spotlight.

"IT'S FAIRLY ROUTINE, RIGHT?"

EVERY TIME THE HEADLINES GET BAD, THE TRAGEDIENNES RISE UP. "There are probably scams in every single tragedy," says Michael Thatcher, CEO of Charity Navigator. "The good ones go undetected. They get away with it."

Though the tragediennes have weaponized emotion, they tend to be strangely emotionless themselves, at least when it comes to other people. Think of Ruksana, sitting for hours in a police car in stony silence, or Tania, vanishing without apology, or Ashley, downloading some terrified parent's NICU photos from the internet. Whether they're doing it for money or fame or out of a pathological need to lie, their attention is always turned inward. Unless a tragedy touches them personally, it might as well be nothing more than a script for them to read aloud.

Because of this, the public hates them. *Hates them*. We can usually find it in our hearts to cheer on a particularly good white-collar grifter or romance scammer, but no one wants to cheer on the tragediennes. They have crossed some invisible ethical line by profiting so callously from death and disaster, and we cannot forgive them. Beneath articles about Tania Head, you can find commenters writing things like "Burn in hell" and "This fat liar deserves death or assisted suicide" and "Tania Head needs an exorcism" and "Disgusting" and "She is a total sociopath" and "There are variations of evil out there and this shows one of the worse kinds." We hate them because they haven't just fooled us, they've cheated the real victims out of so much: money, attention, their own narrative of survival. Who knows how many survivors of the Manchester bombing had their insurance claims delayed because Ruksana was clogging up the system? What about the $11,000 that Ashley collected, which could have gone to real firefighters? How many legitimate 9/11 survivors found their stories drowned out by Tania's melodramatic monologuing?

The tragediennes have always existed, and they always will. In September of 1888, the body of Elisabeth Stride was found lying in a narrow yard in Whitechapel—the third victim of Jack the Ripper. But ten years before her own tragedy found her, Elisabeth used the tragedy of others to survive. When a steamship called the *Princess Alice* collided into another ship, killing about seven hundred people, Elisabeth decided to claim that she'd been part of the disaster. Londoners were raising tens of thousands of pounds for a relief fund—why shouldn't she get a cut of all that cash? So she went around pleading her case: *My husband died on that ship*, she told people, *and so did two of my children.*

One hundred and twenty-four years later and an ocean away, a gunman killed twenty children and six adults at Sandy Hook Elementary School in Newton, Connecticut. Within four hours of the shooting, a woman from the Bronx named Nouel Alba was claiming to be an aunt of one of the slaughtered children. Through social media posts, emails, and even phone calls, she begged for donations to her nephew's "funeral fund," telling people that she'd seen the boy's bullet-ridden body.

"This is so shocking," said a reporter from CNN, "but really the most shocking thing out of all of this is that it's fairly routine, right?" Life goes on, the death toll climbs, and somewhere, the next tragedienne glances over her script, smears her mascara, and waits for the curtain to rise.

BONNY LEE BAKLEY

alias: Florence Paulakis, Sandra Gawron, Leebonny Bakley, Elizabeth Baker, Lorraine Drake, Sylvia Stefanow, Alexandria King Daniela, Christina Scheier

1956–2001

IT WASN'T FAIR, DYING IN HOLLYWOOD. YOUR REPUTATION COULD be trashed before your body went cold, and what could you do about it? Nothing. Less than a week after poor blond Botoxed Bonny Lee Bakley had been found slumped over in the passenger seat of her husband's car, her friends and family were spilling all her secrets to the press. Her mother explained that Bonny "liked to live on the edge." Her half brother told one magazine that she "was not Mother Teresa." Her sister said that she had a habit of stalking rock stars.

The sordid details of her life just kept emerging: her mail-order porn business, her criminal record, her celebrity obsession. All the raw, desperate striving of her life was laid bare, and she could no longer defend herself. And the strangest part was that most of these unflattering details were coming straight from her "grieving" husband, who was feeding them to his lawyer, who was in turn feeding them to the press.

The detectives working on her case couldn't help but notice how thoroughly her husband was trying to destroy her reputation. "It's kind of unfair," mused a spokesman from the LAPD. "Here's a person who's been murdered and now they start painting her as a bad person. The focus of the investigation is not on her past. We have to focus on one thing: Who killed her?"

✳

THE IRONY WAS THAT BONNY WOULD HAVE BEEN THE FIRST PERSON to admit to the celebrity obsession and the mail-order porn, had she not been shot in the head. She was cheerfully honest about her own ambition, and nobody in the world was a more relentless documenter of her life than Bonny Lee Bakley. She'd been recording her phone calls for decades. She kept a well-organized collection of her own nude photographs, which she mailed around the country. You didn't have to read the tabloids to learn about her sordid double life—if Bonny was around, she'd tell you all about her sordid double life herself, and then buy you a drink.

Bonny's obsession with famous men began when she lived with her grandma, and she was only living with her grandma because the first man in her life—her father—was an abusive alcoholic. She was born in Morristown, New Jersey, on June 7, 1956, and grew into a nervous girl, the oldest of six kids. Her father made a habit of striking his pregnant wife in the stomach and burning through their money. According to Bonny's younger sister, her parents gave three of their children up for adoption. At one point, the whole family was so broke that they had to live in a garage, where the kids kept rats as pets. When Bonny was seven, her mother went into labor and headed to the hospital—while back at home, her father attempted to molest her.

And so Bonny was sent to live with her grandmother, either to escape her father, or because her father could no longer afford to raise her. Her grandma was a strange, stingy woman who lived in the woods. She'd grown up during the Great Depression and had a morbid fear of running out of water, and so she wouldn't let Bonny wash her hair. Young Bonny would show up at school with greasy, stringy locks, and the other kids would torment her for it. (As an adult, Bonny reveled in taking long baths.) The television turned into her only means of escape. On TV, all the girls had clean hair, and all the men were handsome. She loved the tough guys that her mom and grandma were also obsessed with: Humphrey Bogart. James Cagney. Elvis Presley. Robert Blake.

Decades later, Bonny was chatting on the phone to a friend—and recording it, of course—when she started to reminisce about her past. "I was the kid that everybody hated in school, 'cause I was, like, poor and couldn't dress good and you know, and everybody always made fun of me because I was, like, a real loner type," she said. "So then you grow up saying, Oh, I'll fix them, I'll show them, I'll be a movie star."

✳

BONNY SOON FOUND OUT THAT BEING A MOVIE STAR WASN'T EASY, but being a nude model *was*—at least for her. She was blond, curvy, and accessibly pretty, more slightly-disheveled-girl-next-door than

Hollywood vamp. (People often described Bonny as looking a little ragged around the edges, like she was wearing thrift-store clothes.) And she loved being naked. When she was a preteen, she and her little sister went swimming at a nudist colony, and though her sister was appalled by the experience, Bonny was hooked. As a young woman, she began placing ads in the backs of nudist magazines, advertising her modeling services. She'd preen and pose and take her paycheck, and then spend it immediately on bus fare and concert tickets so that she could see all her favorite men perform. For a while, she was absolutely obsessed with Frankie Valli. Then she was all about Elvis. Then Jerry Lee Lewis. Other girls may have pinned up these singers' posters on their wall, but Bonny was actively trying to become their girlfriend. She'd befriend their security guards and secretaries; she'd follow them around the country on tour. Once, she even climbed over the walls of Elvis's Graceland estate and clambered up a tree to peer into his bedroom, until a security guard dragged her off the grounds. Undeterred, Bonny later referred to herself as Elvis's "former girlfriend."

After dropping out of high school and earning a modeling certificate from a place called the Barbizon School of Modeling, Bonny moved to New York and joined the endless slog of young women who were trying to become famous actresses. She optimistically told her family that she'd earned her Screen Actors Guild card and that she'd been cast in the sexy drama $9^1/_2$ *Weeks*. Neither was true. As a matter of fact, the high point of her film career was working as an extra in a film called *Turk 182!*, which critic Roger Ebert called "an insult to the intelligence of the audience."

She also tried her hand at singing as a sort of backup plan. If acting didn't turn her into a household name, maybe she could become the next queen of pop. And so she gave herself the stage name "Leebonny" and recorded two bizarre, fatalistic singles called "Just a Fan" and "Let's Not Dream." Her voice is tuneless, and the lyrics are vaguely ominous: *I'm chasing a celebrity/God only knows what he means to me/don't know where I'll ever be/there's no future in it, don't you see?* (Decades later, the singles would be uploaded to YouTube and described as "'70s Stalker Pop.")

Throughout it all, she continued her nude modeling. One day, a Greek man named Evangelos Paulakis found her information in the back of a nudist magazine and reached out to her. He wanted a green card, and he was willing to pay for it. Bonny agreed to marry him—she was late to her own wedding—but when Paulakis began to abuse her, she had him deported. She knew that there were plenty of other fish in the sea who were willing to pay her for her time, her body, and her ring finger. Decades later, once she was finally famous, one *Rolling Stone* reporter wrote, "Depending on the source, Bakley had between nine and more than a hundred husbands."

✳

THE PROBLEM WITH NUDE MODELING WAS THAT THERE WAS ONLY one Bonny, and Bonny could only be in one photo studio at a time. So she began to pivot to mail-order porn, a business with far more potential for growth. With a few sultry form letters and a photocopy machine, Bonny could share her assets with hundreds of men all across the country.

She started placing a new sort of advertisement in her magazines, saying that she was just a lonesome gal looking for a pen
pal—an older, male pen pal, preferably. When a man responded to
her ad, she'd introduce herself in a coquettish letter. (It was a form
letter, but the guy never knew it.) In her letter, she'd mention that
she would be happy to send over a couple of, ahem, *special photos*,
if he would just send her a little cash first. As their correspondence
continued, Bonny would keep careful track of the man's information in order to bilk him out of as much money as possible: his
name, address, phone number; the specific alias that she'd been
using with him; and, of course, his precise desires. One of her
notes read: "loves phone sex."

To keep her clients happy, she built up a robust library of por-
nographic snapshots, not all of them hers. She had photos of big
breasts and small ones, narrow hips and wide ones, and every skin
tone under the sun. Even through form letters, she had a freakish
ability to make men feel special. She toyed with these men, strung
them along, and took their cash—all while making them feel that,
at any minute, she might drop everything and show up at their
door wearing nothing but a trench coat.

Hers wasn't a simple cash-for-photos business. She'd weave
sob stories into her letters, saying that she couldn't afford her rent
that month, or that she had medical bills to pay, or that someone
she loved was in the hospital. Sometimes she'd ask for money so
that she could buy a bus ticket and visit. (Inevitably, something
would come up before the visit could happen.) Her form letters
were coy and girlish: "I don't have anyone to spend the holidays

with, do you? My family lives too far away, could I spend them with you?"

Sometimes she earned nothing more than $10 for a snapshot, but Bonny was an expert at sniffing out the men who were *really* willing to spend money on her. She'd run credit checks on them and figure out their assets; she'd find their Social Security numbers and forge their signatures to reroute their checks, through the mail, to her. If the man was really rich—or really old, with a juicy life insurance policy—she might even go ahead and marry him. (When one of her marks died, his grown children were shocked to find that he had a "fiancée" who was getting part of his estate.) Her form letters were organized into eight levels: at the lowest level, she requested money for nudes, while at the highest level, she asked to be added to the man's will. As Bonny's business grew, she enlisted her relatives to help her lick stamps and stuff photographs of strangers' breasts into envelopes. She made so much money that she was able to buy several houses.

In the fall of 1977, Bonnie married her first cousin, Paul Gawron. Like so many of the other men in her life, Gawron was physically violent with her—even breaking her nose at one point. In other ways, he was submissive. The couple had two children, and Gawron stayed home with them, while Bonny chased celebrities and paid the rent. When her mail-order business grew big enough, Gawron started working under her. She liked to have her form letters written out by hand—it gave them a more personal touch—and so Gawron spent his days carefully copying out lines like "You make me wet when I think about licking your big hairy balls."

"If she had put her mind on something else, she could have been a whiz," he said, years later. "It's just a shame that everything she did was crooked."

✴

WHILE BONNY PAID HER RENT BY STOKING MEN'S FANTASIES, HER own dreams hadn't gone anywhere. If anything, they were more sizzling and urgent than ever, and when she and Gawron finally divorced, she made up her mind that her next husband *had* to be someone famous. After all, hadn't she declared her intentions to the entire world when she recorded "Just a Fan"? *I'll just chase my celebrity/in hopes one day he may notice me . . .*

Bonny chased celebrities with the same organization and drive that she used in her mail-order porn business. She made lists of famous men. She tracked their movements in tabloids like the *Star* and the *National Enquirer*. She wrote down their favorite colors and their go-to cocktail bars. She even ran background checks on them. Why not? If you were serious about something, you had to work for it. In the meantime, she was racking up a bit of a criminal record: she got caught passing a few bad checks, she was arrested in Tennessee on a misdemeanor drug charge, and she was pulled over in Arkansas with five Social Security cards and seven driver's licenses. But none of this distracted her from her goal.

In 1984, Bonny set her sights on the rock star Jerry Lee Lewis, whose nickname was "The Killer." He was everything her grandma had taught her to love in a guy: famous, talented, and dangerous. In fact, by the time Bonny began pursuing him, two of his wives had died under suspicious circumstances. That didn't bother Bonny, though. She already knew that men could be violent. To get closer to The Killer, she befriended his road manager, his sister, and even his wife's secretary. She moved herself and her kids to Memphis to be closer to him and joked about killing his sixth wife so that she could be his seventh. For almost ten years, she chased after him—while continuing to run her mail-order porn business and marrying her clients when it served her—until 1993, when she overplayed her hand. She'd gotten pregnant, possibly by Paul Gawron (they were divorced but still sleeping together), but she told everyone that the child belonged to Jerry Lee Lewis. To prove it, she named her baby—a girl—"Jerilee Lewis." But no one believed her. Jerry Lee Lewis refused to acknowledge the baby, Paul Gawron was sure that little Jerilee was his, and as Bonny's sister Margerry put it, bluntly: "You can't get pregnant from a blow job."

Eventually, Bonny was forced to admit that she probably wasn't going to become Mrs. Jerry Lee Lewis the Seventh, and so she turned her laser-like focus away from the stadium and onto the silver screen. She began spending more and more time in Hollywood, eyeing tough guys like Robert De Niro, Sylvester Stallone, and Robert Redford. Her motives were transparent, if not pure. "I like being around celebrities," she told a friend. "It makes you feel better than other people."

Now in her forties, Bonny seemed just as cheerful and ambitious as ever, even though none of her schemes had really played out and she had no backup plan—unless she wanted to run mail-order porn scams forever. But it wasn't easy being a fortysomething woman in Los Angeles, the city of eternal youth. She got Botox and lied about her age and weight. She managed to weasel her way into exclusive bars and celebrity birthday parties, but she was typically taken for nothing more than an infatuated middle-aged groupie. Still, she told her family and friends back home that she was living the dream. She snagged an invite to Dean Martin's seventy-seventh birthday party, and then called up her family and told them that she was dating him. She even put a man on the phone who sounded a lot like the famous crooner. This was typical Bonny: she could always conjure up glamour and excitement, if only for a night.

Yes, Bonny was great fun at night. Her friends loved hanging out with her. She would buy you a drink, flirt with the most dangerous men in the bar, take you on a fast ride in her car with the license plate 1RSKTKR—Number 1 Risk Taker. If you couldn't be there, she'd call you on the phone and keep you there for hours, telling you all the details. But when daylight came, Bonny would be doing the same things that she did at eighteen: sleeping late, reading the tabloids, arranging her hair, and looking ahead toward the next night, when surely, *finally*, she'd meet the man of her dreams.

✳

ONE SULTRY SUMMER NIGHT IN LOS ANGELES, BONNY WALKED INTO yet another celebrity birthday party—this one for the comedian Chuck McCann—and noticed an older man across the room. He was handsome, in a ruggedly dangerous sort of way, and wearing a sleeveless black shirt. They made eye contact. Something sizzled between them. She slid into the booth where he was sitting.

This man was the actor Robert Blake, and he had been her grandma's crush, not hers. Blake was a child star from the 1940s show *Our Gang* who became even more famous for playing the murderer Perry Smith in the 1967 movie *In Cold Blood* and a tough cop on the 1970s show *Baretta*. Like Bonny, he was a New Jersey native with a troubled childhood. When he locked eyes with Bonny Lee Bakley in 1998, he was sixty-four, but thanks to daily exercise, a face-lift, and some black hair dye, he could pass for a few years younger. He had a reputation for being angry and volatile. His star was on the decline—just low enough for Bonny to pluck it out of the sky.

Though Bonny was thrilled to meet Robert Blake in the flesh, she had already managed to snag a celebrity lover by that point. Okay, so he wasn't a celebrity, exactly, but he was certainly celebrity-adjacent. She was sleeping with Marlon Brando's son, Christian Brando, a troubled young man who had just gotten out of prison after shooting his half sister's abusive boyfriend in the face. Bonny—knowing a captive audience when she saw one—started writing to Christian while he was still behind bars, and then hired a private investigator to track him down once he was paroled. From there, she seduced him. It was aggressive, but effective. Typical Bonny.

But now that she saw the chance to sleep with Robert Blake, she wasn't going to let a little thing like Christian Brando stand in her way. At the party, she slithered up to Blake and started laughing at his jokes. He eyed her up and down and amped up his bad-boy New Jersey accent to impress her. It wasn't long before they were sneaking out of the party to have sex in his SUV. Afterward, Bonny raced to her room to call her sister and her best friend. She'd just slept with a movie star, a real, honest-to-goodness movie star, she told them. Her lifelong dream of a celebrity husband was finally within her grasp. Now she just needed to play it cool, wait for him to call.

He eventually called, and they continued to sleep together, but the affair wasn't as romantic as Bonny had hoped. Blake seemed awfully casual about the whole thing. There was no talk of being soul mates. No discussion of a ring. As the months passed, Bonny wavered: Should she pursue Blake, or stick with Brando? Who was more likely to turn into the famous Hollywood husband of her dreams? And she had a darker question to consider: Who was less likely to hurt her? Both men were handsome, troubled, and violent. Once, Christian yelled at her over the phone, angry about her mail-order porn business. (As always, Bonny was recording the call.) "You're lucky, you know," he seethed. "I mean, not on my behalf, but you're lucky somebody isn't out there to put a bullet in your head."

Bonny spent hours on the phone with her friends, debating the pros and cons of each lover. "I thought, well, when I met Blake, I kinda wanted him, but I kinda didn't, because he wasn't like up to par with the looks, and I thought I was already in love with Christian," she told one friend. "Who would you go for? Blake or Christian? I'd probably feel more safe with Blake."

✳

"More safe," for Bonny, was relative. Because from early on, Bonny harbored the idea that Robert Blake might kill her. Sometimes she even joked about it with friends. He had a violent streak that would flare up unpredictably. When they had sex, Blake would sometimes choke her, or try to rip out her hair—but Bonny took it in stride as one of his fantasies, and if she was used to anything, it was fulfilling male fantasies. Instead of pulling back in fear, she decided to get as close to him as she possibly could. She assured him that if she ever got pregnant, she'd get an abortion. Then she went off her birth control.

When she told Blake that she was pregnant, he went berserk. "You swore to me on your life that no matter what I didn't have to worry, and that was a rotten, stinking, filthy lie and you deliberately got pregnant," he raged on the phone. "Your period ended on August the 20th and you were out here fucking me on the exact day you were supposed to. You did all that. You did it. For the rest of your life you'll have to live with that and for the rest of my life I'll never forget it."

Bonny ignored his fury, and her little girl was born on June 2, 2000. At first, she named her Christian Shannon Brando, claiming she was Christian's child, but then she persuaded Blake to take a DNA test, which proved that the baby was his. (Later, Bonny changed her daughter's name to "Rose Lenore Sophia Blake.") After some hesitation, Blake fell in love with the child, but by then he was starting to truly loathe Bonny. Even though

she was spending a lot of time in Hollywood, she was still technically on parole in Arkansas for the time she was pulled over with
five Social Security cards and seven driver's licenses. Blake knew
this, and so, during one of her visits to Hollywood, he had someone call her probation officer and rat her out. Bonny was dragged
back to Arkansas. Blake kept their baby.

But it was going to take more than a parole officer to keep
Bonny from achieving her goals. She told Blake that she'd expose
him in the tabloids if he didn't marry her. She knew he didn't
love her, but she didn't care. Despite her penchant for dreaming
big, Bonny had always been a bit of a realist. As she'd sung in
1977, over two decades before she met Blake: *Baby, baby let's not
dream/I don't mean to be mean but that's the way it must seem.*

That same year, Blake had given an interview to *Playboy*. He
had played a murderer in *In Cold Blood*, and now he was musing
on the whole idea of murder. "I can conceive of *me* killing somebody," he said, "but that's because I'm a human being, not God,
and I'd hope that somebody would stop me from doing it."

Neither of them knew that decades later, both of their quotes
would take on an ominous new life.

＊

Bonny Lee Bakley and Robert Blake were finally married on
November 19, 2000. Bonny had to buy her own wedding ring,
and Blake refused to spend their wedding night with her. Instead, he forced Bonny to live in a bungalow in the backyard of his
house and made her sign a prenuptial agreement saying that she
wouldn't hang out with "known felons" if their child was around.

Bonny stayed chipper, brushing off the insults as best she could. She relocated her mail-order porn business to the bungalow and sent out Christmas cards to everyone she knew, announcing that she'd just married Robert Blake, and wasn't it fabulous?

But despite her positive attitude, Bonny couldn't deny that Robert Blake was starting to scare her. He collected guns—lots of them—and though he mostly refused to have sex with her, he *did* ask her to pose for a series of sexy photos holding the firearms. He had a bodyguard, Earle Caldwell, and the two of them were clearly up to something. They whispered to each other so much that Bonny initially thought they were lovers. Later, she started wondering if Earle was trying to kill her. Twice, she'd seen him coming at her, holding something that looked like a gun. Both times, he stopped, threw up, and had to be soothed by Blake, who murmured things like, "It's okay, I'll get someone else." It didn't make any sense.

Bonny had no idea that Earle was also writing down shopping lists for his boss: *2 Shovels, Small Sledge, Crowbar, Get Blank Gun Ready, Old Rugs, Duct Tape—Black, Drano, Pool Acid, Lye* . . . She also didn't know that Blake was holding weird "hypothetical" conversations with people about whether or not they'd be willing to kill someone for money. He spoke to two old stuntmen about the idea and even floated it to Bonny's own brother, Joey, who had the sort of sketchy past that apparently made people feel comfortable talking about murder with him. Joey was so disturbed by their conversation that he told his sister, "Blake's gonna get you."

And yet Bonny seemed oddly calm amid the fray. She told

her mother about a fight they'd had during which Blake snarled, "Girl, you better remember who you are fucking with. I'll kill your ass!" At one point, she asked her family, "Think this guy's going to kill me?" Later, she told her sister, "I know he's going to kill me." The idea had turned from a question into a statement.

✳

SPRING NIGHTS IN LOS ANGELES WERE COOL AND SPARKLING. THEY were the sort of nights that made you want to throw on a light sweater and head to your favorite neighborhood restaurant with your lover. On May 4, 2001, Bonny and Blake did just that, driving to a nearby place called Vitello's, an old-school Italian joint that Blake adored. He ate at Vitello's so often that they named a dish after him. *Fusilli alla Robert Blake* was corkscrew pasta with garlic, olive oil, spinach, and tomatoes.

The couple walked in at 7:30 p.m. Blake ordered his fusilli. Nobody remembers what Bonny ordered. Nobody remembers whether the two of them fought, or flirted, or sat in icy silence. But they ate, and paid, and walked out of the restaurant, back to Blake's car. Bonny slid into the passenger's seat. Blake hesitated. He'd left something in the restaurant, he said—a gun.

As Blake would explain later, he had carried a gun to Vitello's because the world was *crawling* with men who wanted to kill Bonny Lee Bakley. She made so many enemies through her mail-order scams that he felt practically obligated to keep a gun on him at all times, he said. And so that night, Bonny waited in the car and Blake walked back to Vitello's to look for the gun that he had so carelessly left behind. And as Bonny sat there, alone under the Hollywood sky, someone walked up to the car and shot her in the head.

Bonny didn't die right away. Blood started leaking from her nose, eyes, and mouth. Her eyes rolled back in her head. She struggled to breathe. In fact, she was still breathing when Robert Blake returned to the car, saw the blood, and ran off, yelping that he needed help. He came back with a neighbor and an off-duty nurse who'd been eating at the restaurant. The neighbor and the nurse went straight to Bonny, trying to save her, while Blake himself stayed away from the car, yelling things like, "What happened?" As the nurse checked her pulse, Bonny took her final, agonized breath. The last person in the world to touch her was a stranger.

There were no signs that she'd fought anyone off or tried to get up from her seat. Later, police would theorize that this meant she knew her killer.

＊

AS BONNY'S BODY WAS WASHED, PAINTED, AND PREPARED FOR burial, Robert Blake lawyered up and began to trash her in the press. His lawyer leaked her taped phone calls, her salacious form letters, and even some painfully personal documents in which she worried about her weight and wondered about getting plastic surgery. Everybody had something to say about Bonny, and most of it was cruel. She was forty-four when she died, and the press didn't let anyone forget that. "The dowdy grifter," they called her.

Bonny was buried in a "mega-cemetery" called Forest Lawn that boasted a view of the Hollywood sign, and was now surrounded by the bones of the celebrities she'd loved so much. A year later, Robert Blake was arrested for her murder. Though many people believed that Blake had killed her—or at the very least, hired someone to kill her—he was acquitted. Several years later, in a civil trial, he was found responsible for Bonny's death and ended up paying her family an undisclosed amount of money. The whole fracas drew comparisons to the trial(s) of O.J. Simpson, which had happened several years earlier—except, as people pointed out, Blake was far less famous, and unlike O.J., no one had ever been fooled into thinking that he was a nice guy.

Today, Bonny's daughter Rose is a model with thousands of Instagram followers and the pretty round eyes of her mother. Robert Blake is nearing ninety years old. In a recent TV interview, he turned to the camera and snarled, "I'm still here, you bastards. I'm still here." No one has ever been officially sentenced for Bonny's death.

It was the saddest ending one could get in Hollywood. After a lifetime of failed attempts to get famous, even Bonny's high-profile murder didn't turn her into a beloved victim. She was too old, too conniving, too *obvious*. Hollywood was a land that rewarded hooded glances, sly flirtations, and cool girls who didn't try that hard, but Bonny's desires were all right there on the surface. She'd sent too many nudes, pursued too many famous men, recorded too many phone calls. She had a terrible habit of telling people exactly what she meant. *I'll fix them, I'll show them, I'll be a movie star. I like being around celebrities. I know he's going to kill me.* By the time she was buried among the bones of celebrities, Bonny Lee Bakley was finally famous—but she was also disgraced.

Still, Bonny would have been the first person to appreciate how everything unfolded after her death. She probably would have sympathized when her sister took $20,000 from the *Star* for an exclusive interview and her mother signed a "lucrative" contract with the *National Enquirer.* In Bonny's world, you took what you could get when you could get it. If someone offered to pay you for your story, you talked. If someone asked you to model, you posed. Bonny knew better than anyone that you should take the cash, soak in the tub, climb the walls of the mansion, and sway to the music while it was still playing—because the night was young, but the dawn was coming.

THE DRIFTERS

1. LAURETTA J. WILLIAMS
2. MARGARET LYDIA BURTON
3. SANTE KIMES

MISCELLANIA

THREE FAKE ETHNICITIES
TWO LINCOLN CARS
ONE RED WIG
TWO ESCAPES FROM PRISON
NUMEROUS INSTANCES OF RACING OUT OF TOWN
ONE SET OF FRECKLES
ONE FAKE MUSTACHE
THREE OMINOUS BOUQUETS OF FLOWERS
ONE FAKE AMBASSADOR
AT LEAST FIVE RUN-INS WITH THE FBI
ONE CELEBRITY DOPPELGÄNGER
A SERIES OF FAKE FAINTING SPELLS
ONE NOVEL CALLED *DYNASTY OF DEATH*
ONE FOLDER TITLED "FINAL DYNASTY"
ONE STUN GUN

LAURETTA J. WILLIAMS

alias: Loreta Janeta Velasquez or Velazquez, Lieutenant Harry T. Buford, Ann Williams, Mary Ann Williams, Mary Ann Keith, Mrs. M. M. Arnold, Mrs. L. J. V. Beard, Señora Beard, Loretta J. Wasson, Mrs. Bonner, Lauretta Clapp, Lauretta Clark, Lauretta Roach, Lauretta Roche, etc.

1842(?)-1923

A BEAUTIFUL CUBAN GIRL WITH DARK, FLASHING EYES STRIDES down the streets of the American South, dressed as a man. The year is 1861. Everyone around her is talking about war. For months, the girl watched in envy as men in gray uniforms joined the movement, their faces alight with purpose. And then she couldn't take it anymore. So she stripped off her skirts, strapped down her breasts, and enrolled as a soldier. After all, she didn't come to America just to wait on the sidelines.

Meet Loreta Janeta Velasquez: the proud Cuban American Confederate soldier who wasn't. Dark-eyed "Loreta" was the alter ego—was *one* alter ego—of a gal named Lauretta, who made up for in spunk what she lacked in honesty. The first time Lauretta appeared on the historical record, she was a teenage sex worker in

New Orleans, working in notoriously rough brothels and getting dragged in and out of court for petty crimes. It was an ignoble beginning, so Lauretta quickly scrubbed away that part of her past and replaced it with a better story: that she was the proud descendant of famous Spanish politicians and artists, born in Cuba and given the crème de la crème of education in American schools. In other words, she was *somebody*, so you should definitely listen to her—and invest generously in her latest scheme.

The real Lauretta was born sometime around 1842, perhaps in Cuba, Texas, New York, or the Bahamas. She changed the names of her mother and father so many times that no one has any idea who they were. Sometimes she called herself Lauretta J. Williams, or Clark, or Roach, or Roche, or Clapp, or Arnold, or Burnet, or Wasson, or Bonner, or DeCaulp—depending on who she was claiming as a father, who she was married to at the time, and whether or not the journalist interviewing her could spell. (When she announced that her last name was actually "Velasquez," one paper spelled it "Velazquex.") As a teenager, she went by Ann or Mary Ann Williams—but "Lauretta" was the name she used the longest.

Her Cuban identity—which she only started claiming later in life—is supported by little more than her word. It's possible that one or both of her parents were Hispanic or Latinx, as there were times when journalists mentioned a trace of an accent in her voice, or a certain "Latin" sensibility in her looks. But she was able to pass as a white American whenever she needed to. When she announced to the world that her *real* last name was Velasquez, it felt more like a rebranding than a revelation.

She was all about the rebranding. For her entire life, Lauretta had tried to shape-shift into someone else, someone *better*, someone with a fascinating past and a future so bright that you should finance it *immediately*. She wasn't always successful. From one angle, she was a grifter of a rather depressing persuasion, who drifted across America for seven lonely decades without ever scraping together much in the way of capital. From another, though, she was a quintessential American heroine: a trickster entrepreneur, a self-made woman, a raconteur with an imagination as long and winding as the Mississippi. To this day, people believe her tall tales.

❋

ON APRIL 12, 1861, THE UNITED STATES OF AMERICA SPLINTERED into the North and the South, and the Civil War began. As the first guns thundered at Fort Sumter, no one could have anticipated the four-year bloodbath that was to follow. In those early days, a lot of people thought the whole conflict was . . . kind of romantic.

Yes, before the bodies piled up, before the battlefield surgeries, before the plundering, the rape, and the brothers killing brothers, many white Americans were caught up in a tizzy of patriotism. Down South, where Lauretta lived, that patriotism was exacerbated by the sense that they were being invaded by the North and must defend what was rightfully theirs. Even the women felt a certain bloodlust stirring in their veins. As one poet roared, in a poem titled "Song of the Southern Women": "The fire that sleeps in our Southern eyes dark/Would lighten in the battle—we're Joans of Arc."

The rhetoric sounds melodramatic today, but the emotion was very real. Many women truly did want to join the army, no matter which side they were on. Not only would they be fighting for a cause they believed in, but the pay was much better than anything a woman in hoopskirts could hope to make on her own. Plus, the job promised freedom and adventure—which, to certain thrill-seeking women, sounded much better than rolling up bandages for the troops. Their presence on the battlefield was a bit of an open secret. Newspapers were always printing thrilling stories about dashing young soldiers who turned out to be women— sometimes even *pregnant* women.

In those days, it wasn't terribly hard to pretend you were someone else. No one carried around a passport or a driver's license. Hardly anyone had a birth certificate. If you said you were Emma Wilson, you were Emma Wilson. If you moved a couple of states over and declared that you were Private Alonzo Gifford, who could say that you weren't? And if you didn't want to risk life and limb but you wanted your share of wartime glory anyway, all you needed was a few yards of cloth—Confederate gray or Union blue, take your pick—and a train ticket to a town where no one knew you.

✳

ONE FINE SEPTEMBER DAY IN 1861, A DAPPER YOUNG CONFEDERATE lieutenant calling himself Harry T. Buford appeared in the streets of Lynchburg, Virginia. The young man looked good in his uniform. *Really* good. And he was walking around with such deliberate swagger that people couldn't help but notice. Women swooned.

Men scowled. In fact, the young soldier was so gaudily dressed that it didn't take people long to realize that this lieutenant was actually a pretty young woman in costume. Harry T. Buford was none other than Lauretta, who had broken away from her days of teenage sex work in New Orleans and was trying on a new identity for size. She peacocked around town, reveling in the attention. "Her dashing manners, fine appearance, gay uniform, and perfect *physique*, had caused her to be 'the observed of all observers,'" one newspaper reported.

The mayor of the town was unimpressed, however, and arrested her on suspicion of being a spy. Lauretta told him that her name was Mary Ann Keith and that she was most certainly *not* a spy. No, she insisted, she was naught but a loyal Confederate girl hoping to fight for what she believed in! See, she'd been married to a Southern man who betrayed her by running away to the Union army, and now she wanted to join up with the rebels to make up for his sins.

News of this overconfident little dandy quickly reached the Confederate capital of Richmond, Virginia, and the authorities there demanded that "Mary Ann Keith" be sent their way for questioning. Lauretta went, obligingly, but instead of turning herself in, she strode into the War Department—still in her fake uniform—and told the clerk that she needed help getting back to her post in Kentucky, as her general there was demanding her presence. The clerk was suspicious, but handed over the necessary documents anyway, and Lauretta escaped without a scratch. On her way out of the office, she forgot that she was disguised as a man—and curtsied.

Before long, the story of Lieutenant Harry T. Buford and his slippery antics was spreading across the country, devoured by readers on both sides of the Mason-Dixon Line. Some people were impressed by Lauretta's bravery, some people were intrigued by the strangeness of the whole thing, but *everyone* was talking about her. With nothing more than a couple of yards of gray cloth and a swaggering walk, Lauretta had achieved something truly impressive: fame. She was the "first celebrity" of the Confederacy, as her biographer William C. Davis wrote, "created wholly by the press."

Lauretta soon returned to New Orleans, where she'd lived as a teenager, but when the city fell to the Yankees in the spring of 1862, she realized that walking around in a Confederate uniform wasn't a great idea anymore. To save her skin, she loudly declared that she was a Union sympathizer—and then stole some jewelry from *real* Union sympathizers, which got her thrown into prison for six months. Local journalists were quite familiar with Lauretta's antics by then, since they remembered her from her days as a troublesome teenager. When she managed to escape from prison, the papers cheered her on. A "wily heroine," one called her. "This celebrated fast one," wrote another.

But her escape was thwarted when she accidentally strolled past the officer who had arrested her in the first place. He did a double take and threw her back into prison. Subdued, she served the rest of her sentence without a hitch and was released in May of 1863. The flowers were blooming, the war was raging, and Lauretta was ready to resume her wandering.

✳

I<small>T WAS OBVIOUS TO</small> L<small>AURETTA BY NOW THAT HER</small> H<small>ARRY</small> T. B<small>UFORD</small>
disguise was an easy way of getting attention. So she made her
way to Jackson, Mississippi, where she waltzed up to the editor
of the local *Mississippian* and pitched him a fantastical story.
The editor was so obsessed with Lauretta's tale that he printed
the whole thing without bothering to fact-check, and the ensuing
piece made Lauretta even more famous.

In it, the *Mississippian* editor wrote about how Lauretta had
been betrayed by her treasonous Yankee husband and had then
decided to join the war herself—where she had an army career
that can only be described as suspiciously star-studded. She led
a troop of soldiers through some of the most famous battles of
the whole conflict, she fought side-by-side with her own father
(who didn't recognize her), she snuck drugs and uniforms past
an enemy blockade, and she was even called an "incorrigible she-
rebel" by one of the Union's major generals. *Incorrigible she-rebel!*
Lauretta must have loved giving herself that title. She also must
have loved how the editor spent plenty of time in the article raving about how amazing she was. "Like most of the women of the
South, her whole soul was enlisted in the struggle for indepen-
dence," he wrote, breathlessly. "Possessing little of the character-
istic weakness of the sex, either in body or mind, [she] vowed to
offer her life upon the altar of her country."

Once the story came out, Lauretta capitalized on her growing
fame by treating herself to a new uniform, parading around the

South, and giving as many additional newspaper interviews as she could. Even though she was claiming to be a soldier, she clearly had no interest in joining the fray now. If she had really wanted to fight, she would have discarded her now-very-public alter ego and snuck into the army in some other disguise. But she stuck with her Lieutenant Buford identity, knowing that people would see "Lieutenant Buford" and think *Lauretta*. She wanted them to think that. She craved the world's attention.

When Lauretta wasn't giving interviews, she was busy with her other favorite hobby: writing letters to powerful men. This was a genius little trick she'd developed—she'd write to someone high up, they'd send back a bland, gracious, *signed* response on their official letterhead, and Lauretta would tuck this response away for her future schemes. Signatures and letterheads, she knew, were extremely valuable. You could flash them quickly in front of someone's eyes and they'd probably be impressed. Once, she wrote to Adjutant General Samuel Cooper, telling him that there were too many healthy young men working noncombatant jobs and that he should force them to join the army or else the South would definitely lose. (She signed her letter, "the female Lieutenant whoes whole soul is Enlisted in her countrys cause.") When he responded—*Thank you for your suggestion*, etc.—she added his response to her growing bundle of letters. One glimpse of the signature *Adjutant General Samuel Cooper*, and Lauretta's marks would be suitably impressed. Why would such a powerful man be writing to this scrappy little woman unless she was someone special?

And then Lauretta fell in love. One day, somewhere in the

wilds of the South, Lauretta met a tall, handsome captain with dreamy gray eyes who called himself Thomas C. DeCaulp. Later, Lauretta would claim that they fell in love as man and woman but fought next to each other as man and man, and DeCaulp didn't realize that his favorite soldier and his beautiful girlfriend were actually the same person until he got wounded and Lauretta walked into his hospital room—still wearing her fake mustache—to reveal herself. It was all terribly romantic (and a bit homoerotic, too), but the truth was much blander. DeCaulp was a minor con man himself: his real name was William Irwin, and he already had a wife, but Lauretta may not have known any of that. As "DeCaulp," he and Lauretta got married in September of 1863, after which he was sent back to battle and Lauretta continued on her merry-go-round of interviews.

Despite Lauretta's grand talk about how she supported the Confederacy with every fiber in her being and every brass button on her fake uniform, she and DeCaulp were loyal, first and foremost, to money. While they were still in their honeymoon period, they decided to run away to the North, where the pay was better. There, DeCaulp joined the Union army, and Lauretta took a job working for an arsenal in Indiana. Of course, making bullets for Northern soldiers wasn't a good look for a Southern girl "whoes whole soul is Enlisted in her countrys cause," so later in life, when she was back in the South, she told people that she had only been working at the arsenal in order to blow the whole place up.

Bullet-work was dreary work, and so soon enough, Lauretta decided that she was going to become a spy—or rather, she was going to convince people that she *had been* a spy. She visited several important Army men and showered them with tall tales, dropping important names and flashing impressive letterheads until one of them handed her a railroad pass that declared her "in secret service" for a single train ride. The pass itself was kind of boring. But Lauretta knew how to spin boring into gold. If you squinted at the paper, it almost looked like Lauretta was a spy, given that whole "secret service" bit. Once again, Lauretta had achieved her goal of not doing the work—or at least, not doing the *traditional* work—but getting the credit anyway.

✳

FOR THE NEXT COUPLE OF MONTHS, LAURETTA AMUSED HERSELF BY pretending to be a spy, putting on her fake uniform when she wanted attention, and chasing her husband from camp to camp. She also got pregnant. In a letter to DeCaulp, she referred to her "present condition"; in another letter, DeCaulp mentions "my Infant." It's likely that Lauretta had her baby sometime in mid-1864. But it's unclear what, exactly, happened to the child, as Lauretta was almost constantly on the move, crisscrossing the country like the Transcontinental Railroad (whose construction had started a year earlier). At one point, she appeared in Nashville pretending to be an army insurance agent, where she passed out alarming flyers that read, "Come one, Come all, for this may be the last opportunity you will have to insure your Limbs and Lives." Other times, she'd publish fake personal ads in the papers that were supposedly directed at her and claimed that her father had died and was leaving her a lot of money, or that she needed to send a representative to Cuba to deal with a dispute over her property. These ads were ingenious, as Lauretta could simply cut them out of the newspapers and show them to people as proof that she owned property or was coming into a large inheritance. Translation: this woman is important. Conclusion: you should definitely lend her money.

In those days, Lauretta was certainly not the only liar making her way around the rubble of the United States. One of her contemporaries was a gal named Caroline Wilson, who liked to claim that she'd lost all of her money by graciously "providing for Union soldiers"—so wouldn't you reward her patriotism with a bit of cash? But the difference between Lauretta and women like Caroline Wilson was that Lauretta almost never resorted to sob stories. Instead of making her marks feel bad for her, she was always trying to impress them. She was always implying that she'd *been* rich or *would be* rich soon. She would claim that she was on the verge of a huge financial breakthrough and *now* was the time to invest if you, too, wanted to be as rich as she was about to be! Her tales were grandiose to the point of unbelievability, but it helped that she was a slick talker—and that she was endlessly confident.

The Civil War ended on April 9, 1865, but Lauretta continued to con. DeCaulp had either died or left her earlier that year, and their child was God knows where, so Lauretta was free to keep roaming. She told people that she was writing her memoirs, and traveled around the country taking money for preorders, despite the fact that the book simply did not exist. In 1866, a steamboat called the *Miami* exploded, killing 120 people, and Lauretta claimed she was one of the surviving passengers for a while—but she was forced to discard that identity when the names of the two living women were published. She got married three times in quick succession: to a man with "long, wavy, flaxen hair" named John Wasson who died shortly afterward, to a prospector named Edward Hardy Bonner who never quite struck it rich, and then to a stagecoach driver named Andrew Jackson Bobo who left town after killing a man. She never divorced Bonner, so she was technically bigamous when she married Bobo—or trigamous, maybe, if DeCaulp was still alive.

She even traveled to Venezuela. After the war ended, certain furious white Southerners wanted to leave the country altogether and start a new South somewhere else. Venezuela looked promising, and so Lauretta traveled there to see if she could get ahead of the trend. The trip looked political on the surface, but—like so many of Lauretta's other schemes—it probably just came down to a desire for cash. Lauretta didn't care about starting a new South, but if someone was going to make a lot of money by starting a new South, she wanted in. Sure, when she was around Southerners, she told them she was a Southerner through and through, but when she was up North, she swore loyalty to the Stars and Stripes. At the end of the day, her only true allegiance was to herself.

✳

When none of her schemes panned out, Lauretta started talking about her memoir again. The Civil War may have been over, but America still had quite the appetite for war stories, and Lauretta was starting to think she could tell a really good one. She was a born storyteller. She could think on her feet, and her tales were so compelling that her listeners often failed to notice how implausible and downright contradictory they were.

But talking and writing were two different things, and Lauretta realized that she needed a cowriter. (Her spelling was questionable . . . and anyway, it's hard to imagine Lauretta dutifully scribbling down her thoughts for three hours every morning.) Since Lauretta believed that Lauretta deserved only the best in life, she decided to hire the best writer in the country to work for her. And so she sent a letter to Mark Twain.

God knows what Mark Twain thought when he opened up the day's mail and read that a bold nobody named Lauretta was asking him to collaborate on a shady-sounding war memoir. He refused her, and when she asked him again, he refused her for the second time. But Lauretta knew that the real truth didn't matter as much as the "truth" she declared in the papers, so she went ahead and made a grand announcement to the press: she was thrilled to announce that she would be collaborating on her memoir with none other than . . . Mark Twain!

She was undaunted when Twain wrote to the papers, furiously denying the collaboration. She didn't blink when the same paper that published his denial *also* printed an enraged letter from a man from her past, a man who knew and hated her. This man had been a friend of her ex-husband Bonner, the prospector, and he wanted the world to know that Lauretta was not to be trusted. "She is without doubt a low, vulgar, unprincipled adventurer," his letter roared. "Her ideas of morals are of the loosest kind, and no one in this country would believe her under oath. In a word, she is what the people in this country call an old blister."

Lauretta may have been a loose-moraled old blister, but she wasn't going to let a little slander stand between her and literary fame. So she signed a contract with William Ramsay of the Southern Publishing Company and somehow found a cowriter to scribble down her narrativizing. Perhaps figuring that a more exotic backstory would help her sell the book, she announced in the papers that she was now and for the first time revealing her *true* identity. She was no longer plain old American Lauretta: instead, she was a high-class, well-educated Cuban citizen named *Loreta Janeta Velasquez*.

Writing the book was hard work—she fought with her publisher over copyright and chased him down the street with a knife as he screamed for the police—but finally, after sufficiently terrorizing everyone she worked with, Lauretta managed to print the memoir that she'd been lying about for so many years. In July 1876, *The Woman in Battle* was released upon an unsuspecting public.

The title was straightforward, yes. But the subtitle gave readers a hint of the chaos within: *A Narrative of the Exploits, Adventures, and Travels of Madame Loreta Janeta Velazquez, Otherwise Known as Lieutenant Harry T. Buford, Confederate States Army. In Which Is Given Full Descriptions of the Numerous Battles in which She Participated as a Confederate Officer; of Her Perilous Performances as a Spy, as a Bearer of Despatches, as a Secret-Service Agent, and as a Blockade-Runner; of Her Adventures Behind the Scenes at Washington, including the Bond Swindle; of her Career as a Bounty and Substitute Broker in New York; of Her Travels in Europe and South America; Her Mining Adventures on*

the Pacific Slope; Her Residence among the Mormons; Her Love
Affairs, Courtships, Marriages, &c., &c.

That subtitle was jam-packed with titilating morsels, designed to make the memoir fly off the shelves. Violence! Sex!
Government secrets! Inside, the book contained a weirdly unflattering portrait of Lauretta in which she looks about fifty-five (she
would have been in her midthirties when it was published), and
the text itself was, unsurprisingly, full of outrageous claims. Even
though Lauretta clearly had a lot of help with the writing, there
was something about the prose that fit her personality well. It was
bold, self-serving, vague, rambling, and full of contradictions. In
the preface, she declares that she will use the plainest, simplest
language she knows, and then plunges into the fray with this em-
purpled first line:

> *The woman in battle is an infrequent figure on the*
> *pages of history, and yet, what would not history lose*
> *were the glorious records of the heroines—the great-*
> *souled women, who have stood in the front rank where*
> *the battle was hottest and the fray most deadly—to be*
> *obliterated?*

The rest of the 600-plus-page tome was so chaotic and inconsistent that it led one historian to wonder if it was a sign of
"incipient mental problems." But Lauretta had been contradict-
ing herself since her very first newspaper interview. She didn't
care about consistency; she cared about fame, shock value, and
cold hard cash. Her entire life up to this point had taught her that

accuracy was far less important than verve and passion; if she just told a story *convincingly* enough, people might forget to fact-check. And so her book proceeds along those lines. She refers to a brother by multiple different names, she claims to have fought a battle on July 18, 1861, and woken up the next morning forty miles away, she openly plagiarizes from another book, she rarely gives anyone's full names (making it difficult to confirm or deny her claims), and she pads the book with long, strange passages about irrelevant things like the flora and fauna of Venezuela. ("The onions are numerous, but small.") She conveniently omits the more embarrassing parts of her life—like her stint as a jewel thief—and focuses instead on a series of suggestive anecdotes about how Southern women were always falling in love with her and her delicious little glued-on mustache. When she talks about the war, she paints herself as a pivotal figure. She says that she had a chance to kill Ulysses S. Grant, but graciously chose not to. She claims that she was there when "Stonewall" Jackson was given his famous nickname. She declares that she met Abraham Lincoln himself. And she insists that if *she* had been allowed to command an army, the entire conflict would have turned out very differently.

Right after her book was published, the editor of a magazine called the *Southern Historical Society Papers* cast doubt on its truthfulness. The Confederate general Jubal Early dismissed it right away as utterly false, due to its "several inconsistencies, absurdities, and impossibilities." As the decades passed, historians continued to eye the book with suspicion. In 1999, one of them declared that it would be impossible to read her memoir "without concluding that she was at the very least an opportunist." In 2016, the first full-length biography of Lauretta announced, "To date there is still no independent, directly contemporaneous eye-witness testimony to support her claims. We have only her word, and given her record with the truth, accepting that word would be folly."

It's easy to say that now that Lauretta is no longer in our midst, wheedling and persuading. But back in the 1800s, Lauretta's word was awfully convincing, especially if she was in the room with you. And so her book sold.

✳

HER BOOK SOLD, BUT IT DIDN'T MAKE HER RICH. NEITHER DID MAR-rying yet another husband. The years turned into decades, and the only thing Lauretta gained, through all her wily scheming and endless traveling, was notoriety. And now, as she approached sixty, her notoriety was turning into a problem.

Confidence tricks are typically a young person's game. They require a great deal of vim and vigor, along with the ability to pivot fast, both mentally and physically. When your investors re-alize that there *is* no Californian hotel being built—as Lauretta's investors did in the spring of 1899—you've got to be able to get out of town, fast. When you're in a room full of men and they start asking you pointed questions about the railroad you claim to be building—as happened to Lauretta in the spring of 1900—you've got to be able to think on your feet so that they don't throw you into jail.

Lauretta managed, but her reputation was starting to precede her. She had grown up in a world where it was easy to con. She could give one story in one town, hop on a train, and give a completely different story in the next place. No one would be the wiser—at least, not for a week or so. But now, thanks to the invention of wire services, newspaper stories could travel across the country much faster than Lauretta could, meaning that the news of her latest scheme could reach her destination before she did. As the world changed beneath her feet, Lauretta found herself less able to convince people, and more likely to be laughed at. She was starting to look kind of strange, too. Her precious bundle of documents had grown so large that journalists would comment on it when they wrote about her.

Still, she did her best. At one point, she lived in Philadelphia for a year without paying a cent. She told everyone that she was a Cuban princess with an ambitious plan to build a railroad using grants from the Mexican government, and she managed to raise thousands of dollars from investors. She also convinced her landlord to give her free rent and persuaded local restaurants and stores to let her dine and shop on credit. She may have been older, but she was still the loquacious Lauretta of yore. "The woman is one of the most plausible and fluent I have ever met," said one of the men she swindled. "She seems to be able to persuade her fellow humans to almost anything."

But as the years went on, that clever, fast-paced mind of hers began to destroy itself. On August 5, 1912, when Lauretta was about seventy years old, she entered the Government Hospital for the Insane in Washington, DC. Upon being admitted, she gave her occupation as "writer" but was listed as "indigent"—in other words, penniless. It was there that her roving ended. Her brain was being devoured by dementia, and she spent the last eleven years of her life inside those hospital walls, while all the identities she had constructed slipped away from her. She died, without fanfare, on January 6, 1923. She never received an obituary.

But who needs an obituary when you've written a 600-page monument to your own real and imagined achievements? Today, the name "Loreta Janeta Velasquez" appears in books with titles like *Immigrant Women* and *Heroines of Dixie* and *They Fought Like Demons: Women Soldiers in the Civil War*. The name even appears on the website for the American Battlefield Trust, where "Loreta" is listed as one of the central characters of the Civil War. There is just enough truth in her book—certain dates, locations, and even descriptions of the weather are accurate—that many people over the decades have chosen to believe her. Her book turned out to be her longest and greatest con.

Lauretta would have loved all this attention. And yet, strangely, her memoir is full of little hints warning the reader not to trust her. "A good deal of the information I gave them was fictitious," she writes at one point, "while the rest was made up from telegrams, the newspapers, and conversations I had overheard." Another time, she writes, "The fact is, that human nature is greatly given to confidence; so much so, that the most unconfiding and suspicious people are usually the easiest to extract any desired information from, provided you go the right way about it." It was as though she was winking at the reader: *Here's how I pulled it off.* Perhaps she was showing us just enough of her hand to ensure that we'd continue to be impressed by her. "Women have the reputation of being bad secret-keepers," she continued, with all her old swagger. "Well, that depends on circumstances. I have always succeeded in keeping mine."

MARGARET LYDIA BURTON

alias: Mrs. Leda McGlashan, Mrs. Margaret E. Mitchell, Mrs. Jasper W. Burton, Mrs. Margaret Edna Burton, Mrs. M. B. Royal, Mrs. L. D. Grayson, Mrs. Edmond Landsden, Margaret Leda Burton, Janet Scott, Mrs. James A. Scott, Jeanette Watson Scott, Janice J. Scott, Janet Royer Gray, Mrs. C. E. Laine, Mrs. H. Adams, Mrs. C. Snowden, Janice Scott, Clara Buxton

1906-1992

THE FRECKLE-FACED WOMAN CALLING HERSELF "JANET R. Gray" was fabulously wealthy and cursed with a tragic past. At least, that's what the affluent citizens of Atlanta were led to believe. Janet had appeared in their midst in the fall of 1954, blown in like a leaf from Washington, DC, where her millionaire husband had recently died. Both of her children were gone, too: one died at birth, and the other was—oh, it was almost too horrible to say out loud—*run over by a school bus* a mere week after Janet's husband passed away. And so here was Janet, come South to lick her wounds. She was friendly, gracious. Everybody liked her. She didn't talk much about her past—though rumors swirled that she was the daughter of a high-ranking US Army general—but after all she'd been through, who could blame her?

Janet wasn't alone when she showed up in Atlanta. She was accompanied by a curvaceous blond teenager who looked much older than her fifteen years. Janet explained that the girl—Candace Victoria Laine, or "Candy" for short—was her niece. She was raising Candy, said Janet, out of the goodness of her own heart, since Candy's real mother was an irresponsible playgirl who lived in Switzerland with her fourth husband. The fine citizens of Atlanta thought this was just wonderful of Janet, though they had to admit that they didn't like Candy all that much. She was a bit spoiled. "Plain snippy," one of them explained. Besides, she didn't act the way a fifteen-year-old should. The way she dressed, the way she flirted, it was all a bit . . . inappropriate. A local hairdresser, who knew all the upper-class gossip, came right out and said it: "She was built like Marilyn Monroe . . . and it was embarrassing when she wore sweaters too small for her."

But Janet was a different story. "Brilliant and attractive," the hairdresser called her. A local dress shop owner mused, "She looked and acted like any well-bred educated woman her age to me." She was kind to people, and she left fabulously large tips. Given the sensitive nature of her past, no one knew exactly how much money she had, but she radiated wealth. Her decorator said that she had excellent taste, that she was "commonplace-looking, but in a chic way," and that he assumed she was rich "just from the tone of her voice." She owned horses and an entire kennel's worth of prizewinning cocker spaniels. She had a closet full of pricey fur coats and had recently installed a swimming pool in her backyard.

Because of all that, it seemed a little strange when she took a job as the manager of a doctor's clinic in nearby Decatur—but, as her decorator said, "I had the impression she just worked for the fun of it."

After three years of living in Georgia, mingling with the wealthy, and tipping generously, Janet got a phone call from work. Her bosses at the doctor's office had hired an auditor to look over their finances, and the auditor had found something pretty disturbing: they were missing almost $200,000. The doctors were sure it wasn't anything serious—probably just a slip of the hand, a trick of the light!—but they wondered if Janet could come into the office the next morning to answer a few questions, just in case.

Janet agreed. The next morning, she called the office bright and early to say that she was definitely planning to come by, but first she had to drive a friend to the airport. A few hours later, when she still hadn't shown up, the doctors called her house and were informed—by a woman calling herself Janet's maid—that Janet was having car trouble, but was still absolutely, positively planning to be there.

Little did the doctors know that at that very moment, "Janet R. Gray" was speeding through the Georgia countryside in a pink getaway car, accompanied by "Candy" . . . and thousands of dollars' worth of cocker spaniels.

✳

"JANET," WHOSE REAL NAME WAS MARGARET LYDIA BURTON, HADN'T always been obsessed with cocker spaniels—but she'd always been infatuated with money. Still, unlike her fellow con artists who were obsessed with money as a way to get power and attention, Margaret never wanted all eyes on her. Her background was elegant, privileged, and unstable, and it seemed to create in her a sort of dueling desire: for wealth, but also for anonymity. She cringed from the spotlight. She felt most at home in the getaway car.

On October 23, 1906, she was born Margaret Lydia Mc-Glashan in the port city of Tianjin, China—a white British subject from a well-to-do family. But her Scottish-born father apparently died young, as he dropped out of the picture by the time Margaret was eleven, and her mother later changed her marital status to "widow." Margaret and her two brothers moved to England with their mother when Margaret was eleven, and then to Canada when she was eighteen, which is where she likely went to college. By the time she was in her early twenties, her family had emigrated to the States, where pressure fell on Margaret to provide for them. By 1930, they were living in New Jersey, where Margaret worked as a bookkeeper, and her mother remained unemployed.

No matter where she was living, Margaret never had trouble finding work, and her employers always seemed to put her in charge of things. She was one of those women who just looked like she could *handle* it: friendly, capable, good at keeping the books and balancing the budget. By the age of twenty-eight, she was off on her own, living in Panama and managing a rug company based out of her Chinese hometown. There, she married a cute American auditor named Jasper W. Burton and gave birth to a baby girl named Sheila Joy. But by 1938, Margaret's company decided to transfer her to Honolulu, and Jasper chose to stay behind. (Years later, Jasper refused to talk about the deterioration of his marriage, but he expressed surprise at what his ex-wife had become. "She didn't own any dogs in Panama," he mused to one journalist, "and she showed no interest in them.")

It was in Honolulu that Margaret committed her first recorded crime. She began embezzling money from the rug company, and when her employers found out, they dragged her to court. In May of 1939, her case went before a grand jury—but before the grand jury could hand down their indictment, Margaret was packing her bags, scrambling onto a ship with her baby under one arm, and sailing off to Los Angeles to live with her mother. The LAPD took over the case and caught Margaret a few months later, but California's governor refused to send her back to Hawaii—perhaps he didn't find Hawaii's extradition request convincing enough—and so Margaret walked free.

With that lucky break, Margaret launched into a crime spree that lasted almost twenty years. She had a mania for lying and embezzlement, for reinvention and risk. And she couldn't seem to sit still. Even though she was perfectly capable of finding a good job and bringing home a steady paycheck, she could never resist skimming a little extra off the top, which inevitably meant that she'd have to leave town and find another job elsewhere. At every new job—which is to say, at every new crime scene—she showed up with a fresh alias and an elaborate backstory. Little Sheila Joy often got an alias, too. For years, the two of them ran from city to city, treating themselves to nice houses and fancy schools for Sheila Joy, and then racing away with the cops in hot pursuit.

In LA, Margaret told people that she was going to open a chain of knitting shops. She collected $9,500 from yarn-crazy investors—and then skipped town. In Vancouver, she filched $5,000 from an employer. In San Antonio, she wrote bad checks. It was in San Antonio, too, that she discovered her love of dogs— specifically, fancy show dogs that cost thousands of dollars. She'd been working for a dog kennel, and before long she was getting into the dog business herself, purchasing so many animals that when she inevitably had to pack up all her worldly possessions and flee town, the FBI described her dogs as, simply, "numerous."

And then she and her daughter moved through New Orleans, Denver, St. Louis, and Norfolk, Virginia—finding work, cheating work, and running out of town. Since Margaret's résumé was starting to look a little patchy, she bolstered it with lies. Once, when applying for work at a clinic, she told her employers that she'd come from a prominent position at Johns Hopkins Hospital. Another time, when asked why she didn't have any references, she claimed that she'd been working for her husband until he shattered her heart by having an affair—which is why she couldn't *possibly* ask him for a reference. And she always impressed her employers with her financial skills. *Let me manage the books*, she'd say. *You won't even need an auditor when I'm through with you!*

To little Sheila Joy, bouncing along in the back seat as her mother tore out of yet another city, everything must have seemed normal. It was the only life she knew—a life where Mom was "Leda McGlashan" one day and "Mrs. C. Snowden" the next. She wasn't sure where her dad was. She didn't even know if he was still alive. Her world was a cyclical one: blow into one town, live happily for a while, blow out again on the wind. Maybe her mother's background—skipping between countries and continents, never putting down roots—was what had trained them both to be so migratory. Perhaps Margaret had learned as a child that to be human was to be nomadic, and being nomadic could be a lot of fun. And now she was passing that lesson along to her daughter.

And so, when the two of them raced out of Norfolk, pursued by an angry doctor who was missing $2,000, Sheila Joy knew the drill. They didn't brake until Atlanta, where her mom decided to be "Janet R. Gray" and gave her the name "Candy." Her mom got a new job in a new clinic and started buying new dogs. Sheila Joy enrolled in a new school, an exclusive private one. Her mom was forty-eight, but gave herself a new age: forty. She gave Sheila Joy a new role: niece. They bought a new house, new clothes. They hired someone to install a swimming pool. Everything was shiny and fresh and pretty—and, of course, none of it would last.

✳

"CANDY" AND "JANET" MELTED EASILY INTO ATLANTA'S HIGH SOCIETY. Their backstory was just colorful enough to be interesting and just sensitive enough to keep people from inquiring too deeply. Sure, their lifestyle outpaced Janet's earnings as a lowly clinic manager, but everyone assumed that they'd come from money. For two and a half years, no one questioned a thing about them, other than the occasional raised eyebrow at Candy's tight sweaters.

When she wasn't in the clinic, Margaret was making quite the splash on the dog-breeding scene. She was obsessed with cocker spaniels and began shelling out thousands of dollars for each new silky-eared pup. Before long, she owned forty-eight of them. (Owned—or stole. Later, when her assets were being auctioned off, angry dog owners around the country claimed that some of Margaret's cocker spaniels were actually *theirs*.) Her favorite dog was a celebrity spaniel named Rise and Shine, who'd won Best In Show at the Westminster Kennel Club Dog Show in 1954. Sheila Joy adored the dog, too, and called him "Shiney."

Unfortunately, Sheila Joy wasn't fitting in all that well at school, and by the end of the 1955–1956 school year, she dropped out. She'd been absent for most of the year due to "poor health," and though her teachers liked her, they thought it was best that she not return since she'd missed so many classes. She hadn't exactly been popular. One of her classmates remembered that "Candy" had always seemed a little lonely. Perhaps it was the strain of living a double life that kept her apart from the rest of the girls. Or maybe it was her age. She had enrolled in the school as a sixteen-year-old, and eventually started pretending to be *fifteen*—even though, by the end of her time in Atlanta, she was almost twenty.

Her mother, though, didn't have any trouble fitting in. The doctors at her workplace loved her brisk, efficient work style. She was *so* brisk and *so* efficient, in fact, that they didn't even notice what Margaret was doing every time a patient paid in cash: brazenly pocketing the bills. It wasn't until about two and a half years had passed, and the doctors called in an auditor to look over the books, that they realized they were missing an awful lot of money.

Margaret couldn't have been all that surprised when the doctors asked her to come into the office. How many times had this happened before? She told them that she'd be there in the morning—and began planning her flight with the ease of a professional escape artist. She rented three moving vans and hired four handymen, and her team got to work overnight. By the time the sun rose, she'd filled two of the vans with furniture and expensive clothes, filled the third van with thirty-eight confused cocker spaniels, and re-homed the remaining ten dogs. Then she hopped into her own car—a pink 1957 Lincoln—and, at 10 a.m. on Tuesday, July 30, when she was supposedly taking a friend to the airport, she slammed down the gas pedal and peeled out of the state. It had been one of the smoothest getaways in the history of getaways. It was brisk. Efficient. Classic Margaret.

The doctors called the police, and the police called the FBI. Since Margaret was presumably taking stolen property across state lines, the case was now a federal offense, and so the FBI set off in hot pursuit. They figured that Margaret and her caravan would be easy to spot. After all, she was driving a hot pink car. She had thirty-eight dogs. This wasn't rocket science, right? An FBI spokesman confidently told journalists that finding Margaret would be like finding "an elephant in a snowbank." But they'd underestimated her well-honed ability to vanish.

As the days went by with no sign of Margaret or Sheila Joy—other than the discovery of the pink Lincoln, which they'd abandoned in Greenville, South Carolina—the FBI was forced to admit that their "elephant in a snowbank" simile hadn't been entirely accurate. The woman was slipperier than they expected. The only clue they found came in the form of her cocker spaniels, which she was leaving behind her like a trail of breadcrumbs. In North Carolina, she met up with her dog trainer and gave him most of the dogs, then bought a new car and kept on driving. The FBI tracked the dogs obsessively and discovered that two of them had died from the heat while traveling, five had been taken back to Atlanta by one of the members of her getaway caravan, and twenty or twenty-five turned up in New Haven, Connecticut, with the trainer. (The numbers vacillated a bit because one of the dogs had birthed a litter of puppies while on the road.) Eventually, the FBI figured out that Margaret had only three dogs left: her beloved Rise and Shine, a silky charmer called Piccolo Pete, and a pup named, fittingly, Capital Gain.

✳

NEWSPAPERS ACROSS GEORGIA WERE SALIVATING OVER THE STORY. You couldn't make this stuff up. The pink getaway car. The niece-who-was-secretly-a-daughter. The cocker spaniels! The *Atlanta Constitution* covered every detail of "Janet's" wild ride, and the good citizens of Georgia found themselves cheering her on, even though she had fooled them. "Amazing," the papers called her, and "audacious," and "flamboyant," and "fascinating." The *Constitution* was flooded with phone calls from curious onlookers who wanted to know more about the case. Had Janet been caught yet? Was it true that she had fled to Peru? "She has become a sort of Jesse James–type heroine," one journalist wrote. Another added, "Now I hope the FBI isn't going to construe this as un-American or anything, but wouldn't it be lovely if they didn't catch Mrs. Janet Gray—at least for a little while?"

Granted, not everyone thought "Janet R. Gray" was a heroine. A group called the Cocker Spaniel Club held a somber meeting to discuss this troubling turn of events, and a journalist who attended the meeting compared the atmosphere to a "wake." The club reported that they were "shaken" by the news that their colleague Janet had turned out to be so evil. "It was like picking up the paper and reading that President Eisenhower was a spy for the Communists," said one member.

Meanwhile, a receptionist at a clinic in Tulsa, Oklahoma, was starting to feel a bit "shaken" herself. She'd just hired a nice older woman named "Madge Burton" as the office bookkeeper, but now she was wondering if she'd made a terrible mistake. Sure, Madge hadn't had any references, but she had an explanation for all of that (it was awful, really—she'd been working for her husband, and he had an affair . . .). And the doctors had been impressed with the way Madge spouted off medical terms. In fact, Madge had declared that the clinic could get rid of their auditor, because she'd be more than happy to take care of the auditing herself.

So everything should have been fine—except the receptionist had just read a story in the *Tulsa World* about how a freckle-faced woman with a blond, buxom daughter recently fled from a clinic in Atlanta after embezzling thousands of dollars. The paper's description of the woman sounded eerily like Madge Burton, and wouldn't you know it, Madge just so happened to have a blond, buxom daughter, too. The receptionist conferred with the doctors. The doctors furrowed their brows. They agreed to call the FBI—just in case.

When an FBI agent walked into the clinic on August 21, he

found "Madge" at her typewriter, working with her usual brisk efficiency. He introduced himself. She froze. And then, with a heavy sigh, she stood and followed him out.

Her long run was over.

✳

AS MOTHER AND DAUGHTER WAITED TO BE EXTRADITED BACK TO Atlanta, the details of Margaret's extensive criminal history leaked out in the press. Along with the arrest warrants waiting for her in other states, she had all sorts of smaller, weirder debts: she owed $60 to her getaway car driver, $1,695 to a clothing store in Atlanta, $59.50 for a fancy hat. She even owed $30 to a photographer who'd documented a party she threw "for her dog-loving friends." In jail, she received two mysterious bouquets—gladioli and chrysanthemums—from a couple of men in North Carolina, accompanied by an ominous note: "Thanks for the going over you gave us. It's nothing compared to the going over you're going to get." No one ever figured out who sent the note, but it was a subtle sign that Margaret's trail of destruction was longer than even the FBI suspected.

For a woman who'd lived so extravagantly, Margaret's remaining assets weren't worth all that much: about $40,000 total. Her debtors were distressed to learn that they probably wouldn't ever be fully repaid. Still, everything she owned was auctioned off: her house, her horses, her furs, her dresses, her silverware, her jade figurines, and even that infamous pink 1957 Lincoln. Her three remaining spaniels were taken to a kennel in Tulsa, as members of the American Spaniel Club scraped together $1,555 to purchase

Rise and Shine and give him back to his trainer. In Atlanta, hundreds of curious people drove past Margaret's old house to gawk at the swimming pool and the fancy kennel—the detritus of the life of "Janet R. Gray."

Margaret refused to talk to the press, but local journalists dug up bits and pieces of her past anyway. They discovered that her long-lost ex-husband, Jasper Burton, lived a mere sixty miles away in Athens, Georgia, where he worked as the night manager at a hotel. He was overjoyed to learn that his daughter was nearby—he hadn't seen her since she was two years old—and the two of them were tearfully reunited. Jasper refused to talk to journalists about what, exactly, might have turned his ex-wife into such a pathological scammer. His only complaint was that the papers were making Sheila Joy out to be some sort of glamorous bad girl, and he didn't think that was fair. She was "quiet, refined and intellectual," he explained to journalists. "She most certainly is not the 'flashy siren' type."

Exactly one month after fleeing from Atlanta, all the charges against Sheila Joy were dropped. Authorities were pretty sure she was just an innocent passenger, driven hither and thither by her masterminding mother. Journalists asked her how she was feeling, and her voice shook as she wondered aloud if she'd ever see her mother again. Margaret's younger brother Ian, who was now a movie producer in Hollywood, showed up to rescue Sheila Joy, telling journalists that his sister was a "kind, gentle person who faints when she sees blood." His explanation for her scamming was that it was nature, not nurture: she had an "unfortunate quirk" in her character, he declared. If it weren't for that quirk, he said, "she would be a wonderful, wonderful person. In fact, she is anyway."

✳

By the time Margaret's trial started on December 9, 1957, the federal charges against her had been dropped due to a technicality. They'd charged her with interstate transport of stolen property, a charge that required at least $5,000 worth of stolen goods to be involved, but her dogs, furs, dresses, and pink Lincoln hadn't technically been *stolen*—they'd just been purchased with stolen cash. Now, she was only facing charges from DeKalb County, where the Decatur clinic was located . . . and from San Antonio, Los Angeles, Norfolk, Vancouver, and Honolulu. There were people across the country who hadn't forgotten the ways that Margaret, Janet, Madge, Leda McGlashan, Mrs. C. Snowden, and all the rest had wronged them.

The DeKalb County trial was shaping up to be quite the dramatic event—one of the doctors testified that he'd "lost [his] faith in humanity" because of her crimes—but it was declared a mistrial when a juror heard his pastor talking about Margaret from the pulpit. Really, who *wasn't* talking about her? She was Georgia's top news story for the year. One journalist visited her in jail after Christmas, and found her skulking around in pale blue satin pajamas, reading a novel called *Dynasty of Death*.

Her new trial started in February of 1958, and she showed up looking "slightly pale but chipper." She told the courtroom that her employers had been evading their taxes and so had *forced* her to keep their money in her bank account. She said that she only skipped town because she was afraid of the IRS. And she declared that her lavish lifestyle wasn't funded by anything nefarious—no, she bought the house and the swimming pool and the fur coats by selling furniture and the occasional cocker spaniel. When she wasn't protesting her innocence, she was fainting dramatically. She told a doctor that she'd suffered from fainting spells for the past fifteen years, but people were understandably a bit skeptical every time she swooned to the floor. The prosecutor, especially, didn't feel all that sympathetic toward her faints or her feints, and compared her to a "confidence man in a Texas oil swindle."

The jury agreed with the prosecutor. They found her guilty of two counts of larceny and two counts of forgery (she fainted upon hearing the verdict) and the judge sentenced her to two to five years in prison (she fainted upon hearing the sentence). "An actress to the last," one paper called her. It was the first time in her almost twenty-year swindling career that she hadn't been able to escape.

✳

AFTER TWO WELL-BEHAVED YEARS BEHIND BARS, MARGARET WAS released. By then, most of the other charges against her had been dropped. San Antonio, Norfolk, Vancouver, and Honolulu decided that it would be better to just deport her back to England than to bother with prosecution. Still, Los Angeles wanted to try her for her old knitting-shop swindle, and so they extradited her to the Golden State and gave her 240 days in a county jail. She served her time, and by the spring of 1960, she was free to be deported. Authorities put her onto an ocean liner called *Bremen* and shipped her off to England, the land of her adolescence.

Perhaps Margaret felt some relief about returning to a land where, as far as we know, she had a clean slate. She seemed to have experienced a change of heart while in prison. She'd pled innocent in Georgia, but by the time she was being tried in California, she went ahead and pled guilty—as though she'd realized that after two decades of swindling, she couldn't press her luck any further. There would be no more getaway cars for her. The pools and the hats and the dogs were long gone.

Or were they? On the ship's records, she listed her occupation as "housewife." She was certainly *not* a housewife, though. She and Jasper were long divorced, and she'd gotten out of county jail less than a week earlier, so it's hard to imagine that she already had a new husband. Perhaps she was already dreaming about new backstories, new escape routes.

✳

AMAZING. AUDACIOUS. FLAMBOYANT. FASCINATING. MARGARET quickly faded from the spotlight after being deported, but there was no denying she'd made her mark. Even though she caused a lot of people serious trouble, others found it hard not to root for her. "The great masquerader," one journalist called her. "A legend in her own time," wrote a second. "The remarkable Mrs. Burton," wrote a third, "whose exploits and escapes read like a paperback novel."

Just two years before Margaret's capture, a novel full of exploits and escapes *was* published, though its antihero was a man, not a woman. Reviews of *The Talented Mr. Ripley* called the scammer Tom Ripley a "heroic and demonic American dreamer," and he quickly became something of the ur-scammer, a fictional con artist that every subsequent real con artist would be compared to. It's strange that no one directly compared Margaret to Tom Ripley, though newspapers seemed to do so subconsciously, giving her titles like *The Remarkable Mrs. Burton* and *The Mysterious Mrs. Gray*. Readers clearly saw something of the American dreamer in her, too. She wasn't born an underdog, but she managed to be a bit antiestablishment anyway—weaseling her way into high society with a padded résumé and a fake name. And speaking of America, it was impossible to deny her skill at that most American of plot twists: the getaway. In a way, she was like John Dillinger, or Clyde Barrow—one of those great American thieves able to wreak havoc and then peel out of town at a moment's notice. But unlike Dillinger and Barrow and Ripley, she did it all in a pink car.

In fact, perhaps her penchant for the getaway is exactly why Margaret never became a famous American criminal. She never did become the subject of a paperback novel. She gave one brief interview to a journalist after her arrest, during which she held her cards close to her chest, giving responses like "It's hard to say" and "We just happened to wind up there." Even the photographer she liked to hire for her dog parties remembered how slippery she was. "Come to think of it," he said, "she always made a point of staying out of the pictures."

In 1972, a reader wrote to the *Atlanta Constitution* with a nagging question. "What ever happened to the Mrs. Gray that had all the dogs and took all that money from the doctors in Decatur a few years ago? I seem to recall that she got away somehow, but I don't know for sure." The paper responded: "In May 1960, at the age of 53, she sailed to England under deportation orders. No one seems to have heard of her since." Margaret did eventually return to the United States, where she settled down in Los Angeles and passed away in 1992 as "Margaret Evans," having apparently married again . . . or adopted another alias. But at the time, no one outside of her friends and family noticed.

Her desire for anonymity and her love of a good car chase were legacies that she passed on to her daughter. Back in 1957, when the charges against her were dropped, Sheila Joy told journalists that her biggest desire was to simply escape. "I want to become 'Miss Anonymous,'" she said. "If it's necessary to get away from people, I'd like to switch from car to car until we get away from all the curious people. But I'm afraid I'm not as good at that as Mommie."

SANTE KIMES

alias: Shante Kimes, Santee Kimes, Sante Louise Singhrs, San-
dra Singhrs, Sandra Singhres, Sandra Singer, Sandra Chambers,
Sandra Louise Powers, Mrs. Eddy Walker, Sandra Walker, Sandy
Kimes, Louise Walker, Marjorie Walker, Santa Louisa Powers, San
Tag Singhrs, Sandra Seligman, Sandy Jacobson, Donna Frances
Lawson, Eva Guerrero, etc.

1934–2014

IT WAS DARK WHEN KENNETH KIMES FINALLY WENT HOME TO HIS
mother, holding a massive bouquet of flowers. He'd just killed a
man. Now he was ready to celebrate.

The man's body would be found the very next day, and Kenny
and his mother would go on the run. But just then, Kenny felt
amazing, with the flowers spilling out of his arms and the adrena-
line rushing through his veins. He hadn't wanted to commit another murder, but now that the body was wrapped in plastic and
the blood was scrubbed from the kitchen floor, he was reminded
yet again that his mom always knew best. Always. He'd spent a
hundred dollars on her flowers, just because, and he'd been feeling so electric that he even slipped his number to the girl at the

checkout counter. Now he was going to head home, give the flowers to his mom, and kiss her on the cheek. He really was her "soulmate son," as she liked to call him. Her "honey bunny." They had blood on their hands, sure, but blood washed off. It was so easy to get away with things if you were just smart about it, and his mother was the smartest person in the world.

✳

ASHES TO ASHES, DUST TO DUST.

Sante Kimes was born into a land destroyed by drought. She was a poor kid from Oklahoma who came screaming into the world on July 24, 1934, right smack in the middle of the Dust Bowl. Her mother, Mary Van Horn Singhrs, was Dutch, and her father, Prame Singhrs, was Indian. Sante would grow up to lie to almost every man who ever crossed her path, but the first man in her life lied to her: yes, her dad was bit of a con man himself, spinning stories about how he'd worked as an army captain in India, a doctor in China, and a magician in Russia. He claimed that he was a raja—an Indian prince—or at least, he was *supposed* to be a raja, but the title had been stripped away from him in a family quarrel. But when Prame emigrated to America, his sleight of hand was no match for the raging dust storms he found there. There was no work in Oklahoma, so Prame and his family migrated to California, but there was no work there, either. So they came right back to their parched home state.

When Prame died in 1940, Mary moved to Los Angeles with her four children, hoping life would get easier for them. It didn't. According to Sante, her mother was an abusive alcoholic who always brought strange men home. Her two older siblings ran away as soon as they could, while middle-child Sante grew into a terrifying creature who tormented her little sister by sticking lit matches under her fingernails. (At least, that's what her little sister Retha claimed—but just like her father and her sister, she was an unreliable narrator.) Before long, Sante was begging on the street. Sometimes she found solace by hanging out at a local coffee shop, and the kind couple who owned the place befriended her. They must have seen something in her—some raw intelligence, a glimmer of potential—and eventually they told Mary Singhrs that they had relatives in Carson City, Nevada, who would be happy to adopt her daughter. Mary agreed, and Sante was put on a northbound bus.

Her new parents were named Edwin and Mary Chambers, and they officially adopted her when she was eleven years old. She now had a newer, whiter life, and by all accounts she enjoyed it—or at least took advantage of it. At first, kids teased her for her name, "Sante Singhrs," but stopped when the adoption papers changed her name to "Sandy Chambers." She started powdering her face to disguise her olive skin tone, and her Nevadan classmates found her smart, funny, beautiful, and intriguingly strange. There was something closed off about her, though, despite all that. She had trouble making girlfriends, even though she attracted boys easily. She had a best friend and a boyfriend, and she ruled both of them with an iron fist. From the beginning, Sante wanted to control everyone she came across.

Much later, Sante would paint her time in Nevada with a darker brush. Sometimes she said that her adopted dad, Ed Chambers, had raped her. Other times, she claimed that the two of them had had a consensual sexual relationship. *Something* happened to alienate her from the Chambers family, but we don't know what it was. Later, Ed Chambers would say, tersely, that Sante and the Chambers had a "parting of the ways situation."

After high school, her boyfriend—a sweet young man named Ed Walker—was planning to get married to his beautiful, exciting, control freak of a girlfriend, but Sante shocked him by suddenly marrying an army officer. She'd convinced the army officer to propose by telling him she was pregnant (she wasn't), but when he was honorably discharged from the army and became a high school teacher, she divorced him in a flash. She wanted to be a glamorous army officer's wife, not the wife of a humble high school teacher. With her divorce still fresh, she showed up on Ed Walker's doorstep, ready to reunite. They were married on November 9, 1957, a year and a half after her first wedding.

Sante was only in her early twenties, but she knew exactly what she wanted out of life: a rich husband, and all the power and control that came with wealth. To achieve this, she pushed Walker harder and harder in his work. There was something magical about her pressure, and before long, Walker *was* the rich husband she'd dreamed of, a respected young developer in Sacramento with all sorts of exciting projects simmering away. There was just one problem. His houses kept burning down, and the insurance money always seemed to end up in Sante's pockets.

Sante had grown up without money, and her relationship to money as an adult was morphing into something obsessive and pathological. She had to have it, and she couldn't be trusted with it. One year, she stunned her husband by spending \$13,000 on Christmas gifts. Another time, she got arrested for shoplifting a hair dryer. And money wasn't the only thing she obsessed over. As their marriage progressed, Sante grew more and more controlling of Walker's behavior. She was paranoid about keeping the house clean and nagged her husband when he wore casual clothes. She began sleeping with other men, and she made sure that Walker knew it. When their son Kent was born in 1962, Walker showed up at the hospital to meet him—only to find that one of Sante's lovers was already there.

It was as though she needed a hundred backup plans: backup men, backup money, backup schemes. She had an "absolute paranoia about being poor," her husband said, once. The smell of dust was forever in her nostrils. She was always running away from the storm. Or maybe she was the storm.

✳

BY THE TIME SHE WAS IN HER MIDTHIRTIES, SANTE HAD REINVENTED herself. She'd divorced Ed Walker, who clearly wasn't going to be a multimillionaire anytime soon since his buildings kept burning down, and now she was living in Palm Springs with little Kent. She'd added an accent to her name—Santé—and told everyone that she was French. In Palm Springs, she kept herself busy with a series of delightful hobbies: shoplifting fine liquors, stalking her ex-husband, dragging his new girlfriend around by the hair while calling her a whore, and driving extravagant cars right off the lot. But the real reason she was in Palm Springs was to catch herself a millionaire.

Santé-from-France didn't quite fit in with the moneyed folks of Palm Springs. In fact, many of them assumed that she was a sex worker: she treated lingerie as outerwear, she'd recently gotten breast implants, she wore extremely thick makeup, and she was always buzzing around the local millionaires. But Sante didn't care what the moneyed folk thought of her, because the local millionaires adored her. They loved her spontaneous attitude, her generosity with the cocktail shaker, and her voluptuous beauty. When she was all done up, she bore an uncanny resemblance to the actress Elizabeth Taylor. (The resemblance was so strong that sometimes people would ask Sante for her autograph, and she always obliged.)

When one of her millionaires showed up to take her on a date, he'd be greeted by the disturbingly charming sight of eight-year-old Kent, dressed up as a little butler and offering to make him a drink. As her son mixed screwdrivers in the corner, Sante would sweep into the room, all curves, big hair, and white teeth. The millionaire would sit down on her stolen sofa and sip from her wide selection of purloined liquor, reveling in the heat of her attention. As their relationship progressed, she'd start to turn the screw: she'd manipulate him out of thousands of dollars, and eventually she'd bring around a new millionaire to drive him wild with jealousy. Still, he would inevitably stick around until the bitter end, just like Ed Walker had. Little Kent knew how her millionaires suffered, because he suffered, too. "Nothing felt as good as basking in the charged warmth of her love," he wrote later. "Nothing hurt as much as having it taken away."

It was 1970 when Sante finally locked down one of her Palm

Springs millionaires. His name was Ken Kimes, he was a divorced fifty-three-year-old motel developer, and just like her, he was from a poor family of Oklahoma crop-pickers. He was a bit of a grifter, too: he'd managed to register as Native American and received regular checks from the government. And he was totally enamored with Sante. She peacocked around him in white (his favorite color), wearing gardenia perfume (his favorite scent), and she *always* kept his cocktail glass full. Sante would later claim that they got married in 1971, though there's no record of their marriage until a decade later. The two of them were never quite on the same page about paperwork. Ken had two kids from his previous marriage, and perhaps because of them—or maybe because he never really trusted his new woman—he always kept his money just slightly out of Sante's reach.

That's not to say that he was unwilling to spend money on her. They blew through his checking accounts in a spectacular fashion, vacationing in the Bahamas, buying houses in Honolulu, Las Vegas, Santa Barbara, and La Jolla, and gambling away millions at Vegas casinos. She reciprocated by flattering his ego to an extreme degree. Once, she branded him as an "ambassador," and took him to Washington, DC, where they crashed four exclusive political soirees in a single night, including one thrown by Vice President Gerald Ford himself. Sante wore all white, and glued a rhinestone to her ear, claiming it was an Indian custom. The next day, their faces were all over the papers, and they were being grilled by the FBI, but they managed to weasel away from the drama with nothing more than a bit of notoriety.

Though Sante would later describe her relationship with

Ken as a "magical love affair," the two of them fought all the time, and their fights were brutal and bizarre. One night, young Kent heard his stepfather screaming for him, and raced into the kitchen to find the two of them in the middle of an epic battle. Sante, in her nightgown, was furiously urinating on the floor as a sort of preemptive strike. She then began slapping her husband, who slapped her back for a while, until she climbed into his lap seductively, pretending that all was forgiven, burying her hands lovingly in his hair—and then ripping out his brand-new hair plugs. As Ken howled in pain, Sante tried to rush out of the room, only to slip in her own urine. At that point, her son tackled her, and she bit him on the wrist. The next morning, Kent woke up to find Sante and Ken smiling at each other as if it had all been nothing more than a bad dream.

The years passed this way, in fighting and drinking and spending, but Ken still seemed no closer to signing over all his wealth to Sante. So in 1975, she decided to try a new approach. Kent, who was twelve at the time, noticed that his mother was gaining a little weight, though she disguised it well with her flowy white outfits. He didn't think much of it. She often complained of stomach troubles. And so he was blindsided when, one day, Sante went to the hospital and returned with a baby boy.

✳

THE BABY, KENNETH KAREEM KIMES, WAS ALL PART OF SANTE'S marry-a-millionaire plan. Now that she and Ken Sr. had a biological son, he'd *have* to leave all of his millions to her. Besides, she needed someone new to control. Kent was growing up fast and beginning to extricate himself from the family. So Sante began to home in on her younger son, who she called Kenny.

Kenny's early years were spent in Hawaii, where drama (and arson) abounded, as they always did when Sante was around. His mother spoiled him but wouldn't let him play with other children. In this rarefied, lonely environment, he grew into a strange boy who could be tyrannical or terrified, depending on what was happening around him. On the rare occasion when he was allowed to go on a playdate, he might start crying, saying that he hated his mom. The next day, he'd be perfectly fine. From an early age, his relationship with his mother was marked by confusion. Sante let him shower with her until he was at least seven years old, saying she wanted to teach him that the human body was beautiful.

Kenny's main companions were his mother's maids—young girls from Mexico and El Salvador hired by Sante to clean house and watch over her little son. The maids didn't talk much, and nobody bothered to ask how they were doing. For the most part, they faded into the background, shadows against the scrim of Sante's erratic temper. Because if the Kimes household was characterized by anything, it was by Sante's temper—her screaming, her seductions, her schemes. She thrived on chaos, and if the house fell quiet, she'd create chaos, just to revel in the noise.

Sante adopted the same tactic with the law, creating such a legal tumult wherever she went that lawyers and law enforcement were often tempted to throw up their hands and be done with the case so that they wouldn't have to deal with her anymore. In February 1980, she and her husband were drinking in a piano bar in a DC hotel when she stole a $6,500 mink coat from another woman in the bar. When the woman noticed that her mink was missing, every-one in the bar immediately thought of the sketchy Elizabeth Taylor lookalike who'd skulked out of there earlier. Sante and Ken Sr. were arrested. But they skipped town on bail, and Sante managed to drag the case on—bolstered by doctors' letters claiming she was far too ill to travel back to the courtroom—for five years. "Peace deprivation," Kenny called these tactics, later. "A constant influx of drama and insanity until you think you might be the crazy one."

The drama and insanity meant that there were always law-men and lawsuits following Sante like fans swarming after Eliza-beth Taylor. There was the fur coat case. The constant arson. Her tendency to drive fancy cars right off the parking lot. There were always frantic notices about her appearing in the papers, like the summons that would pop up in the *Honolulu Adviser* from time to time: "TO: KENNETH K. KIMES and SANTE KIMES aka SINGHRE KIMES, YOU ARE HEARBY NOTIFIED THAT SEARS, ROEBUCK AND CO. . . . has commenced an action in Civil No. 58812 for TORT against you . . ." (God knows what Sante had done to poor Sears.) Sante was used to this sort of legal rumbling in the background. She knew how to block it out with the sound of her cocktail shaker or her own clanging voice. But what she didn't know was that behind the scenes, a far more se-rious case was building against her, because someone had finally broken out of her control.

✳

ON AUGUST 3, 1985, SANTE WAS WATCHING TV IN HER LA JOLLA condo when the police kicked in her front door. She and her husband were arrested, right in front of ten-year-old Kenny. Within days, headlines were screaming in disbelief: "COUPLE CHARGED WITH SLAVERY."

Slavery? Everyone was shocked—everyone, that is, except Sante's maids. The young girls from Mexico and El Salvador— the ones who'd been there all along, fading into the background, cleaning up the urine from the floor, and sobbing against their locked bedroom doors late at night—had been held, by Sante, completely against their will. But one of them had finally escaped and gone to the police, who turned the case over to the FBI.

Sante adored having maids—what signified wealth quite like having *maids?*—but she also adored having total and complete control over people. So she'd drive down to Mexico or Central America in search of young girls from poor families who didn't speak much English. When she found the right sort of girl, she'd promise her a job in America, a green card, and a salary so generous that the girl would be able to send money back home. And then Sante would smuggle the girl back across the border in the trunk of one of her fancy stolen cars.

In America, the girls would find out that Sante had lied. She never paid them a cent. She wouldn't let them call home. She would lock them in their rooms at night and tell them that if they called the police, the police would rape them. She would abuse them relentlessly, beating one girl with a coat hanger, burning another with a hot iron, and throwing boiling water on a third. If she needed to terrify them even more, she'd pull out a gun and wave it around. And in return for the privilege of being Sante Kimes's maid, she expected ironclad obedience and total silence.

To achieve this, she wrote pages and pages of rules in terrifying caps lock: "IF YOU PAY ATTENTION TO THE FAMILY AND YOU DON'T GO TO THE DOOR AND YOU DON'T ANSWER THE TELEPHONE FOR ANY REASON, DON'T DO THESE THINGS, then everything is going to be very beautiful and you are going to have a very happy life. IF YOU DON'T PAY ATTENTION, IT IS GOING TO BE A HELL, HELL FOR YOU." She also wrote instructions for Kenny's tutors and babysitters, telling them to keep an Orwellian eye on the girls. One of her instructions read, simply, "Maid: CONTROL! CONTROL! CONTROL! CONTROL! CONTROL! CONTROL! CONTROL! CONTROL!"

But now her control over the girls had splintered. As she prepared for trial, her defense team hired a psychologist to explain away her behavior, and his explanation was less than flattering. "Clinically speaking, this is a person who 'snaps' from time to time," he said, describing her as someone who suffered from a "hysterical lack of control" and "repressed anger." (One of the FBI agents who worked on this case had a less reserved opinion: "Sante Kimes was the cruelest, most self-centered, conniving, and bizarre woman I had ever met in thirty years as an Agent.") Sante was busy working on her own, more ad hoc defense: she pretended to be sick and got transferred to a local hospital, where she managed to escape, possibly by seducing her guard. She fled to a friend's house and immediately took a bubble bath. A few days later, she was recaptured, disguised as a homeless woman. "The best female con I've ever seen," said another FBI agent.

Ken Sr. managed to strike a plea deal, saying that he'd known about the abuse all along and hadn't done anything to stop it, so by the time the trial began in Las Vegas on February 10, 1986, Sante was the sole defendant. She argued that her house's horrors—its locked doors, locked gates, and lists of rules—didn't have anything to do with *slavery*, but were merely precautions she put in place to protect her baby Kenny from being kidnapped by her husband's evil ex-wife! But the jury didn't buy her version of events, and she was found guilty of "forcing involuntary servitude," "unlawfully transporting illegal aliens," and "escaping from federal custody." For that, she was given five years in prison, plus a $300 fine—which was more than she'd paid her maids, ever. (The maids were forced to file a $35 million civil suit against her, a suit that Sante managed to get her insurance company to pay.)

Sante had also been given an additional three- to nine-year sentence for her 1980 theft of the mink coat, but she weaseled out of that punishment in her typical exhausting-but-ingenious fashion. She left the courtroom just before her verdict was read, pretended to get hit by a car, went to the hospital, and then skipped town. Next, she argued that since she wasn't present in the courtroom when her verdict was read aloud, her Sixth Amendment rights had been violated, as she never heard the conviction against her. The fatigued authorities allowed her to plea-bargain her way into a misdemeanor charge of petty theft. She was given a year in jail, credit for time served, and a $10 fine.

By December 11, 1989, she was a free woman once more, and

she put the whole nasty business behind her as though it was no more significant than a parking ticket.

✳

SANTE CELEBRATED HER FREEDOM BY DRINKING CHAMPAGNE IN THE bathtub and devouring her favorite food: french fries with extra ranch dressing. And then she was back to her old life of screaming at her husband, terrifying her sons, and enslaving people. In prison, she had written saccharine letters begging the judge to release her because she would never so much as think the word "slavery" again, but now that she was free, she put that whole *I'm a changed woman* act behind her. She stopped smuggling in "maids" from Mexico, and instead started haunting homeless shelters, promising the residents that they could sleep at her house for free in exchange for a little light cleaning. ("CONTROL! CONTROL! CONTROL! CONTROL! CONTROL! CONTROL! CONTROL! CONTROL!") She was never charged for exploiting the homeless. Prison had taught her a valuable lesson: whatever you do, don't get caught.

Kenny wasn't happy to have his mom back. When Sante was in prison, he'd had the space to blossom into a social, silly kid, but when she came roaring back into his life, all his potential was crowded out once again by the chaos she brought with her. He adored his mom, but he also wanted to be free of her, and the cognitive dissonance threatened to break him. He became sullen. Violent. He got into steroids and bodybuilding—and darker hobbies. At fifteen, he tried to strangle his mother with a rope. At sixteen, his older brother found him in the kitchen, pouring a mysterious clear liquid into his parents' cocktail glasses, with a copy of *The Anarchist Cookbook* on the counter. Sante responded to his growing aggression by isolating him even more: she forced him to finish high school in the Bahamas, away from all his friends, and eventually manipulated him into dropping out of college.

Years later, tabloids would claim that Kenny and his mother didn't just love each other—they were *in love* with each other. There certainly was a strange static between them. Nobody understood that static more than Kent, Sante's first son, who'd been in Kenny's shoes so many times before. He too had felt the pull of Sante's love. It was like a beam from an alien spaceship, alluring and perilous. But Kent eventually managed to escape. He married a nice girl, stopped answering (most of) Sante's calls, got a job, lived a normal life. Kenny never had that chance. He got beamed right up.

✳

FOR YEARS, SANTE HAD SHOWN THAT SHE WASN'T AFRAID OF VIO-lence. She'd rip out your new hair plugs if you disagreed with her. She'd throw boiling water on you if she thought you were being disobedient. Once, she sued her own insurance company and began threatening its executives with stories of children who were kidnapped and dismembered. Though con artists are often described as nonviolent criminals, Sante did her very best to prove otherwise. And one year after she was released from jail, she may or may not have killed someone with a hammer.

One of Sante's many, many lawyers was a man named Elmer Holmgren, whose job wasn't so much "file Sante's paperwork" as it was "burn down Sante's Hawaii house for insurance money." By September of 1990, Holmgren had done just that. But when he drunkenly told a friend about the arson, the friend went to the police, and the police forced Holmgren to become a double agent. They weren't so much interested in *his* crime. They wanted to catch Sante.

Somehow, Sante—with her unnerving, all-seeing eye—found out that Holmgren was working for the police. But instead of confronting him, she invited him on a vacation to Costa Rica. Holmgren accepted her invitation, though he had a bad feeling about the trip. He told his son to notify the authorities if he didn't get in touch in three days.

The three days passed with no word from Holmgren. In fact, his son never heard from him again. No one ever found out exactly what happened to the lawyer, and his body was never discovered. But Sante's older son had a sneaking suspicion about who was responsible for his disappearance. One day, Kent overheard Sante and Ken Sr. drunkenly arguing about a murder. They were disagreeing about who, precisely, had killed an unnamed somebody with a hammer while driving around Los Angeles in a rental car. They never named the victim, but Kent was positive they were talking about poor Elmer Holmgren.

If Ken Sr. had killed for Sante—or simply chauffeured Sante around while she killed—it wouldn't have been all that surprising. Over the course of their relationship, Sante had worn Ken Sr. down to a nub of a man. He was pickled in booze, and his fortune had been frittered away on gambling, legal fees, and french fries with extra ranch dressing. (To be fair, Sante didn't always pay for the french fries. Sometimes she'd create a scene and storm out of the restaurant to avoid the bill.) For almost two and a half decades, she kept Ken Sr. clinging to the pendulum of her love: seducing him, humiliating him, babying him, terrifying him. On March 28, 1994, Ken Sr. finally escaped her the only way he could—by dying of a massive aneurysm.

Sante was quick to rewrite their history. "Our incredible love affair lives on and on," she gushed, a year later. "He was the most loving husband, and we had the greatest love affair and marriage of all time. We could not keep our hands off of each other, even after 30 years! My wonderful papa! On the last day of his life and of our incredible, wondrous love story, after 30 years of our magical love affair, he turned and embraced me, in front of everyone and he said: 'I love you Mama Kimes!' And then he died."

As soon as her wonderful papa was six feet underground, Sante set about the unromantic task of finding the millions of dollars she was sure he'd hidden from her over the years. But she herself had practically eradicated his fortune already, and his will had been written in 1963—seven years before he met her. He had never updated it. The will left everything to the two children from his first marriage. Sante fought it tooth and nail by hiding Ken Sr.'s death from his other children for almost two years, forging his signature on documents and checks, and desperately searching for some secret offshore account full of millions—but none of it worked. Her longest con, catching a millionaire, had failed her.

For Sante, this was the worst thing in the world. Without the promise of easy money, she grew meaner and more desperate. It was like she could smell the dust storms of her youth growing closer and closer. So she grabbed her younger son and ran for her life.

✳

WITH KEN SR. DEAD AND KENT ESCAPING INTO HIS OWN LIFE, Sante and Kenny grew closer and closer. If Kenny had tried to resist his mother's advances earlier—by going away to college, by trying to strangle her—those days were behind him. Now, he was all in: Mommy and Kenny against the world. They dove into a series of moneymaking schemes, desperate to find their next windfall. She moonlighted as a "longevity consultant" named Princess Sante, while he sold black-market Cuban cigars. Once, when they were out shoplifting lipsticks, they got caught—and told the detective who caught them that they were dating.

By September of 1996, mother and son were in the Bahamas, trying to convince a reluctant local banker to give them a loan. The banker, fifty-five-year-old Syed Bilal Ahmed, refused. He thought they were too shady to do business with. Unfortunately for Ahmed, he was right. When Sante realized that Ahmed wasn't persuadable, she invited him over for cocktails—cocktails laced with Rohypnol, the infamous date-rape drug. When Ahmed lost consciousness, mother and son took turns holding him down in a bathtub. It took longer to kill him than they expected. At one point, Ahmed opened his eyes underwater. The next day, Kenny threw his body into the ocean. And then Sante and Kenny continued on their merry way.

Life was good—in a manic, obsessive, desperate way. Mother and son would take long midnight drives into the desert, stopping for burgers when they got hungry, or else they'd drink wine, smoke cigars, and talk for hours about the past. Other times they spoke of darker things. Now that Sante had discovered how easy it was to simply murder one's problems away, she wanted to do it again. She was having trouble with an old friend of hers named David Kazdin, who lived in Los Angeles, and she told Kenny that they should consider disposing of Kazdin, too. Years earlier, Kazdin allowed Sante to slap his name on the deed of her Las Vegas house, in order to hide the house from an angry lawyer who wanted to seize it. But in January of 1998, Kazdin realized that Sante had taken out an expensive mortgage on the house, cashed some of it, transferred the house from Kazdin to one of her homeless "maids," taken out an insurance policy on it, and then burned the whole thing down. Needless to say, Kazdin wasn't pleased that his name was linked to any of this illegal behavior. Sante knew he was angry, and she was worried that he might go to the authorities, so she told her son that her old friend was going to have to die.

At first, Kenny felt exhausted by the thought. Another murder? How many more would there be? But he'd learned long ago that it was far easier to obey Sante than to fight her. So he agreed. Gratefully, Sante tried to make the murder as easy on her baby boy as possible, demanding that one of her homeless "maids," a drifter named Sean Little, help Kenny dispose of the body. She convinced Little to do it with "nice food, cocktails, and fake friendliness," as Kenny later remembered.

On March 13, 1998, the trio woke up at the crack of dawn: "To psych ourselves out and get in the right mindset," Kenny recalled. He filled his backpack with gloves, duct tape, trash bags, and a gun. "Good luck!" chirped Sante, as the men left. It was like she was sending them off to kindergarten. "Do a good job!"

Kazdin was visibly nervous when he let Kenny into his house, even though Kenny assured him that he was just there to chat about the loan, and hey, a cup of coffee wouldn't hurt, either. As Kazdin walked to the kitchen sink, Kenny shot him in the back of the head. Then he and Sean Little wiped up the blood from the floor, wrapped Kazdin's head and feet in trash bags, and tossed his body into a dumpster near the Los Angeles airport. By this point, Kenny's exhaustion had burned away with the sunrise, and he felt invincible. He'd done exactly what he'd been trained to do. He'd obeyed his mother.

This called for flowers.

✳

KENNY'S ELATION DIDN'T LAST LONG. A HOMELESS MAN DISCOVERED Kazdin's body the very next day, and Sante and Kenny were forced to scramble out of town, pursued by the FBI, the LAPD, and other cops in multiple states. "Mommy and Clyde," tabloids would call them, later. They drove a green Lincoln Town Car that Sante had purchased with a bad check in Utah. She'd stolen so many cars in her day that she probably didn't think twice about it, but that car would eventually be their downfall.

While on the run, Sante heard a juicy piece of gossip involving her favorite type of person: a millionaire. But this time, the millionaire was a woman. There was a wealthy widow in New York City, Sante heard, who lived in a mansion worth nearly $8 million. The place had a ballroom, a garden on the roof, and a Renoir in the bathroom. Best of all, the owner was eighty-two years old—easy prey, Sante thought. Maybe *this* was the millionaire she'd been waiting for her whole life, this frail, malleable woman, who probably walked with a cane and was perhaps suffering from a convenient bout of dementia? And so, on June 13, 1998, mother and son set out for New York City, drawn like moths to the flame of wealth.

✳

Dementia? Eighty-two-year-old Irene Silverman was sharp as a tack. She'd grown up dirt poor and never forgot it; even now, with her ballroom and her rooftop garden and her Renoir, she loved nothing more than getting paid in cash. She and Sante were quite similar, in a way: both were the brainy, scrappy daughters of immigrants, both had a flair for the theatrical and a taste for the finer things in life. Unlike Sante, though, Irene Silverman had achieved real wealth—and kept it. She'd worked as a chorus girl in New York City before marrying the banker Sam Silverman, who left her his fortune when he died in 1980. She kept chilled champagne in her purse and threw legendary parties. She had bright red hair and wore bright red glasses. At only five feet tall, she might have looked vulnerable, but she had grit for days.

Her mansion, located a block away from Central Park in Manhattan's Upper East Side, was far too big for a tiny former dancer, and so she remodeled the lower floors into expensive apartments and rented them out to people like the actor Daniel Day Lewis and the singer Chaka Khan. She screened all her renters carefully. As a former chorus girl, she could spot a creep from a mile away. But she had one weakness. When she received a call from someone calling herself "Eva Guerrero" who claimed that she knew one of Irene's good friends and that she wanted to rent an apartment for her boss, "Manny Guerrin," Irene decided to lease him apartment 1B. When Manny himself showed up at Irene's doorstep on June 14, she was skeptical at first. He had no references, he didn't even have an ID, and she told her maintenance man that Manny looked like he just got out of jail. But he had the first month's rent ready for her: $6,000, all in cash. Irene softened, and let him in.

She regretted this almost immediately. Manny never did produce a single reference. He wouldn't make eye contact with anyone. He hid his face from the security camera in her hallway. He eavesdropped on her maids. He'd stand at the peephole in his apartment and stare out of it for hours. And he kept sneaking an overdressed, middle-aged woman into his room. After a week of this unnerving behavior, Irene asked him to leave—and he refused.

By now, Irene's staff were urging her to call the police, but Manny Guerrin wasn't the first shady man that Irene Silverman had dealt with in her eighty-two years on this earth. Instead, *she* started spying on *him*, looking for definitive proof that she could bring to the cops.

Meanwhile, Sante was creeping about behind the scenes, secretly living with her son in his one-bedroom apartment and trying to figure out a way to get Irene to sign over her entire mansion. She'd managed to snag a copy of the deed for Irene's house and the correct forms for a property transfer; she even put on a red wig and pretended to *be* Irene while convincing a notary public to sign the deed transfer documents. But the most important task, in her mind, was getting Irene's Social Security number, and the old woman was proving a hard nut to crack. At least three times, Sante called Irene to say that she'd won a free Caribbean vacation, and if Irene would simply provide her Social Security number over the phone, the trip would be hers! Again and again, Irene denied her. She was no fool—and this drove Sante crazy. "The more arduous and the more complicated it got, the more desperate we became," said Kenny, later, "and the more morbid-minded we became."

On the night of July 4, Irene had a few friends over for dinner. It was a Saturday. She told them that she was planning to evict "Manny" on Monday. As they spoke, Irene pointed to the monitor that showed the footage from her security camera. A young man was walking into the building, deliberately hiding his face from the camera. One of her friends remembers feeling a sudden, overwhelming sense of evil.

✳

THE NEXT MORNING, MOTHER AND SON WAITED SILENTLY INSIDE IN their apartment. It was a holiday weekend, and once the last maid left to run errands, the entire mansion fell quiet. Upstairs, Irene puttered about in her slippers, taking care of the morning's business. Eventually, she came down to the lower floors, down the hallway that passed apartment 1B. "Get ready," Sante hissed. When Irene was close enough, Kenny burst out of the apartment, grabbed her, and dragged her back inside.

Sante was waiting there with a stun gun.

"Bitch," Sante cried, hitting Irene over the head. "Bitch, bitch." There was a bit of foam at the corner of her mouth. It was as though she was furious at Irene for having the audacity to resist her control, the audacity to be everything that she was not. "Do it!" she hissed at Kenny. He'd been obeying his mother for his entire life. It was too late to stop now. And so he bent over the struggling woman, placed his hands around her neck, and began to squeeze.

✳

IT WAS THE GREEN LINCOLN TOWN CAR THAT ULTIMATELY BETRAYED them—the one Sante had stolen in Utah. After they'd wrapped Irene's tiny body in trash bags, cleaned up the blood (there wasn't much), put her in the trunk of their stolen car, and tossed her into a dumpster somewhere in New Jersey, Sante and Kenny took themselves out for coffee and pastries. But later that night, the FBI and the NYPD stopped them outside of a hotel. The two of them panicked, assuming that they were being arrested for Irene's murder. Sante tried to get rid of her bag—which contained Irene's passport, checks, keys, Social Security card, and bank information, along with $10,000 in cash—as Kenny wet himself in terror. But they were only being arrested for buying the Town Car with a bad check. When Kenny realized that, he was so relieved that he offered to buy the officers a drink.

Their twisted luck didn't last. Several days later, an NYPD detective happened to be watching a TV report about how someone called "Manny Guerrin" was wanted in connection with the disappearance of Irene Silverman, and he realized that "Manny" looked an awful lot like the "Kenny Kimes" he already had in custody. After a lifetime of weaseling out of trouble, one bad check was all it took to put Sante away.

Off to jail they went. Five months later, Sante and Kenny were slapped with an 84-count indictment that was both damning and legally audacious: they were being charged with murder, among other felonies, despite the fact that there wasn't a single piece of physical evidence tying them to Irene's disappearance. There were no fingerprints, no blood, no forensic anything, and most importantly, there was *no body*. The search for Irene was exhaustive—investigators scoured fields and parks and garbage dumps and airports—but her diminutive corpse never turned up. Because of this, the case against Sante and Kenny would have to be entirely circumstantial.

As they waited for their trial to begin, Sante and Kenny tried to clean up their image in the press. They wanted the world to see them as an affectionate mother-and-son duo whose antics—cross-country crime sprees, skulking around mansions, getting arrested outside of hotels—were the totally normal activities of moms and sons who just loved hanging out together! To achieve this, their lawyers allowed the TV show *60 Minutes* to swing by and ask them a few questions. This was a big mistake. Before the disastrous interview was cut short by the lawyers, the two of them managed to come across as creepy, out of touch, and Oedipal in the extreme. They held hands, as Kenny told the interviewer, "I think [my mother] is a beautiful person spiritually and intellectually—and physically."

It was a gross question, but everyone asked it anyway: Were they . . . *a couple*? In pretrial hearings, the two were always whispering and touching each other, and when they were arrested, the cops openly asked Kenny if he was sleeping with his mother. (Later, Kenny would reminisce about this moment in his prison diary. "What was I supposed to do? Say thank you for your brilliant comment? . . . It's not my fault that she looks young and beautiful at her age.") Kenny's older brother, Kent, strongly believes that their relationship was never sexual—just unhealthy, stifling, and stunted—but no one could deny that the aesthetics, at least, weren't great. Sante might have thought that holding hands with her adult son on national television made her look cozily maternal, but the rest of the world thought she looked deranged. And the authorities certainly weren't distracted by her mommy-and-me act. By August 1999, the two were also charged with David Kazdin's murder in California.

The Silverman trial started on Valentine's Day of 2000. In the courtroom, Sante embarked on her usual round of histrionic accusations, fake health crises, and—when all else failed—loud screams. As the prosecution hammered their case home with 125 witnesses and 350 pieces of evidence, Sante would shriek things like, "Your Honor, how can we have fairness?" and "I'm afraid of you, I'm afraid of this corrupt system, I'm afraid of the gossip, the lies, that have been fed about my son and me!" Once, she turned around to face the gallery, holding up a newspaper with the headline "Poll: Cops Out of Control—Need Federal Monitors," while shrieking, "We're innocent! For God's sake, help us!" In return, the judge, Rena Uviller, would yell at Sante to calm down. Once, the courtroom exploded into laughter when Uviller referred to Sante's "performance—I mean, your statement."

Sante could blame the "corrupt system" all she wanted, but the mountain of circumstantial evidence against her and Kenny was damning. There were witnesses linking them to Irene. There were wigs, masks, loaded guns, knockout drugs, handcuffs, and cassette recordings of Irene Silverman's phone calls, all found in their belongings—along with an empty stun gun box, a duffel bag large enough to hold a body, a can of Mace, heavy-duty garbage bags, duct tape, clothesline, hypodermic syringes, and rubber gloves.

But most damning of all were the notebooks. Sante had always been a note taker and a list maker—"CONTROL! CONTROL! CONTROL! CONTROL! CONTROL! CONTROL! CONTROL! CONTROL!"—and even during the trial, she took endless notes, as though she believed that if she could write it down, she could make it happen. But her old notebooks were full of lists that she'd written about Irene, and those lists were now being used as evidence. There were lists of weapons to buy. Lists of information to gather (schedules of Irene's staff, layout of Irene's building, Irene's blood type, Irene's favorite movies, Irene's Social Security number, whether or not Irene had a burglar alarm). Lists of pamphlets to read (*Document Fraud and Other Crimes, How to Build a Practical Firearms Suppressor*). There was even an ominous folder titled "Final Dynasty," which contained a forged deed selling Irene's mansion to a shell corporation set up by Sante. The lists were a "virtual roadmap," the prosecution argued, "to the commission of the offenses charged."

It was enough. On May 18, 2000, the two were convicted of 118 counts: second-degree murder, robbery, forgery, eavesdropping, and more. The jury's verdict took over twenty minutes to read aloud. "Mom, it'll be okay," Kenny called to her, midway through the verdict. Despite statements of innocence that the *New York Times* called "bizarre, rambling and sometimes vulgar," and the *New York Post* called "rambling, bitter and sometimes comical," the two were sentenced to life in prison and then some: $120^2/_3$ years for Sante, $126^1/_3$ years for her son.

Sante seemed shocked that the system had finally overwhelmed her, despite all her twisting and turning, her relentless conniving. She spluttered and rambled so much in response to her sentence that Kenny screamed at her, "Mom, don't talk!" She kept talking. "Mom!" he cried, agonized. "Mom! Stop!" She didn't stop. At that point, Kenny put his hands over his ears. He should have known that with Sante, there would never be silence.

✳

It was over—but not in Sante's mind. Larry King interviewed her from prison, where she spouted vague, conspiratorial statements about how cops planted all the evidence and how people "in England" were calling their trial the "worst, unjust mistake in the history of the United States." She said the jury was "brainwashed." She repeatedly accused a shadowy "they" of targeting her. She said that police were "murdering the Constitution." She claimed that there was "no crime" and that the whole thing had been equivalent to "a big Hitler lie." And she had the audacity to say that she and Irene had been friends since 1994 and that Irene had *asked* her to help sell her mansion.

While Sante talked on and on, Kenny was growing desperate. The two of them were about to be extradited to California to stand trial for David Kazdin's murder, and in California, they'd be facing the electric chair. It was bad enough that *he* might be executed, but the thought of his mother getting the death penalty was unbearable. And so he made his move. When a reporter came to prison to interview him, he sprang at her during a break in the interview, pressed a pen against her neck, and held her hostage for four hours, demanding that Sante not be extradited. (The correctional officers eventually tackled him, and the reporter escaped unharmed.) His demands didn't work, and they were taken back to Los Angeles, where Sante had begged on the streets as a child and where Kenny had scrubbed David Kazdin's blood off the kitchen floor. In Kenny's mind, there was now only one way left to save his mother: betrayal.

On November 19, 2003, the front page of the local edition of the *LA Times* reported that Scott Peterson would stand trial on charges of murdering his pregnant wife Laci, that Michael Jackson's Neverland Ranch was being scoured for evidence of child molestation, that the previous day had been the 25th anniversary of the Jonestown massacre, and that Kenny Kimes had just pled guilty to the murder of David Kazdin.

In the courtroom, Kenny wept as he testified against his mother, and Sante wept as she listened to her son. He told the jury about the way he held Syed Bilal Ahmed underwater. He talked about throwing David Kazdin's lifeless body into the dumpster. And he described just how long it took for Irene Silverman to die while he squeezed his hands around her tiny neck.

In response, Sante was ready with her typical cocktail of denial and conspiracy theory. She raved that David Kazdin had been her best friend and so *obviously* she wouldn't have killed her best friend. She insisted that Kenny was only testifying against her because the prosecutors "broke him" by having him "tortured and coerced." But the jury believed her son. Both were given a second sentence of life without parole and, in perhaps the cruelest cut of all, were sent to opposite ends of the country to live out their days: Sante to the Bedford Hills Correctional Facility in New York, Kenny to the Richard J. Donovan Correctional Facility in San Diego. Almost three thousand long, lonely miles between the mother and son who had once been so inseparable.

After giving up all the details of their crimes in the courtroom, Kenny went back to his cell and turned to his journal with vicious self-loathing. "Just spent the last ten minutes vomiting," he wrote. "I ratted my mom out. If I didn't, we would both go to death row."

✹

ONLY DEATH WOULD EVER FREE KENNY FROM HIS MOTHER'S clutches. Sante Kimes died of natural causes on May 19, 2014. She was almost eighty years old. She'd been working tirelessly on her freedom for the past decade, and right before she died, she was busy making plans to be interviewed by *Inside Edition*—where, presumably, she would declare her innocence yet again. As usual, she expected the show to conform to her own agenda. She asked the producers to send her lipstick, foundation, eyeliner, and a curling iron. "It's important how I look in the interview," she wrote to them. "First impressions mean everything."

With his mother gone, Kenny felt like he could finally start unburdening himself. He began exchanging letters with a writer named Traci Foust. The two of them fell in love. But then Traci got sick, fast, and when she died in 2018 from complications of flu and pneumonia, Kenny's agony finally brought him to his senses. He realized that what he was feeling—the pain, the ferocious sense of loss—was exactly what the families of his many victims had felt. He wrote an essay about it and published it online from behind bars, with help from the writer Jonna Ivin-Patton. In the essay, he declares that he has "finally found a moral compass." Today, he is working with Ivin-Patton on a full-length memoir.

As her son gears up to speak out on his own, Sante herself is finally quiet. *Ashes to ashes, dust to dust.* When her con-artist father died, his obituary was full of glittering lies about how he was a magician and a prince. His daughter's obituary was full of darker compliments. "A talented and obsessive thief," the *New York Times* called her. "As a law enforcement official said at the time of her arrest, Ms. Kimes was 'the most ingenious, evil con artist' he had seen 'in a long time.'" It was impossible to insult Sante without complimenting her, or to compliment her without insulting her. Kent, the son who got away, spends some time in *his* memoir remembering what a wonderful mother she could be, every now and then. When she was in a good mood, Sante would give away $100 bills to strangers, take her boys on high-speed car chases, and throw them elaborate birthday parties full of stolen merchandise. She could be a whirlwind of excitement. But she could never stop whirling.

It must have been exhausting to be Sante Kimes: forever grasping at control, juggling identities, scribbling down her endless lists, terrified of what might happen if she stood still. There were so many Santes that, in a way, there was no real Sante. "This lady had a difficult time discerning what was real and what wasn't real," said one of her many, many lawyers. "She was known by every name there ever was," remembered another. She spent her entire life trying to outrun the storm—but the storm finally overtook her, and returned her to the dust.

CONCLUSION

CONFIDENT

A REN'T THEY FABULOUS? THE GRAND PIANOS, THE FAST CARS, the diamonds. The celebrity chasing. The knack for summoning up spirits. The sense of getting-away-with-it glee. The persuasive smiles, the hypnotic eyes. The bottomless confidence.

Or is all that just another trick of the light? If we strip away the fabulous details, the reality of confidence art is bleak and terrible. The women in this book have pushed people to the brink of suicide. They've drained the bank accounts of the vulnerable. One of them was a sexual abuser; another was involved in so many murders that you can find her listed on Wikipedia as a serial killer. They've dragged their children into dangerous situations, abandoned their children, and turned their children into con artists, too. Between them, they've caused oceans of tears, taken millions of dollars, and earned centuries of jail time.

To achieve these nefarious ends, the con woman weaponizes confidence itself. The word has two meanings. She wields both, a double-edged sword. "Confidence" means "belief in oneself," but it can also mean "belief in something," and the con woman asks us to believe in *something* (a vision, a future, a fairy tale, a scheme), while convincing us because of her belief in *herself* (she's poised, she's cool, she's rich, she doesn't back down). For the victim, both meanings come into play, too. They have confidence in the thing that she is selling, at first, but when they realize they've been swindled, their confidence in themselves is shaken. Shattered, really. Often the victims of cons don't come forward at all, too humiliated to bear the harsh public judgment that comes when they admit: *Yeah, I believed her.*

But if you follow the hard glitter of the con women for long enough, you'll stumble across a surprisingly tender truth. When humanity is operating at its finest, we approach the world with trust, not suspicion. We have hope for the future, we believe in things greater than ourselves, we have faith in our neighbors. We take people at their word. Our confidence—the very thing that she uses to trick us—is the best part of us.

This is how she gets us, of course. This is what makes us vulnerable. If we wanted to kill the confidence woman, we'd simply have to stop having confidence in anything and anybody. We'd have to lock our doors and slam our windows shut and peer apprehensively at each other from slits in the blinds. But is that worth it? The confidence woman just may be the small, bitter price we pay for the ability to trust other people. Better to risk her tricks than to close ourselves off to one another for good.

And let's be blunt. Does anyone *really* want to live in a world without the confidence woman? Look how fabulous she is. The cars. The diamonds. The persuasive smile. Other people may fall for that sort of thing, but she won't get us this time. We're wiser now. Too confident to lose. Let's let her in, hear what she has to say.

ACKNOWLEDGMENTS

I'D LIKE TO FIRST THANK THE WOMAN WHO MAKES ALL THIS criminal-women content happen: my fabulous red-haired agent, Erin Hosier, who just *gets* me and is achingly cool to boot.

Speaking of fabulous red-haired women who make things happen: thank you to my beautiful mom, Rhonda, not only for giving me feedback on some of these chapters, but for always cheerleading my writing. Thank you to my whole beloved family, for everything, forever, especially my baby sister, Anna, who is the epitome of the *good* kind of confident woman.

Thank you to everyone at Harper Perennial: Rebecca Raskin, my lovely, con-women-obsessed editor; Jamie Lynn Kerner, who designed the incredible cover; Carol Burrell, my copyeditor, and Amanda Hong, my production editor, for saving me from all sorts of embarrassing errors; the talented folks in publicity and marketing; and everyone else who worked on this slippery book.

Thank you to everyone who allowed me to interview them for this book. Charlie Stack, hero of the Rose Marks chapter—thank you! Thank you to Fred Schwartz, Rose Marks's attorney. Michael Marks—thank you for speaking to me about your mom. Across the Atlantic, thank you to Detective Constable Pete

Gartland and Detective Sergeant Matt Hussey for giving me the details of Ruksana's swindle, and big thanks to Tom Keating at the City of London Police for facilitating. Thank you to Michael Thatcher, President and CEO of Charity Navigator, for chatting with me about the tragediennes.

Thank you to my brilliant translator, Irene Lo, who helped me *immeasurably* with the Wang Ti chapter—and who is now, plot twist, my sister-in-law!

Thank you to Hope Dunbar, Special Collections Archivist at the E. H. Butler Library at Buffalo State, for digging up those articles on Roxie Rice's time spent in Buffalo. What would authors do without archivists? We'd write shorter, dumber books, that's what.

Thank you to ProQuest and newspapers.com, my old friends, as well as to anyone who has ever faithfully scanned an old newspaper into an electronic database. Oh, and thanks to the Columbia library stacks, where seemingly every book in existence is to be found if you just have the courage to walk down the very long, very dark aisles . . . all alone . . . looking for something with a title like *The Last Days of the Romanovs* or *Criminal Minds and Wait, Is That a Pair of Psychopathic Eyes Peering From Behind the Shelf?*

Thank you to the readers of *Lady Killers* and the listeners of *Criminal Broads*. It's an honor to tell you these stories. (I feel like you will ALL appreciate Mary Ann Scannell's energy.) Thank you to my fellow writers for providing me with the accountability and Zoom cocktail hours that a quarantine writer needs, especially Ximena, Emilie, Jo, Meredith, and Lavonne.

I'd like to dedicate the Margaret Lydia Burton chapter to my canine brother-in-law, Bradley Cocker Pitt. I hope you like hearing about your fellow cocker spaniels! You're even more handsome than Rise and Shine.

Charlie! My love, thank you for *everything*. I can't possibly fit all my gratitude into one paragraph. Thank you for the endless cups of coffee, for giving me the time and space to finish my work, and for wrangling a certain adorable yet loud infant when I'm on a deadline. You've been inspiring me to work harder since we were nineteen. I hope that by the time you read this, we're living in a mansion . . . okay, fine, a two-bedroom. I LOVE YOU.

And last, and smallest, but certainly not least: Cecil, my baby, we wrote this book together, didn't we? You were with me in every coffee shop and for every chapter, all through the nine months of writing it. I revised the book with you lying peacefully next to me on the couch, a tiny though very tall newborn. And I am copyediting it and writing these acknowledgments when you are two days away from your six-month birthday! You're very wild and wriggly now, and are currently sitting between my legs, leaning over my thigh, trying with a mighty will to reach the keyboard. I'm sorry for not taking *all* of your edits ("bzzzzph" was a compelling suggestion, I admit). But thank you for being here with me. They say babies are distracting, but honestly, I couldn't have done it without you. I love you forever and ever!

NOTES

INTRODUCTION: CHARMING

xi **"If you meet her, you will like her"**: Quoted in *Daily News* (New York), "The Pocketbook Drop . . . and Other Con Games," December 18, 1977.

xiv **A recent psychology study**: Rebecca L. Mitchell, Katherine K. Bae, Charleen R. Case, and Nicholas A. Hays, "Drivers of Desire for Social Rank," *Current Opinion in Psychology*, 33, June 2020, 189–195.

xiv **Social climbing actually strengthened their immune systems:** "Climbing the Social Ladder Can Strengthen Your Immune System, Monkey Study Suggests," *Science* magazine, November 24, 2016.

JEANNE DE SAINT-RÉMY

3 *Collier d'esclavage*: Jonathan Beckman, *How to Ruin a Queen: Marie Antoinette, the Stolen Diamonds and the Scandal That Shook the French Throne* (London: John Murray, 2014), 101.

4 **Seventeen million dollars:** Historical Currency Converter, accessed June 12, 2019, https://www.historicalstatistics.org/Currencyconverter.html. According to the website, "2,000,000 French livres tournois [1663-1795] in year 1772 could buy the same amount of consumer goods and services in Sweden as 17,215,769.930655662 US dollar [1791-2015] could buy in Sweden in year 2015."

4 **They couldn't afford it:** As Thomas Carlyle wrote of the time, "The age of Chivalry is gone, and that of Bankruptcy is come." Thomas Carlyle, *The Diamond Necklace* (Nabu Press, 2010), 30–31.

5 **Difficult to look at:** Jacques Claude Beugnot, *Life and Adventures of Count Beugnot* (London: Hurst and Blackett, 1871), 2.

5 **Waiting in the wings:** In her memoirs, Jeanne writes, "People were incessantly telling me, I heard it from every quarter, that, with a small degree of

favour, it might be easy to regain possession of [the Valois country home]."
Jeanne de La Motte, *Memoirs of the Countess de Valois de La Motte* (London:
J. Ridgway, 1791), 7.

5   **$8,000 annually:** The pension for Jeanne and her siblings was 800 livres a
year, which ends up being roughly $8,000 in 2019.

6   **Fresh flowers:** Antonia Fraser, *Marie Antoinette* (New York: Doubleday,
2001), 178.

6   **Striving for more:** "Everyone was struggling to clamber up to a niche from
where they could peer with satisfaction at those beneath them," writes one
historian, while "those above struggled to fend off the inundation of scrab-
blers from below." Beckman, *How to Ruin*, 24.

8   **"Demon":** Beugnot, *Life and Adventures*, 9.

8   **"Without being aware":** Ibid.

8   **Pregnant:** Note that historians disagree about who, exactly, got Jeanne
pregnant. In Iain McCalman's essay "The Making of a Libertine Queen:
Jeanne de La Motte and Marie-Antoinette," in *Libertine Enlightenment:
Sex, Liberty and Licence in the Eighteenth Century*, ed. Peter Cryle and Lisa
O'Connell (New York: Palgrave Macmillan, 2004), McCalman says it was a
local bishop.

8   **Noble La Mottes:** McCalman, Ibid., 118.

9   **Kicked them out:** Frantz Funck-Brentano, *The Diamond Necklace* (New
York: Brentano's, 1900), 82.

9   **Palace . . . English mares:** Ibid., 85–86.

9   **"Weak and vain":** Henry Vizetelly, *The Story of the Diamond Necklace*
(London: Vizetelly & Co., 1881), 36.

9   **Prime minister:** Beckman, *How to Ruin*, 64.

10   **Seduced him masterfully:** "Decking herself out in her finest feathers, putting on her most coquettish airs, and making the [room] redolent with the
odour of her perfumes." Vizetelly, *The Story*, 39.

10   **"Egyptian Elixir" . . . "demonic Masonries":** Carlyle, *The Diamond
Necklace*, 89.

11   **To attract Marie Antoinette's attention:** Beckman, *How to Ruin*, 43.

12   **"Master" . . . "slave":** Ibid., 73, 78.

13   **The fateful night . . . found out:** Ibid., 88.

14   **Lavish dinner parties:** Beugnot, *Life and Adventures*, 34.

15   **"A secret negotiation":** Jeanne Louise Henriette Campan, *The Private
Life of Marie Antoinette* (London: Richard Bentley and Son, 1883), 375.

15   *Marie Antoinette de France:* Ibid., 376.

16   **"Greatest and the best of queens":** Beckman, *How to Ruin*, 128.

16   **"Born to be my torment":** Campan, *The Private Life*, 7.

16   **Gowns:** Beugnot, *Life and Adventures*, 37.

16   **Mechanical bird:** Vizetelly, *The Story*, 162–163.

16   **Carriage:** McCalman, "The Making of a Libertine Queen," 124.

17   **"Balloon mania":** *Mércure de France*, 17 February 1784, reprinted in J. Jobé, *The Romance of Ballooning: The Story of the Early Aeronauts* (New York: Viking Press, 1971), 31.

17   **More money than most of France's nobles:** Beckman, *How to Ruin*, 126.

18   **"Talk of a diamond necklace" . . . She dropped her napkin:** Beugnot, *Life and Adventures*, 72.

20   ***The Royal Bordello***: Corinna Wagner, *Pathological Bodies* (Berkeley: University of California Press, 2013), 21.

20   **Much of France was now convinced:** Robert Darnton, *The Forbidden Best-Sellers of Pre-Revolutionary France* (New York: W. W. Norton & Company, 1995), 78.

20   **"Come and weep with me":** Funck-Brentano, *The Diamond Necklace*, 323.

21   **French court was admitting:** Beckman, *How to Ruin*, 246.

21   **"At this juncture":** Funck-Brentano, *The Diamond Necklace*, 9. Funck-Brentano is quoting Campan here.

21   **True mastermind:** Vizetelly, *The Story*, 248.

21   **"It is the blood":** Funck-Brentano, *The Diamond Necklace*, 341.

21   **June of 1787:** Vizetelly, *The Story*, 304.

22   **"The public must at length":** La Motte, *Memoirs of the Countess*, 5.

22   **Believed that the visitors were sent by the queen:** Vizetelly, *The Story*, 220.

22   **"The noted Countess de la Motte":** *Jackson's Oxford Journal* (Oxford, England), August 27, 1791.

23   **Bringing down the monarchy:** McCalman, "The Making of a Libertine Queen," abstract.

23   **"A catalyst":** "Popular entertainments . . . and modern scholarly studies are united in seeing this scandal . . . as both a catalyst of the French Revolution and a moulder of its outcomes." Ibid., 112.

23   **"The queen's death must be dated from then":** Frantz Funck-Brentano, *La Mort De La Reine* (Paris: Hachette, 1901), 9.

24   **Nobody who dealt with the necklace . . . over a hundred years after it was created:** Beckman, *How to Ruin*, 294–302.

CASSIE CHADWICK

25   **Born: Elizabeth Bigley . . . Elizabeth Springsteen:** C. P. Connolly, "Marvelous Cassie Chadwick," *McClure's Magazine*, XLVIII, no. 1, November 1916. Alice M. Bestedo: "Without Education or Beauty, Mrs. Chadwick Fascinated Men," *The Daily Province* (Vancouver, British Columbia, Canada), December 14, 1904, 4. Elizabeth Springsteen: "Unable to

Secure Bail Will Return to Cleveland," *The Berkshire Eagle*, December 9, 1904, 12.

25   **Fake $20 bills:** "Policeman Talks of Chadwick Bills," *The Washington Post*, February 25, 1906, 12.

25   **"Cassie Chadwick Nerve Tonic":** Connolly, "Marvelous Cassie Chadwick."

26   **Intelligent, in her own odd way:** "The Story of Mrs. Chadwick, The High Priestess of Fraudulent Finance," *The Washington Post*, December 25, 1904, 6.

26   **"Possessed of a mania from childhood to acquire great wealth quickly":** "Want to Kill a Sensation," *Detroit Free Press*, October 12, 1907, 1.

27   **"Sharp scolding":** "Mrs. Chadwick's History, Record of Woman's Strange Power, and the Marvelous Gullibility of Financiers," *The Inter Ocean*, December 8, 1904, 2.

27   **The letter was so convincing:** Connolly, "Marvelous Cassie Chadwick."

27   **Calling cards:** "Her Great Graft," *The Topeka State Journal*, December 9, 1904, 4.

27   **Took pains to act "eccentric" in court:** "Chadwick Affair Near Its Climax," *Chicago Daily Tribune*, November 29, 1904, 1.

28   **Threw Cassie out:** "From Farm to Prison, Then to Life of Ease," *Chicago Daily Tribune*, December 4, 1904, 2.

28   **"At that time . . . I began to think she was unbalanced":** "Mrs. Chadwick Spends Night in Prison," *The Berkshire Eagle* (Pittsfield, MA), December 9, 1904, 12.

28   **She told him all about her various troubles:** "Without Education or Beauty, Mrs. Chadwick Fascinated Men," *The Daily Province* (Vancouver, British Columbia, Canada), December 14, 1904, 4.

29   **Learned to make her gums bleed on command:** "The Story of Mrs. Chadwick, The High Priestess of Fraudulent Finance," *The Washington Post*, December 25, 1904, 6.

29   **Needle:** "Active Mind, Cute Lisp and Winning Smile Paved Way to Riches for Cassie," *The Knoxville Journal*, August 29, 1958, 4.

29   **"Hemorrhage of the lungs":** "From Farm to Prison, Then to Life of Ease," *Chicago Daily Tribune*, December 4, 1904, 2.

29   **"La Rose" . . . "some kind of demi-social, dubious resort":** Connolly, "Marvelous Cassie Chadwick."

30   **"To her no man was great, and most men were fools":** Ibid.

30   **Prominent Cleveland politician:** "From Farm to Prison, Then to Life of Ease," *Chicago Daily Tribune*, December 4, 1904, 2.

30   **A cool $40,000 in forged notes:** "Chadwick Woman Now Under Guard," *The Times Dispatch* (Richmond, VA), December 8, 1904, 2.

30   Florida G. Blythe: "Chadwick Woman's Life Is a Marvel in Millions," *The Minneapolis Journal*, December 19, 1904, 15.

31   Detailed description of her: "Bertillion: Measurements Are Taken of Mrs. Chadwick," *Courier-Journal* (Louisville, KY), December 31, 1904, 2.

31   Cassie suggested that he try massage: Connolly, "Marvelous Cassie Chadwick."

32   Emeralds . . . tray: "Cassie Was a Charlatan, a Crook, But a Lady, Too," *The Pittsburgh Press*, August 14, 1946, 21.

32   "She had a mania for fancy clocks": "The Remarkable Financial Operations of a Remarkable, Mysterious Woman," *Courier-Journal* (Louisville, KY), December 11, 1904, B10.

33   "No beggar was ever turned away from her door": Connolly, "Marvelous Cassie Chadwick."

33   "This is your Christmas gift": Ibid.

33   "She had everything she wanted": "Mrs. Chadwick Spends Night in Prison," *The Berkshire Eagle* (Pittsfield, MA), December 9, 1904, 12.

34   The notes were forged: "The Story of Mrs. Chadwick, the High Priestess of Fraudulent Finance," *The Washington Post*, December 25, 1904, 6.

36   "I deemed it my duty to protect her": "Mrs. Cassie Chadwick Love Child of Andrew Carnegie," *The Atlanta Constitution*, December 12, 1904, 1.

38   Suicide wouldn't fix anything: Connolly, "Marvelous Cassie Chadwick."

39   "Woke up": Ibid.

39   "Oh, this is awful, awful, awful": "Husband and Daughter Are Left Penniless," *The Austin Statesman*, January 1, 1905, 1.

39   "Torture and transactions and transactions and torture": "In Tears: Aged Banker Talks of the Chadwick Loans," *Courier-Journal* (Louisville, KY), December 6, 1904, 1.

39   "Every time she looked at me I became dizzy": "Bank Wrecked by a Woman," *San Francisco Chronicle*, November 29, 1904, 1.

39   "I know nothing of the woman or her dealings": "Mystery of Chadwick Case Grows," *San Francisco Chronicle*, November 30, 1904, 1.

40   "Anti-panic proclamation" . . . "How much did she get of you?": Connolly, "Marvelous Cassie Chadwick."

41   "Please deny reported suicide": "On His Bed: The Aged Banker Tells of Loans to Mrs. Chadwick," *Courier-Journal* (Louisville, KY), December 1, 1904, 2.

41   "For nerve": *The Berkshire Eagle* (Pittsfield, MA), December 9, 1904, 4.

41   The marshal who arrested her found her lying in bed: "Uncle Sam Nails Cassie Chadwick," *Chicago Daily Tribune*, December 8, 1904, 1.

41   "I steadily looked into her hypnotic eyes": "Those Brown Eyes of

Fascinating Cassie," *Edmonton Journal* (Edmonton, Alberta, Canada), December 30, 1904, 5.

42   **"I am a very much maligned and persecuted woman":** "Barren Walls of Prison Cell Confront Her," *The Nashville American*, December 9, 1904, 1.

42   **She forgot all about the cramp:** "Verdict Is Guilty," *Detroit Free Press*, March 12, 1905, 1.

42   **"Would you not feel glad to know":** "Cassie L. Chadwick Arrested on the Charge That She Aided in Embezzlement by Bankers," *The San Francisco Call*, December 8, 1904, 1.

43   **"It may never be known how much money she borrowed":** "Find Mrs. Chadwick Guilty Seven Fold," *The Inter Ocean* (Chicago, IL), March 12, 1905, 5.

43   **A million dollars stowed away in Belgium:** "Cassie Chadwick Dead," *Lancaster Intelligencer* (Lancaster, PA), October 12, 1907, 2.

43   **Conspiring to defraud the United States by banking fraud:** "Mrs. Cassie L. Chadwick Convicted on Seven Counts," *The Buffalo Sunday Morning News* (Buffalo, NY), March 12, 1905, 1.

43   **"Let me go! Oh, go! Oh my God, let me go!":** "Verdict Is Guilty," *Detroit Free Press*, March 12, 1905, 1.

43   **"Witch of finance":** "Mrs. Cassie Chadwick Dead; Notorious Swindler Goes to Grave With Lips Sealed," *The Washington Times*, October 11, 1907, 9.

43   **"Queen of Swindlers":** "Cassie Chadwick Dead," *Lancaster Intelligencer* (Lancaster, PA), October 12, 1907, 2.

43   **"The most talked of woman in the world":** "Find Mrs. Chadwick Guilty Seven Fold," *The Inter Ocean* (Chicago, IL), March 12, 1905, 5.

43   **"Without Education or Beauty, Mrs. Chadwick Fascinated Men":** "Without Education or Beauty, Mrs. Chadwick Fascinated Men," *The Daily Province* (Vancouver, British Columbia, Canada), December 14, 1904, 4.

43   **"Strange Power":** "Mrs. Chadwick's History, Record of Woman's Strange Power, and the Marvelous Gullibility of Financiers," *The Inter Ocean*, December 8, 1904, 2.

44   **"Good clothes are the tools of the grafters' trade":** "Grafters Crowd the Metropolis," *San Francisco Chronicle*, December 12, 1904, 2.

44   **"Suppress":** "Government Puts Ban on 'Cassie Chadwick' Money," *St. Louis Post-Dispatch*, August 8, 1908, 2.

44   **"This is the only occasion known that Mrs. Chadwick ever professed an interest in religion":** "Mrs. Chadwick Baptized in Ohio Penitentiary," *Courier-Journal* (Louisville, KY), October 9, 1907, 3.

44   **Blamed her illness on her taste for rich food:** "Mrs. Chadwick Dying," *The Washington Post*, October 10, 1907, 3.

44   **Her son and two of her sisters:** "Cassie Chadwick Dead," *Lancaster Intelligencer* (Lancaster, PA), October 12, 1907, 2.

44   **The prison doctor claimed she died of neurasthenia:** "Financial Witch Is Dead," *The Dayton Herald* (Dayton, OH), October 11, 1907.

45   **"Chinese Cassie Chadwick":** "Chinatown in Tears Over 'Wooey' Game," *Los Angeles Times*, June 30, 1906, II1.

45   **"Roumanian Cassie Chadwick":** "Clever Woman Got $200,000 by Scheming," *St. Louis Post-Dispatch*, December 16, 1906, 6.

45   **"Russian Cassie Chadwick":** "Russian Cassie Chadwick," *The Washington Post*, December 18, 1907, 9.

45   **"Italian Cassie Chadwick":** "Italian Cassie Chadwick," *Nashville Tennessean and the Nashville American*, August 8, 1911, 2.

45   **"German Cassie Chadwick":** "Pretty Widow Dupes Berlin," *Detroit Free Press*, March 5, 1917, 7.

45   **"Apt pupil of Mrs. Chadwick":** "Called Apt Pupil of Mrs. Chadwick," *The Washington Post*, September 1, 1906, 1.

45   **"How could a woman of no particular brilliancy":** "The Remarkable Financial Operations of a Remarkable, Mysterious Woman," *Courier-Journal* (Louisville, KY), December 11, 1904, B10.

46   **"Her securities have, in nearly every instance, been mythical":** "Her Career Astounding," *The Wilkes-Barre News* (Wilkes-Barre, PA), December 10, 1904, 5.

46   **Even her husband eventually went bankrupt:** "Dr. Chadwick Is Bankrupt," *Detroit Free Press*, August 15, 1908, 2.

46   **Insisted even on his deathbed that Cassie *was* Andrew Carnegie's daughter:** "Almost with [Beckwith's] dying breath he declared his faith in the shadow of Cassie Chadwick's birth." From Connolly, "Marvelous Cassie Chadwick."

46   **"She was great, even in an evil way, as it was":** "Those Brown Eyes of Fascinating Cassie," *Edmonton Journal* (Edmonton, Alberta, Canada), December 30, 1904, 5.

WANG TI

47   **China, 2008:** Details of the wedding taken from "Yang Wei and Yang Yun Tie the Knot . . . Finally," Triple Full (a gymnastics blog), November 6, 2008, and "Gymnastics-Wedding About Love Not Money, Says China's Yang," Reuters, November 11, 2008.

47   **Hot air balloon:** "Dazzling Firework Lowers the Curtains of Yang Wei's Wedding. The Wedding Trilogy Displays Ultimate Romance," Sina Sports, November 7, 2008. Translated by Irene Lo, accessed November 13, 2019, http://sports.sina.com.cn/o/2008-11-07/00174056354.shtml.

48   **Made good money:** "Exposing Details of Wang Ti's Fraud Case: Scamming 26 Million to Buy Luxury Cars for Xiao Qin," Anhui News, December 24, 2013. Translated by Irene Lo, accessed November 13, 2019, http://www.ahtv.cn/c/2013/1224/00189939_2.html.

49   **Called themselves the "Mrs. Group":** "Wang Ti Gets Life Sentence for Fraud. Numerous Olympic Champions and Sports Stars Were Scammed," Anhui News, December 24, 2013. Translated by Irene Lo, accessed November 13, 2019, http://www.ahtv.cn/c/2013/1224/00189885_all.html.

49   **Bogged down with legal troubles:** "Wuhan Ejected from Soccer League," People's Daily Online, November 10, 2008.

49   **"Beijing is not a livable city":** Edward B. Barbier, "Nature and Wealth: A Parable from Beijing," *China-US Focus*, November 10, 2015.

49   **Building huge domes:** "Inside Beijing's Airpocalypse—a City Made 'Almost Uninhabitable' by Pollution," *The Guardian*, December 16, 2014.

50   **Sometimes the sun itself was blotted out:** "Beijing Olympics Were the Most Polluted Games Ever, Researchers Say," *The Telegraph*, June 22, 2009.

50   **The most expensive Summer Olympics of all time:** "Beijing Games to Be Costliest, but No Debt Legacy," Reuters, August 4, 2008.

50   **Held back the rain:** "How Beijing Used Rockets to Keep Opening Ceremony Dry," *Independent*, August 11, 2008.

50   **She attended a star-studded wedding:** "Exposing Details of Wang Ti's Fraud Case: Scamming 26 Million to Buy Luxury Cars for Xiao Qin," Anhui News, December 24, 2013. Translated by Irene Lo, accessed November 13, 2019, http://www.ahtv.cn/c/2013/1224/00189939_2.html.

50   **"Pony God":** "Coach Scouted 'Pony God' Xiao Qin at the Kindergarten When He Was 4 Years Old," People's Olympics, August 12, 2008. Translated by Irene Lo, accessed November 13, 2019, http://2008.people.com.cn/BIG5/7654995.html.

50   **"I get to take a vacation!":** "Xiao Qin Claims Pommel Horse Title at Beijing Olympics," Gov.cn (the "official web portal of the Central People's Government of the People's Republic of China"), August 18, 2008, accessed November 8, 2019, http://www.gov.cn/english/2008-08/18/content_1074043.htm.

51   **"We had both drunk a bit":** "Master Con Woman Who Scammed Beijing's High Society," *Telegraph* (London), January 3, 2014.

51   **"That red one is going to be yours":** The details of Qin wooing Wang Ti are taken from "Exposing Details of Wang Ti's Fraud Case: Scamming 26 Million to Buy Luxury Cars for Xiao Qin," Anhui News, December 24, 2013. Translated by Irene Lo, accessed November 13, 2019, http://www.ahtv.cn/c/2013/1224/00189939_2.html.

52   **Sleek Audi TT:** "Master Con Woman Who Scammed Beijing's High Society," *Telegraph* (London), January 3, 2014.

52   **Most citizens never dreamed of owning an automobile until the early 1980s:** "High Speed Scandal: Ferrari Incident Rocks China," *The Daily Beast*, July 13, 2017.

52   **"Men love Audi like women love Dior":** "Car Brands Represent Status, Stereotypes in China," *China Daily*, April 22, 2014.

52   **Sent by her estranged husband:** "Exposing Details of Wang Ti's Fraud Case: Scamming 26 Million to Buy Luxury Cars for Xiao Qin," Anhui News, December 24, 2013. Translated by Irene Lo, accessed November 13, 2019, http://www.ahtv.cn/c/2013/1224/00189939_2.html.

53   **Offshore companies:** "Leaked Records Reveal Offshore Holdings of China's Elite," *International Consortium of Investigative Journalists*, January 21, 2014.

53   **Masterminded a cover-up of the whole incident:** "How Son's Death in a High-Speed Car Crash Led to Powerful Chinese Official's Fall from Grace," *South China Morning Post*, December 23, 2014.

53   **"A very delicate matter":** "Master Con Woman Who Scammed Beijing's High Society," *Telegraph* (London), January 3, 2014.

54   **Bought her new pal a BMW:** "Exposing Details of Wang Ti's Fraud Case: Scamming 26 Million to Buy Luxury Cars for Xiao Qin," Anhui News, December 24, 2013. Translated by Irene Lo, accessed November 13, 2019, http://www.ahtv.cn/c/2013/1224/00189939_2.html.

54   **"I thought these athletes dressed tastelessly":** "Master Con Woman Who Scammed Beijing's High Society," *Telegraph* (London), January 3, 2014.

54   **"She was not stunning":** Ibid.

54   **Latest mobile phone:** Ibid.

55   **His *other* girlfriend would buy it for him:** "Exposing Details of Wang Ti's Fraud Case: Scamming 26 Million to Buy Luxury Cars for Xiao Qin," Anhui News, December 24, 2013. Translated by Irene Lo, accessed November 13, 2019, http://www.ahtv.cn/c/2013/1224/00189939_2.html.

55   **It drew criticism in the press:** "Yang Wei Defends 'Lavish' Wedding to Yang Yun," *International Gymnast Magazine*, November 11, 2008.

56   **Registered under someone else's name:** "Exposing Details of Wang Ti's Fraud Case: Scamming 26 Million to Buy Luxury Cars for Xiao Qin," Anhui News, December 24, 2013. Translated by Irene Lo, accessed November 13, 2019, http://www.ahtv.cn/c/2013/1224/00189939_2.html.

57   **Helping him pay off his massive credit card debts:** "Wang Ti Gets Life Sentence for Fraud. Numerous Olympic Champions and Sports Stars Were Scammed," Anhui News, December 24, 2013. Translated by Irene Lo,

accessed November 13, 2019, http://www.ahtv.cn/c/2013/1224/00189885
_all.html.

57   **Shuangshuang got a cut of the profits:** "Exposing Details of Wang Ti's
Fraud Case: Scamming 26 Million to Buy Luxury Cars for Xiao Qin," Anhui News, December 24, 2013. Translated by Irene Lo, accessed November 13, 2019, http://www.ahtv.cn/c/2013/1224/00189939_2.html.

58   **Planning to marry her:** "Fake Princeling 'Scammed Stars Out of Millions,'" *South China Morning Post*, June 28, 2012.

58   **The owner showed up and introduced himself:** "Wang Ti Gets Life
Sentence for Fraud. Numerous Olympic Champions and Sports Stars Were
Scammed," Anhui News, December 24, 2013. Translated by Irene Lo, accessed November 13, 2019, http://www.ahtv.cn/c/2013/1224/00189885
_all.html.

59   **Never materialized:** "Woman Took Celebrities for 55m Yuan, Court Says,"
ShanghaiDaily.com, June 27, 2012.

59   **Killing herself:** As Wang Ti said at her trial, "At that time, I was about to
kill myself with a knife. I asked them to call the police but they wouldn't do
it. They kept me there and just kept asking for money." "Wang Ti Gets Life
Sentence for Fraud. Numerous Olympic Champions and Sports Stars Were
Scammed," Anhui News, December 24, 2013. Translated by Irene Lo, accessed November 13, 2019, http://www.ahtv.cn/c/2013/1224/00189885
_all.html.

60   **"Will We Ever Be Over Anna Delvey?":** "Will We Ever Be Over Anna
Delvey?" *W Magazine*, October 4, 2019.

60   **"At some point between the Great Recession, which began in 2008, and
the terrible election of 2016":** "The Fiends and the Folk Heroes of Grifter
Season," *The New Yorker*, June 5, 2018.

60   **"Old-fashioned grift":** "Why Are We Suddenly Surrounded by 'Grift'?"
The New York Times Magazine, December 4, 2018.

60   **"Distinctly American ethos":** "The Distinctly American Ethos of the
Grifter," *The New York Times Style Magazine*, September 12, 2019.

62   **"I don't have to lie anymore":** "Wang Ti Gets Life Sentence for Fraud.
Numerous Olympic Champions and Sports Stars Were Scammed," Anhui
News, December 24, 2013. Translated by Irene Lo, accessed November 13,
2019, http://www.ahtv.cn/c/2013/1224/00189885_all.html.

62   **"I don't know":** "Numerous Olympic Champions Were Scammed by
Xiao Qin's Ex-Girlfriend," *NetEase Sports*, December 25, 2013. Translated by Irene Lo, accessed November 13, 2019, http://sports.163.com
/13/1225/08/9GU5IOFM00051C89.html?f=jsearch.

63   **"It's hard to earn money":** "Wang Ti Gets Life Sentence for Fraud. Zou

Kai: We Won't Be Able to Get the Money Back," Sohu Sports, December 29, 2013. Translated by Irene Lo, accessed November 13, 2019, http://sports.sohu.com/20131229/n392590757.html.

63   **Sentenced to life in prison:** "Criminal Ruling of Punishment Reduction of Wang Ti's Fraud Case," *China Judgments Online*, August 8, 2019. Translated by Irene Lo, accessed November 13, 2019, http://wenshu.court .gov.cn/website/wenshu/181107ANFZ0BXSK4/index.html?docId= 4d3c0a37bf2346e2865daaa100b4c348.

63   **A terrible car accident she'd caused in early 2010:** "Xiao Qin's Ex-Girlfriend Commits Fraud of $60 Million. Victims Are Mostly Sports Stars," *Phoenix New Media*, December 24, 2013. Translated by Irene Lo, accessed November 13, 2019, http://news.ifeng.com/gundong/detail _2013_12/24/32410171_0.html?_from_ralated.

63   **Wang Ti is currently scheduled to get out of prison:** "Criminal Ruling of Punishment Reduction of Wang Ti's Fraud Case," *China Judgments Online*, August 8, 2019. Translated by Irene Lo, accessed November 13, 2019, http://wenshu.court.gov.cn/website/wenshu/181107ANFZ0BXSK4 /index.html?docId=4d3c0a37bf2346e2865daaa100b4c348.

63   **Relies on part-time jobs to make a living:** "Olympic Champion Disappeared for 4 Years Because of His Girlfriend's 58 Million Fraud, Now Is a Chubby Man Living a Miserable Life," Sohu, October 8, 2019. Translated by Irene Lo, accessed November 13, 2019, http://www.sohu.com /a/345411586_100078945.

THE SPIRITUALISTS

67   **"A silly woman":** Reuben Briggs Davenport, *The Death-Blow to Spiritualism* (New York: G. W. Dillingham, 1888), 36.

68   **Millions of followers:** There's some debate over how many followers, exactly, Modern Spiritualism had at its peak. Spiritualists themselves always tended to estimate their followers as more than they really had. Today, you'll see a lot of people cite "eight million" as the number of Spiritualists that existed by the end of the 1800s, but skeptics at the time found that number highly implausible. See Joseph McCabe, *Spiritualism, a Popular History from 1847* (London: T. Fisher Unwin Ltd., 1920), 64–66.

68   **"Innocent little children":** Davenport, *Death-Blow*, 36.

68   **In those early days . . . even an apple:** Intro material taken mainly from Tori Telfer, "The Female Persuasion," *The Believer*, 122, December/January 2019.

69   **1848 was the perfect year:** For more on just what a perfect year 1848 was, see McCabe, *Spiritualism*, 9–26.

70   **2,000 "writing mediums":** Ibid., 57.

70   **Strumming the banjo:** Or the drums, accordion, harp, triangle, fiddle, or tambourine . . . Frank Podmore, *Modern Spiritualism: A History and a Criticism, Volume 1* (London: Methuen & Co., 1902), 247.

70   **Empty vessels:** Ann Braude, *Radical Spirits: Spiritualism and Women's Rights in Nineteenth-Century America* (Bloomington: Indiana University Press, 1989), 23–24.

71   **"Your linen clean and neat":** George W. Hudson, *The Marriage Guide for Young Men* (Ellsworth, ME: published by the author, 1883), 116.

71   **Plucky little servant:** "Strange Record of Mrs. May S. Pepper, 'Medium'; Broken Homes and Bitter Enemies in her Former Haunts," *The Brooklyn Daily Eagle,* January 15, 1905, 1.

72   **New dress . . . nephew:** Kerry Segrave, *Women Swindlers in America, 1860–1920* (Jefferson, NC: McFarland, 2007), 15–16.

72   **"He wasn't real":** "Strange Record of Mrs. May S. Pepper," 1.

72   *Medicine:* Ibid., 5.

73   **"Psychic gifts":** "Medium Owns to a Milkmaid's Past," *Los Angeles Herald,* January 24, 1905, 7.

73   **Talk on the phone, drive a horse named Charley, eat candy:** "Heard 'Bright Eyes' Over Telephone," *New York Times,* August 28, 1907, 4.

73   **Cash checks:** "Spirits Wouldn't Work in Court," *New York Times,* September 7, 1907, 4.

73   **"Wrecked homes and ruined lives":** "While in Pulpit Her Life Exposé is Prepared," *The San Francisco Examiner,* January 16, 1905, 4.

73   **Cash . . . houses:** "'May Pepper' Dies in Boston," *Times Union,* April 28, 1919, 2.

74   **"LIGHTHOUSE":** M. E. Cadwallader, *Mary S. Vanderbilt, a Twentieth Century Seer* (Chicago: The Progressive Thinker Publishing House, 1921), v.

75   **The exposures began:** McCabe, *Spiritualism,* 63.

75   **Hollow-legged tables:** Ibid.

75   **Irish Catholics:** Ibid., 32.

75   **Elsie Reynolds . . . "sluggers":** Segrave, *Women Swindlers,* 9.

75   **Rectum:** M. Brady Bower, *Unruly Spirits: The Science of Psychic Phenomena in Modern France* (Urbana: University of Illinois Press, 2010), 171.

76   **"Resembling an orchid":** Baron von Schrenck-Notzing, *Phenomena of Materialisation,* translated by E. E. Fournier d'Albe (London: Kegan Paul, Trench, Trubner & Co. Ltd, 1923), 116.

76   **"I introduced the middle finger":** Ibid., 84.

77   **Indentured servant:** Hattie's book is often taken to be at least somewhat autobiographical, which is why historians think that Hattie had likely risen

to the position of author and cosmetics mogul from a past as an indentured servant.

78   **"Serious humors":** Ad in *Hartford Daily Courant*, June 20, 1860, 1.

78   **Enormous undertaking:** "First Black Author Published in 1859," *Democrat and Chronicle* (Rochester, NY), November 11, 1982, 5C.

79   **Communing with her dead father:** R. J. Ellis and Henry Louis Gates, "'Grievances at the Treatment She Received': Harriet E. Wilson's Spiritualist Career in Boston, 1868–1900," *American Literary History* 24, no. 2, 2012, 253.

79   **"Strictly genuine, honest and highly qualified mediums":** Thomas R. Hazard, "The Philosophy and Phenomena of Modern Spiritualism," *The Watchman*, vol. 4. no. 6 (Chicago), February 1884, 7.

79   **"Enterprise and generosity":** "The Red Man's New Year," *Spiritual Scientist*, January 14, 1875.

79   **Several years...her death:** Ellis and Gates, "Grievances," 246–7, 250.

79   **National Spiritualist Association of Churches:** "National Spiritualist Association of Churches (NSAC)," *Encyclopedia of Occultism and Parapsychology*, Encyclopedia.com, accessed November 2, 2019, https://www.encyclopedia.com/science/encyclopedias-almanacs-transcripts-and-maps/national-spiritualist-association-churches-nsac.

80   **Black mediums often slipped through the cracks:** "Many black women mediums, especially those who were working-class, did not leave personal papers or records that documented their public and private lives." LaShawn Harris, "Dream Books, Crystal Balls, and 'Lucky Numbers': African American Female Mediums in Harlem, 1900–1930s." *Afro-Americans in New York Life and History*, 35, no. 1, 2011: 74–110.

81   **"Trail of sorrow":** Harry Houdini, *A Magician Among the Spirits* (New York: Harper & Brothers, 1924), 66.

81   **Said she was the daughter:** "Diss Debar's Own Story," *New York Times*, May 1, 1888, 8.

81   **Tried to kill a doctor:** "Ann Odelia Diss de Bar [sic]: A Modern Female Cagliostro," *The Belleville Telescope*, December 5, 1901, 7.

81   **Asylum:** Houdini, *A Magician*, 69.

81   **Pulled someone's hair . . . pretended to be dead:** Edmund Richardson, "Nothing's Lost Forever," *Arion*, 20, no. 2, 2012, 19–48.

82   **Eleanor Morgan:** "Like a Meteor," *Boston Daily Globe*, August 2, 1891, 1.

82   **Vera P. Ava:** "Ava or Diss Debar," *St. Louis Post-Dispatch*, December 11, 1892, 25.

82   **"Order of the Crystal Sea":** "A Diet of Fruit and Nuts," *The Sun* (Baltimore, MD), November 16, 1898, 2.

82   **Force God Himself to appear:** Ibid.

82   **India . . . South Africa:** "A Figure Not Laughable, But Terrible—DISS DEBAR—A Great Criminal with Grotesque Mask," *New York Times*, September 5, 1909, 47.

83   **"Merely a jocose" . . . "spectacle":** Ibid.

83   **"Foreign gentleman of 35":** Segrave, *Women Swindlers*, 27.

83   **"Christ returned to earth":** "Only Perfect Man," *The Baltimore Sun*, October 12, 1901, 1.

83   **"In the presence of the Lord":** Segrave, *Women Swindlers*, 29.

84   **"Any such revelation of the truth":** "The 'Theocratic Community,'" *Coventry Evening Telegraph*, October 11, 1901.

84   **"Quite powerless":** "Theocratic Unity; Horos and His Converts," *The Advertiser* (Adelaide, Australia), November 19, 1901, 9.

84   **"Soiled, draggled white silk toga":** "Mere Child the Witness," *Boston Daily Globe*, October 18, 1901, 14.

84   **"Made it impossible" . . . "Beast!":** "Theocratic Unity; Horos and His Converts," *The Advertiser* (Adelaide, Australia), November 19, 1901, 9.

85   **"A scarcely audible voice":** Ibid.

85   **"The most heartless manner":** "Notes From London," *The Age* (Australia), November 15, 1901, 7.

85   **Detroit:** "Notorious Woman Is Located," *Great Falls Tribune*, April 14, 1907, 9; and Segrave, *Women Swindlers*, 32.

85   **New Revelation:** "Dis Debar [sic] Founds a New Cult Here," *New York Times*, August 26, 1909, 16.

85   **Didn't eat meat:** "Third Degree for Ann," *The Washington Post*, August 29, 1909, 11.

85   **"I need no introduction":** "Diss de Bar [sic] Lets Things Be Known," *Detroit Free Press*, August 30, 1909, 2.

86   **"The present whereabouts":** "Master Crooks and Criminals Deluxe: Ann O'Delia Jackson, Reputed Daughter of King Louis of Bavaria and Lola Montez," *The Washington Post*, November 16, 1913, MT4.

86   **"You are driving me into hell":** Davenport, *Death-Blow*, 36.

86   **In the fall of 1888 . . . cracking her toes onstage:** Maggie's confession was printed in "Spiritualism Exposed," *New York World*, October 21, 1888.

87   **"I have explored the unknown":** Davenport, *Death-Blow*, 37.

88   **2,500 members:** Email between the author and the secretary of the NSAC, February 25, 2020.

88   **Some young people:** "Meet the Young People Who Believe They're Communicating with the Dead," BBC.co.uk, March 5, 2019, accessed February 22, 2020, https://www.bbc.co.uk/bbcthree/article/eabdc0ed-70c0-4af2 -8295-96ebfc4dc613.

FU FUTTAM

89   **3 Musketeers bar:** Introduced to the US market in 1938, according to Mars.com. "History in the Making," Mars.com, accessed November 5, 2019, https://www.mars.com/about/history.

89   **A martini (newly legal):** Newly legal because Prohibition ended on December 5, 1933, baby!

89   **Fu Futtam, scientific East Indian Yogi:** All ads in this section are from the classified section of the *New York Amsterdam News*, October 18, 1933.

90   **Right there in New York:** George J. Lankevich, *New York City: A Short History* (New York: New York University Press, 2002), 163.

91   **Born in Kingston, Jamaica:** Naturalization record for Dorothy Matthews, May 18, 1937. The National Archives and Records Administration; Washington, D.C., Petitions for Naturalization from the U.S. District Court for the Southern District of New York, 1897-1944, Series: M1972; Roll: 1242.

91   **Japanese:** Though papers in the 1930s attribute Fu's Asian heritage to all sorts of different countries, she herself told journalists that her father's dad was Japanese. This seems to be the most trustworthy account. "Sufi's Widow Tells of Contact with Dead Mate," *The Chicago Defender*, October 22, 1938, 3.

91   **Chinese:** "A Bank Is Her Monument: She Led Business Parade Long Before Women's Lib," *Afro-American*, February 14, 1976, A6.

91   **Everyone was pretending:** Claude McKay, the Harlem Renaissance writer, spent some time studying Harlem's occultists, and noticed that most of them marketed themselves as having some connection to the Middle East or to Asia. This trend is also easy to spot if you scroll through any of the Spiritualist classified ads of the time.

91   **"DE Larz, The Girl from India":** From the classified section of *New York Amsterdam News*, October 18, 1933.

91   **"Moderately rich uncle":** "Widow Carries on Cult Leader's Work," *Philadelphia Tribune*, October 20, 1938, 2.

91   **By fifteen, she had emigrated:** Naturalization record for Dorothy Matthews.

91   **"Seeing visions and dreaming dreams":** "Link Forbes Girl's Death with Spirits: Delves Into Mysticism," *New York Amsterdam News*, November 25, 1939, 5.

92   **Killed in a car crash:** Ibid.

92   **Pink for celestial happiness:** Claude McKay, *Harlem: Negro Metropolis* (New York: Harcourt Brace Jovanovich, 1968), 76.

92   **"Like drug addicts":** Ibid.

92 **"Modern 'miracle workers'":** "Million Dollar Take," *New York Amsterdam News*, May 25, 1940, 13.

92 **Decent paycheck:** LaShawn Harris, "Dream Books, Crystal Balls, and 'Lucky Numbers': African American Female Mediums in Harlem, 1900–1930s." *Afro-Americans in New York Life and History*, 35(1), 74–110.

92 **"One of the few businesses in Harlem which has actually flourished":** "Million Dollar Take," *New York Amsterdam News*, May 25, 1940, 13.

92 **The most successful:** "Madame Fu Futtam Is the Top-Ranking Occultist." McKay, *Harlem*, 79.

93 **"As universally read in Harlem as the Bible":** "Million Dollar Take," *New York Amsterdam News*, May 25, 1940, 13.

93 ***Madam Fu-Fu's Lucky Number Dream Book*:** You can see the cover online at https://www.luckymojo.com/madamfufusdreambook.html. Accessed November 5, 2019.

93 **This whole ritual *must* be done . . . "while burning Mme. Fu Futtam's special blessed candles":** "Million Dollar Take," *New York Amsterdam News*, May 25, 1940, 13.

93 **"Voluptuous dream book publisher":** "Mme. Fu Futtam Wed to Sufi Adul [sic] Hamid," *New York Amsterdam News*, April 23, 1938.

93 **"A young and comely spiritualist":** "Madame Talks of Sufi," *New York Amsterdam News*, November 20, 1937, 1.

93 **"Crystal gazing Mme. Fu Futtam":** "'. . . he done her wrong': Stephanie Puts Finger on Sufi," *New York Amsterdam News*, October 28, 1939, 15.

94 **Stephanie was about ten years older than Fu:** Stephanie's background is taken from Shirley Stewart, *The World of Stephanie St. Clair: An Entrepreneur, Race Woman and Outlaw in Early Twentieth Century Harlem* (New York: Peter Lang Publishing Inc., 2014).

94 **Sixty percent of Harlem's economic life:** "The Black Mafia Moves Into the Numbers Racket," *New York Times*, April 4, 1971.

95 **Retired from the racket as a millionaire:** "Harlem Romance," *Afro-American*, July 25, 1936, 13.

95 **"The story of Sufi Abdul Hamid and Mme. Stephanie St. Clair":** "'. . . he done her wrong': Stephanie Puts Finger on Sufi," *New York Amsterdam News*, October 28, 1939, 15.

95 **Born Eugene Brown:** Sufi was either born in Lowell, MA, or Philadelphia, PA. Of course, being Sufi, he wanted to claim a more exciting birthplace—thus the Egypt rumor. *Encyclopedia of the Harlem Renaissance, Volume 1 and 2, A–Z*, edited by Cary D. Wintz and Paul Finkelman (New York: Routledge, 2004).

95 **"Sufi Abdul Hamid":** Sufi's background is taken from McKay, *Harlem*, 185.

96 **Unemployed white workers from all over the city:** Ibid., 188.

96   **"I couldn't imagine collaborating with the Nazis"**: Ibid., 203.

96   **"Hothead"**: Winston McDowell. "Race and Ethnicity During the Harlem Jobs Campaign, 1932–1935," *The Journal of Negro History*, 69, no. 3/4, 1984, 140.

96   **They fell in love fast**: "'. . . he done her wrong': Stephanie Puts Finger on Sufi," *New York Amsterdam News*, October 28, 1939, 15.

96   **The two were wed secretly**: "Sufi-St. Clair 99-Yr. Marriage by Contract, Off: Ex-Numbers Queen Declares They Have Been Apart 4 Weeks," *Afro-American*, December 4, 1937, 1.

97   **"Feasibility of the plan"**: "Madame Talks of Sufi," *New York Amsterdam News*, November 20, 1937, 1.

97   **"As they do on the continent"**: "'. . . he done her wrong': Stephanie Puts Finger on Sufi," *New York Amsterdam News*, October 28, 1939, 15.

97   **A gambler. A player**: Ibid.

97   **Burgeoning dream book business**: "Bride, 3 Months, Urged Sufi on to Death Flight: But Dream Book Lady Predicts He'll 'Rise' in 90 Days," *Afro-American*, August 6, 1938, 3.

98   **She went raging to the papers**: Stephanie's story can be found in "Sufi Wooed St. Clair in 'Darkened Room': Ardent Lover Changed Over Into Mad Mate," *New York Amsterdam News*, January 29, 1938, 3.

98   **Fertilizing business**: "Madame Talks of Sufi," *New York Amsterdam News*, November 20, 1937, 1.

98   **"The woman is insane"**: Ibid.

98   **"He was just 'conning' my confidence"**: "Sufi Wooed St. Clair in 'Darkened Room': Ardent Lover Changed Over Into Mad Mate," *New York Amsterdam News*, January 29, 1938, 3.

98   ***Bang, bang, bang***: "Mme. Sufi Up for Sentence," *New York Amsterdam News*, March 19, 1938, 1.

99   **Two to ten years**: "Mme. Fu Futtam Wed to Sufi Adul [sic] Hamid," *New York Amsterdam News*, April 23, 1938, 5.

99   **"The pair should really knock the spirits for a loop"**: Ibid.

99   **Distributing a customized lucky numbers book**: Ibid.

99   **"He was so kind, so true"**: "Sufi's Pilot Told to Get More Gas," *Afro-American*, August 6, 1938, 3.

100 **"More tranquil business of preacher of oriental mysticism"**: McKay, *Harlem*, 79–80.

100 **"After eight years of strife and struggle"**: "Seek Sufi's Fortune as Followers Begin Fight Over Cult: Pick Carter to Succeed Sufi," *New York Amsterdam News*, August 6, 1938, 1.

100 **"IS LIFE A PROBLEM?"**: Ad from *New York Amsterdam News*, May 28, 1938, 17.

100 **Word on the street was that Fu had invested:** "Sufi Opens Rival 'Heaven,'" *New York Amsterdam News*, April 16, 1938, 1.

100 **The Temple flung open its doors on Easter Day:** The story of the Temple's opening ceremony is from "Bishop Sufi A.A.M.M.S.A.H. Unveils His Universal Buddhist Holy Temple to Public," *New York Amsterdam News*, April 23, 1938, 5.

101 **"Suddenly, without any apparent cause, it went out":** Sufi's premonitions are from "Sufi's Pilot Told to Get More Gas," *Afro-American*, August 6, 1938, 3.

101 **Planning to take a flight straight to Egypt:** "Sufi's Widow in Memorial," *New York Amsterdam News*, August 26, 1939, 2.

102 **Fell back to the ground, dead:** "Cult Leader and Pilot Die in Crash," *New Journal and Guide*, August 6, 1938, 1.

102 **Red dress:** "Sufi's Pilot Told to Get More Gas," *Afro-American*, August 6, 1938, 3.

102 **Rise from the dead in ninety days:** "'Sufi' Cult God Killed," *Afro-American*, August 6, 1938, 1.

102 **"Inscrutable half-smile" . . . "She was born smiling":** "Old Hymns Stir Sufi Mourners," *Afro-American*, August 13, 1938, 6.

102 **"Harlem was about to have its first black prophetess":** "Harlem to Have Black Prophetess," *Star-Phoenix* (Saskatoon, Saskatchewan, Canada), August 1, 1938, 1.

103 **"Harlemites want to know":** "Mme. Fu Futtam Slipped Up on Forecasting Doom of Sufi," *New York Amsterdam News*, August 6, 1938, 1.

103 **"Tranquility! It is the Light":** "Sufi Hamid Successor Is Picked," *New York Amsterdam News*, January 7, 1939, 2.

103 **"How contacts are made to hidden soul forces":** From an ad in *New York Amsterdam News*, October 22, 1938, 23.

103 **"Little Mother of Silent Devotion":** "Widow Carries on Cult Leader's Work," *Philadelphia Tribune*, October 20, 1938, 2.

103 **Her chauffeur confirmed:** "Mme. Fu Futtam 'Talks' with Dead Hubby, Sufi," *New York Amsterdam News*, October 15, 1938, 7.

103 **"Before Eve was 'She' was":** "Sufi's Widow in Memorial," *New York Amsterdam News*, August 26, 1939, 2.

104 **"It is quite possible that the young man":** "Link Forbes Girl's Death with Spirits: Delves Into Mysticism," *New York Amsterdam News*, November 25, 1939, 5.

105 **She wore a long veil in court:** "Sufi's Widow Jailed for Fraud," *New York Amsterdam Star-News*, March 22, 1941, 1.

105 **"Mission":** "Delay Hearing in Case of Mme. Futtam, Sufi's Widow," *New York Amsterdam Star-News*, March 29, 1941, 1.

105 **Mysteriously dismissed:** "Error Revealed in Hamid Story," *New York Am-sterdam Star-News*, October 31, 1942, 5.

105 **The store was a huge success:** "Old Egyptian Secrets Told in New Doro-thy Hamid Book," *The New York Age*, August 20, 1949, 10.

105 *Flight to Power:* Ibid.

105 **"Fu Futtam's Religious Store":** "'Flight to Power', 'Dream Book' Pub. by Fu Futtam's Religious Shop," *The New York Age*, April 8, 1950, 10.

105 **"Fu Futtam's Mirror Guide Green Card":** From ad in *The New York Age*, December 11, 1954, 21.

105 **You could buy her merchandise at religious stores:** "'Flight to Power', 'Dream Book' Pub. by Fu Futtam's Religious Shop," *The New York Age*, April 8, 1950, 10.

106 *Free reading $3 purchase:* One of Fu Futtam's last ads, as far as we know, from *New York Amsterdam News*, August 6, 1966, 42.

106 **Dorothy Hamid:** Ancestry.com, *U.S., Social Security Death Index, 1935–2014* [database online]. (Provo, UT: Ancestry.com Operations Inc., 2014).

ROSE MARKS

107 **Alias:** "Colorful Testimony Kicks Off Psychic Trial," *South Florida Sun Sentinel*, August 29, 2013, 1.

107 **A little storefront, all lit up:** Descriptions of Rose's Manhattan storefront from USA v. Marks, Transcript of Jury Trial Proceedings, Vol 3, p 70, Au-gust 28, 2013 and Vol 7, p 32, 4 September 2013.

108 **One of New York's ritziest neighborhoods:** The actual address, should you care to walk by it someday, was 21 W. 58th St., New York, NY.

108 **Bracelet:** Charlie Stack (former Fort Lauderdale Police Detective, Eco-nomic Crimes Unit), interviewed by Tori Telfer, March 19, 2019.

108 **Human sacrifice:** USA v. Marks, Transcript of Jury Trial Proceedings, Vol 3, p 129–130, August 28, 2013.

108 **There's an ATM across the street:** The description of what went on at Joyce Michael Astrology is taken from the opening statements of Rose's trial by Assistant United States Attorney Roger H. Stefin. Ibid., p 8–23, August 28, 2013.

109 **May 3, 1951:** Ancestry.com, *U.S. Public Records Index, 1950–1993, Volume 2* [database online] (Provo, UT: Ancestry.com Operations, Inc., 2010).

109 **A different set of skills:** Michael Marks (Rose Marks's son), interviewed by Tori Telfer, July 7, 2019.

109 **That marriage didn't work out:** Ibid.

110 **Rose worked as the breadwinner:** Here's Rose's lawyer, Fred Schwartz: "But I don't think there's any question from the books we have read, the information on the Romani culture, that it's a patriarchal culture. . . . At the

end of the day, the men are the ones who make the decisions, who control where shops are set up, how shops are set up, which members of the family work in a particular shop, and things of that sort. And that was the case with Rose and her husband Nicholas until Nicholas died in 2006." USA v. Marks, Sentencing Hearing, p 21, March 3, 2014.

110 **Never a chance, either:** Unless otherwise indicated, Rose's background information is taken from "Psychic Accused in $25 Million Fraud Says She Is Portrayed 'as Some Kind of Monster,'" *South Florida Sun-Sentinel*, December 29, 2012.

110 **The women in the family worked, and the men oversaw the work:** USA v. Marks, Transcript of Jury Trial Proceedings, Vol 3, p 7, August 28, 2013.

110 **Jewelry:** Ibid., Vol 4, p 20, 41, 58–59, August 29, 2013.

111 **"When I met her, she could hardly read":** Fred Schwartz (Rose Marks's defense lawyer), interviewed by Tori Telfer, March 1, 2019.

111 **Five, ten, fifteen times as much money:** At one point, her daughter-in-law had been asking a client for sums like $9,000 and $24,000; when Rose stepped in, she convinced a client to send her $370,000. USA v. Marks, Transcript of Jury Trial Proceedings, Vol 6, p 20, September 3, 2013.

111 **"She had more vast knowledge":** Ibid., Vol 5, p 81, August 30, 2013.

111 **"She was very good at what she did":** Ibid., Vol 8, p 23, September 6, 2013.

112 **"It was beyond depression":** The details from Jude Deveraux's life, including this quote, are taken from her testimony in Ibid., Vol 10, p 71–160, September 10, 2013.

113 **"Never seen another human being as angry":** Ibid., p 89.

113 **Rose had hired a private investigator:** Ibid., Vol 8, p 119, September 6, 2013.

113 **A smooth divorce:** "Novelist Says She Faced Threats," *South Florida Sun Sentinel*, September 12, 2013, 8A.

113 **A modest $1,200:** "Author Writes Off Lost Money," *South Florida Sun Sentinel*, September 13, 2013, 2B.

113 **Pills, alcohol, gambling:** USA v. Marks, Sentencing Hearing, p 53, March 3, 2014.

113 **She became a regular at the Seminole Hard Rock Casino:** "Novelist Says She Faced Threats," *South Florida Sun Sentinel*, September 12, 2013, 8A.

113 **Angry all the time:** Michael Marks (Rose Marks's son), interviewed by Tori Telfer, July 7, 2019.

113 **A "pathological gambler":** Fascinatingly, the *DSM*-IV includes "has committed illegal acts such as . . . fraud . . . to finance gambling." That part was dropped in the *DSM*-5. Substance Abuse and Mental Health Services

Administration, *Impact of the DSM-IV to DSM-5 Changes on the National Survey on Drug Use and Health* [Internet] (Rockville, MD: Substance Abuse and Mental Health Services Administration (US), 2016), Table 3.38, DSM-IV to DSM-5 Gambling Disorder Comparison, https://www .ncbi.nlm.nih.gov/books/NBK519704/table/ch3.t39/.

114 **"I lost control over everything"**: USA v. Marks, Sentencing Hearing, p 61, March 3, 2014.

114 **"Get out on the street and hustle clients"**: Ibid., p 23, March 3, 2014.

115 **"Maybe the toughest S.O.B. I've ever met in my life"**: "In Fortune Teller Probe, Fort Lauderdale Cop Emerges as a Tough But Gentle Hero," *South Florida Sun Sentinel*, August 24, 2011.

116 **"Pinkey"**: "Jailed South Florida 'Psychic' has Written a Book in Prison but Profits Will Go to Her Victims," *South Florida Sun Sentinel*, April 7, 2017.

116 **$100,000 in a single month**: "Jurors Weigh 'Psychic' Case," *South Florida Sun Sentinel*, September 26, 2013, 7A.

117 **The British solicitor**: "Widow: I Paid Psychic for Hope," *South Florida Sun Sentinel*, September 3, 2013, 1A and 7A.

117 **Japanese woman . . . Turkish man**: "Last of Psychic Fraud Family Gets $3^1/_2$ Years," *South Florida Sun Sentinel*, March 29, 2014, 9A.

117 **The American woman**: "Psychics Took Advantage of Woman, Says Ex-Husband," *South Florida Sun Sentinel*, August 29, 2011, 1A and 6A.

117 **"Five is your number"**: USA v. Marks, Transcript of Jury Trial Proceedings, Vol 9, p 32, September 11, 2013.

117 *Don't discuss this with anybody:* Ibid., Vol 3, p 18, August 28, 2013.

117 **"Calm down, calm down, you're getting hysterical"**: Ibid., Vol 4, p 150, August 29, 2013.

117 **Their lives would be utterly destroyed:** All of the Marks women used the same rhetoric. During the trial, one victim quoted Nancy Marks as saying, "Do not gamble with your life . . . your life is going to be destroyed if you don't continue this." Ibid., Vol 3, p 80–81, August 28, 2013.

118 **Gift cards:** Ibid., Vol 5, p 3–4, August 30, 2013.

118 **Watch:** Ibid., Vol 4, p 146, August 29, 2013.

118 **Supposed soul mate ended up in bed with another woman:** Ibid., Vol 7, p 130, September 4, 2013.

118 **"Sacrifice" it:** Ibid., Vol 6, p 160, September 3, 2013.

118 **"Michael the Archangel"**: "Three 'Psychics Admit Fraud," *South Florida Sun Sentinel*, March 19, 2013, B3.

118 **The psychics were never able to tell the truth from the lies:** Unless otherwise indicated, the information in this entire section is from Charlie Stack (retired Fort Lauderdale Police Detective), interviewed by Tori Telfer, March 19, 2019.

118 **Dreaming of suicide:** USA v. Marks, Sentencing Hearing, p 15, March 3, 2014.

119 **"He's now worth millions of dollars":** USA v. Marks, Transcript of Jury Trial Proceedings, Vol 10, p 93, September 10, 2013.

119 **She walked Deveraux through the process of in-vitro fertilization:** USA v. Marks, Sentencing Hearing, p 37, March 3, 2014.

120 **Had her son:** Obituary for Sam Alexander Montassir, *The Washington Post*, October 8, 2005.

120 **"Perhaps I could break away and meet you":** USA v. Marks, Transcript of Jury Trial Proceedings, Vol 4, p 82, August 29, 2013.

120 **"I hesitate to call her anymore":** "Author Writes Off Lost Money," *South Florida Sun Sentinel*, September 13, 2013, 2B.

121 **Fish and hunt:** Obituary for Sam Alexander Montassir, *The Washington Post*, October 8, 2005.

121 **The truck driver, going sixty miles an hour, never saw him:** The story of Sam's death is from USA v. Marks, Transcript of Jury Trial Proceedings, Vol 10, p 115–116, September 10, 2013.

121 **Rose arranged the funeral:** USA v. Marks, Sentencing Hearing, p 38, March 3, 2014.

121 **Weeping in the fetal position:** USA v. Marks, Transcript of Jury Trial Proceedings, Vol 10, p 117, September 10, 2013.

123 **"It was like someone hit me with a hammer":** Ibid., p 127, September 10, 2013.

123 **Fortune-telling itself isn't illegal:** From Rose's trial: "Fortune telling by itself . . . is not illegal. Doing palm readings or tarot card readings for a fee is not a crime. However, it becomes a crime if people are lied to or deceived or tricked into giving up large sums of money under false pretenses." Ibid., Vol 3, p 7, August 28, 2013.

123 **"Twisted enough to make me say: Wow!":** "Operation Crystal Ball: Gullibility in Astrology, Ponzis," *South Florida Business Journal*, August 17, 2011.

124 **"The fire, the 9/11 fire":** USA v. Marks, Transcript of Jury Trial Proceedings, Vol 18, p 54, September 25, 2013.

124 **"Gold coins":** From "INDICTMENT as to Rose Marks . . ." filed August 11, 2011.

124 **Millions of dollars in restitution:** "Woman Gets Four Years in Scam," *The Palm Beach Post*, January 14, 2014, B2.

125 **"It's ridiculous":** USA v. Marks, Sentencing Hearing, p 19, March 3, 2014.

125 **"Whatever Joyce Michael told me to do, I did":** USA v. Marks, Transcript of Jury Trial Proceedings, Vol 3, p 133, August 28, 2013.

125   **"I was doing things I wouldn't normally do":** Ibid., Vol 9, p 24, September 11, 2013.

126   **Struggling to breathe:** "'Psychic' Gets 10 Years for Fleecing Millions from Clients," *South Florida Sun Sentinel*, 6A.

126   **"We grew old together":** USA v. Marks, Sentencing Hearing, p 61, March 3, 2014.

126   **"I think that she probably started making promises to her clients":** Michael Marks (Rose Marks's son), interviewed by Tori Telfer, July 7, 2019.

127   **"Her offenses have been very much a part of our culture":** Letter from the Marks and Eli families to Judge Marra, June 16, 2016.

127   **Inspired her to write her own:** "Jailed 'Psychic' Isn't Reading Minds, but Writing Book," *South Florida Sun Sentinel*, April 9, 2017, 18A.

127   **Art of boxing:** USA v. Marks, Transcript of Jury Trial Proceedings, Vol 11, p 16, September 11, 2013.

127   **"When something rotten happens to me":** "FAQ," judedeveraux.com, accessed November 5, 2019, https://judedeveraux.com/faq/.

128   **"Psychic Mediums Are the New Wellness Coaches":** "Psychic Mediums Are the New Wellness Coaches," *New York Times*, March 19, 2019.

128   **"Mystical services market":** "Venture Capital Is Putting Its Money Into Astrology," *New York Times*, April 15, 2019.

128   **"It's kind of like . . . the mafia":** Michael Marks (Rose Marks's son), interviewed by Tori Telfer, July 7, 2019.

THE ANASTASIAS

131   **Bayonet:** Greg King and Penny Wilson, *The Resurrection of the Romanovs: Anastasia, Anna Anderson, and the World's Greatest Royal Mystery* (Nashville: Turner Publishing Company, 2010), 7.

131   *Berliner Illustrirte Zeitung*: This was the October 23, 1921 issue.

132   **Turned red and began to shake:** King and Wilson, *Resurrection*, 88.

132   **"The originator of all mischief":** Robert K. Massie, *The Romanovs: The Final Chapter* (New York: Random House, 1995), 166.

132   **"In naughtiness she was a true genius":** King and Wilson, *Resurrection*, 23.

133   **"Fertile soil":** Massie, *Final Chapter*, 144.

133   **And then *hundreds*:** "Кто тут в цари последний?" *Nasha Versia*, July 23, 2018.

133   **One Anastasia . . . exposed her:** For more on the 1918 imposters (though we know very little about them), see King and Wilson, *Resurrection*, 71.

134   **A world that was desperate for happy endings:** Ibid., 2.

135   **She had noble ancestors:** Ibid., 269.

135   **Curling up with a book somewhere:** Ibid., 274.

135   **Incest:** Ibid., 274.

135 **"Someone grand, someone important":** Ibid., 287.

136 **He left scars:** Ibid, 285

137 **"My reason cannot grasp it":** Massie, *Final Chapter*, 173.

137 **"I saw immediately that she could not be one of my nieces":** Ibid., 167.

137 **Crown Princess Cecilie:** Quotes from Massie, *Final Chapter*, 168.

137 **"There is not the slightest resemblance":** King and Wilson, *Resurrection*, 162.

138 **She didn't look like Anastasia:** This is noted in Pierre Gilliard's book *The False Anastasia*, quoted in Massie, *Final Chapter*, 175.

138 **Russian Orthodox church:** King and Wilson, *Resurrection*, 155.

138 **Studying photographs:** Ibid., 95.

139 **Went on believing:** From King and Wilson: "The reality of the 'unmasking' faded in the face of desire, ignored, distorted, and dismissed by her supporters until it was reduced to an absurdity, a mere footnote to her story." Ibid., 314.

139 **"Pave the streets":** Massie, *Final Chapter*, 169.

140 **"She was difficult to live with":** "Former Chicagoan Lays Claim as Grand Duchess Anastasia," *Chicago Tribune*, August 26, 1963, 14, section 2.

140 **Robert Speller and Sons . . . she was Anastasia:** "Despite Skeptics, Newport's Anastasia Clung Quietly to Her Story," *Providence Journal-Bulletin* (Rhode Island), February 16, 1997.

141 **Exploded with anger:** King and Wilson, *Resurrection*, 239

141 **The article wasn't all positive:** All details from *Life* magazine article can be found in, well, "The Case for a New Anastasia," *Life* magazine, October 18, 1963, 104A–112.

141 **Alexei had been killed:** Massie, *Final Chapter*, 159.

142 **Filled with tears:** "The Case for a New Anastasia," *Life* magazine, October 18, 1963, 112.

142 **Nikolai Sokolov:** Massie, *Final Chapter*, 18.

142 **Most people:** Ibid, 11.

143 **"We felt the parts of no fewer than nine bodies":** "Soviet Writer Tracks His Greatest Mystery," *The Philadelphia Inquirer*, May 8, 1989, 10-A.

143 **"So badly damaged":** Massie, *Final Chapter*, 41.

144 **Neighbors complained:** King and Wilson, *Resurrection*, 244.

144 **Soon overflowing:** Ibid., 249.

144 **"Annie Apple" . . . wine:** "Anastasia: The Mystery Resolved," *The Washington Post*, October 6, 1994.

145 **"Maybe I am not me":** King and Wilson, *Resurrection*, 248.

145 **No one had been murdered at all:** Ibid, 251.

145 **"I am certain at the end":** "Anastasia: The Mystery Resolved," *The Washington Post*, October 6, 1994.

145 **"Sane, if highly strung":** King and Wilson, *Resurrection*, 296.

145 **"Borderline personality . . . unlikely that she was actually clinically insane":** Ibid., 283–4.

146 **"Believed by virtually no one":** "Final Verdict: The Legend of Anastasia Will Not Die," *Chicago Tribune*, November 12, 1995, Section 7, 22.

146 **"Absolute nonsense":** "Service Held for Eugenia Smith, Who Said She Was Czar's Daughter," *The Boston Globe*, February 17, 1997, F15.

146 **DNA confirmed that these were the bones:** Michael D. Coble, Odile M. Loreille, Mark J. Wadhams, et al. "Mystery Solved: The Identification of the Two Missing Romanov Children Using DNA Analysis." *PLoS ONE*, 4, no. 3, 2009, e4838, https://doi.org/10.1371/journal.pone.0004838.

147 **Shot him in the chest:** Sources differ on some of the exact details of the execution. For example, some say that the Tsar was shot in the face, or that Alexei was the last child to be killed, or that Yurovsky read out a slightly different statement. And unsurprisingly, multiple men tried to claim the honor of killing the Tsar—not just Yurovsky. Of course, the general narrative is consistent: we know that they were all killed, and that it was horribly gruesome. I've constructed this scene mostly from Simon Sebag Montefiore's *The Romanovs: 1613–1918* (New York: Alfred A. Knopf, 2016), 647–648.

147 **Crushing their faces:** King and Wilson, *Resurrection*, 330.

148 **Vomit:** Montefiore, *The Romanovs*, 649.

148 **"Filipino's grandmama":** "Filipino's Grandmama Could Be Russia's Anastasia," Inquirer.net, May 13, 2012.

148 **Franziska had actually been Anastasia all along:** "Did Grand Duchess Anastasia Survive the Bolshevik Bullets? Explosive New Book Claims Fresh Evidence Shows the Russian Princess Really DID Escape to the West," *Daily Mail*, March 2, 2014.

148 **"Amateur genealogist":** "Anastasia Again," NewportRI.com, July 9, 2018.

148 **"Eugenia was also a prolific artist":** "Anastasia or Imposter? Local Author Digs Deeper," *Times Union* (Albany, NY), May 29, 2018.

149 **"People look for exceptional events":** "Anastasia: The Mystery Resolved," *The Washington Post*, October 6, 1994.

ROXIE ANN RICE

151 **Alias:** Mrs. Kenneth Houston, from Lt. Frank Burns, Commander, Robbery-Burglary Division, Metropolitan Police Department, City of St. Louis, Police Report, January 1, 1975, Complaint #2982. Dr. Andiza Juzang, from "Girl Says She Was Sports Drug Courier," *St. Louis Post-Dispatch*, January 22, 1975, 1E. Roxie Ann Christian, Roxie Houston, and Lara Borga, from "Woman Extradited to Face Charges," *Albuquerque*

Journal, November 28, 1975, E-8. Roxanne A. Harris, from "Woman Admits Posing as M.D.," *Buffalo Courier-Express*, December 3, 1978.

152   **Didn't actually know where the country of Ghana was located:** "Drug Case Shakes Gridders," *Chicago Defender*, January 23, 1975.

153   **It didn't make sense:** All details of the meeting between Rick Forzano and "Dr. Andiza Juzang" from "Laughter Dwindles in NFL Over Roxie's Story," *St. Louis Post-Dispatch*, January 23, 1975, 1C.

153   **Roxie was born:** Birthdate from Lt. Frank Burns's police report. Unless otherwise indicated, all of Roxie's background information from "Roxie Ann Rice a Good Student, Mother Recalls," *St. Louis Post-Dispatch*, January 26, 1975.

154   **Tricked a local woman:** "Woman Extradited to Face Charges," *Albuquerque Journal*, November 28, 1975, E-8.

154   **Got pregnant:** "Background of Alleged NFL Drug Courier Obscure," *The Daily Capital News* (Jefferson City, Missouri), January 25, 1975, 8.

154   **Gun battle:** "Roxie's Mother Saddened by Pro Grid Drug Caper," *Kansas City Star*, January 26, 1975, 4S.

154   **Black Americans were breaking records right and left:** "African-American History Timeline: 1970 to 1979," ThoughtCo.com, July 2, 2019, accessed November 4, 2019, https://www.thoughtco.com/african-american-history -timeline-1970-1979-45445

155   **Fred Christian:** Fred Christian's story from "Roxie Regarded as Hollywood Material," *St. Louis Post-Dispatch*, January 24, 1975, 2C and "No 'French Connection' Here . . ." *Beckley Post-Herald and Raleigh Register*, combined Sunday edition, February 2, 1975, 24.

158   **Quit her job:** "Roxie Ann Rice a Good Student, Mother Recalls," *St. Louis Post-Dispatch*, January 26, 1975.

159   **Ken Houston's credit card:** Details of Roxie's encounter with Hugh Robnett from Lt. Frank Burns's police report.

160   **His credit card:** "Houston Player Says Miss Rice Stayed with Him," *Kansas City Star*, January 23, 1975, 19.

161   **Roxie told them that back in September:** Roxie's story, as per the 39-page police report, from "Roxie's Story—Fact or Fiction?" *The Press Democrat* (Santa Rosa, California), January 24, 1975, 31, and "19-Year-Old Girl Gives Names, Etc., Tells of NFL Drug Ring," *Mt. Vernon Register-News*, January 22, 1975, 1-C.

163   **The laughter died:** "Laughter Dwindles in NFL Over Roxie's Story," *St. Louis Post-Dispatch*, January 23, 1975, 1C.

163   **"She seemed too interested in water poisoning":** "Houston Player Says Miss Rice Stayed with Him," *Kansas City Star*, January 23, 1975, 19.

163   **Press privileges:** "Roxie: From Fat and Unwed to Mysterious and Fa-

mous," *Beckley Post-Herald and Raleigh Register*, combined Sunday edition, January 26, 1975, 29.

164 **"I was taken in by her"**: "Roxie Finds No Defense in NFL's Security," *Cumberland Evening Times*, January 23, 1975, 19.

164 **"Enough substance to warrant a full-scale investigation"**: "Government Scrutinizes Drug Story," *New York Times*, January 24, 1975, 22.

164 **San Diego Chargers**: "Roxie Rice . . . Is She Telling the Truth About NFL?" *Kansas City Star*, January 23, 1975, p 17.

164 **"Hollywood material"**: "Roxie Regarded as Hollywood Material," *St. Louis Post-Dispatch*, January 24, 1975, 2C.

165 **This ominous mystery**: "No 'French Connection' Here . . ." *Beckley Post-Herald and Raleigh Register*, combined Sunday edition, February 2, 1975, 24.

165 **"She's an intelligent girl"**: "Roxie Ann Rice a Good Student, Mother Recalls," *St. Louis Post-Dispatch*, January 26, 1975.

165 **"Sociopathic hysteria"**: "Girl in Drug Quiz Reportedly Cuts Her Wrist," *Chicago Tribune*, January 27, 1975, 6.

165 **Bail**: "Roxie Rice Free on Bail," *The Kansas City Times*, February 1, 1975, 1D.

165 **"They told me to do it"**: "No 'French Connection' Here . . ." *Beckley Post-Herald and Raleigh Register*, combined Sunday edition, February 2, 1975, 24.

165 **"Completely innocent"**: "Players Cleared in Rice Probe," *St. Louis Post-Dispatch*, February 7, 1975.

166 **"Doing this on her own"**: "Roxie Called 'Con Woman,'" *The Kansas City Times*, February 8, 1975.

166 **"Malice in Wonderland"**: "Overreaction Sets In with Soccer Community," *St. Louis Post-Dispatch*, February 10, 1975.

167 **An unusual source**: "Roxie Called 'Con Woman,'" *The Kansas City Times*, February 8, 1975.

167 **The entire magazine oozed with images**: All details from *Ebony* magazine, November 1974 issue.

168 **"It was a definite comedown"**: "Roxie Ann Rice Plea Results in Fine, Probation," *The Pantagraph* (Bloomington, Illinois), March 28, 1975, B-3.

168 **Extradited to New Mexico**: "Woman Extradited to Face Charges," *Albuquerque Journal*, November 28, 1975, E-8.

168 **Served concurrently**: "Man in Heroin Case Given Prison Terms," *Albuquerque Journal*, January 29, 1976, B-6.

168 **One of her old, familiar lies**: "Woman Accused of Posing as MD," *Buffalo Courier-Express*, October 11, 1978.

168 **$28,000**: Ibid.

169 **Give birth there at a discount:** "Dec. 1 Trial Set for Roxie Rice," *Buffalo Courier-Express*, October 18, 1978.

169 **"Wide range of accents":** "Woman's Tie to NFL Hoax Solid," *Buffalo Courier-Express*, October 14, 1978.

169 **"She's a smart girl":** Ibid.

169 **"A woman with a very vivid imagination":** "Players Cleared in Rice Probe," *St. Louis Post-Dispatch*, February 7, 1975.

169 **"She's not a dummy":** "NFL Grass Plot For Real or Just a Pot-On?" *Philadelphia Daily News*, January 23, 1975, 59.

170 **"She didn't have any props":** "Roxie Regarded as Hollywood Material," *St. Louis Post-Dispatch*, January 24, 1975, 2C.

170 **"It's awful, awful strange":** "No 'French Connection' Here . . ." *Beckley Post-Herald and Raleigh Register*, combined Sunday edition, February 2, 1975, 24.

THE TRAGEDIENNES

171 **Headlines:** "Scots Fraudster's £180,000 Fake Terror Claims: Evil Conwoman Filed Bogus Reports," *Express*, December 20, 2018. "GRENFELL VULTURE: £180k Insurance Ghoul Caged for Scamming Spree," *The Sun*, December 20, 2018. "Vile Fraudster Claimed Compensation for Grenfell Tower Fire and Manchester Bombings," *Mirror*, December 19, 2018. "Callous & Heartless," *Daily Record*, December 20, 2018. "'Disgraceful' Edinburgh Woman Jailed over Fraudulent Grenfell Tower and Terror Attack Insurance Claims," *Edinburgh Evening News*, December 19, 2018.

171 **Pakistan:** "'Callous' Scot Jailed over Grenfell Fraud," *Scottish Daily Mail*, December 20, 2018.

171 **Father . . . sister:** "Opinion of Lady Wise in the Petition of Her Majesty's Advocate against Mohammed Younas and Farzana Ashraf," Outer House, Court of Session, February 8, 2018.

171 **Kingpins:** "Drug Kingpins Duck £4.5m Court Orders," *Evening News* (Edinburgh), 31 December 2015.

172 **2012:** "We charged her with offending between 2012 and 2017. Now it's very possible that she was offending well before 2012. In fact, when I looked at her electronic devices, there were some things on there that I wasn't happy with that went back as far as 2007, but I couldn't prove that any of those things were fraudulent purely because so long had elapsed." Pete Gartland (Detective Constable, City of London Police, IFED), interviewed by Tori Telfer, July 9, 2019.

172 **A little cave:** Information about Ruksana's life from "'Callous' Scot Jailed over Grenfell Fraud," *Scottish Daily Mail*, December 20, 2018, and Pete

Gartland (Detective Constable, City of London Police, IFED), interviewed by Tori Telfer, July 9, 2019.

173 **Louis Vuitton . . . gold:** Email between author and Tom Keating, Media and Communications Officer, Corporate Communications, City of London Police, July 12, 2019.

174 **Clinging to each other:** "A Year After Grenfell Tower Fire, Pain and Anger Still Resonate," *New York Times,* June 13, 2018.

174 **Ruksana's ears perked up:** "She'd been using a tried and tested method which had been working quite well, but it was almost like she'd been about to run out of excuses about how to make these claims, and this new opportunity that presented itself was something that she grasped and just took on." Pete Gartland (Detective Constable, City of London Police, IFED), interviewed by Tori Telfer, July 9, 2019.

174 **Headlines:** "Woman Suspected of Fire Donation Scam: O.C. Investigators Say She Possibly Made Up Husband Fighting Holy Blaze to Collect Gifts," *Los Angeles Times,* September 11, 2018. "Deputies Arrest Woman, Accuse Her of Scam to Collect Money: Fake Pregnancy Part of a Con, Authorities Say," *Orange County Register,* December 19, 2018. "California Woman Fabricated Firefighter Husband to Scam Donors: Police," *The Daily Beast,* December 19, 2018. "Wedding Planner, 28, Is Jailed for Posing as a Firefighter's Wife to Collect More Than $2K from Good Samaritans during 2018 California Wildfires after Faking Three Pregnancies by Stuffing a CUSHION Up Her Blouse," *Daily Mail,* March 4, 2019.

174 **A brutal Southern Californian blaze:** "Holy Fire in Riverside and Orange Counties Is 100 Percent Contained," *The Press-Enterprise* (Riverside, CA), September 13, 2018.

175 **"Shane works for Cal Fire":** "Woman Pleads Guilty to Posing as Firefighter's Wife in Holy Fire Scheme, Gets Jail Time," *Los Angeles Times,* March 4, 2019.

175 **Happy to meet up with donors:** "OC Woman Accused of Using Holy Fire to Scam More Than $11K in Donations from People," *ABC7 Eyewitness News,* September 10, 2018.

175 **Helpful list:** "San Clemente Woman Suspected of Fabricating Firefighter Husband to Collect Cash, Donations," *The OC Register,* September 7, 2018.

176 **Better to retreat from real life:** Information about Ashley's early life is taken from her appearance on *Dr. Phil,* November 1, 2018.

176 **Headlines:** "'America's Darkest Day': See Newspaper Headlines from Around the World 24 Hours after 9/11," *Business Insider,* September 10, 2019.

179 **"Personally":** "In a 9/11 Survival Tale, the Pieces Just Don't Fit," *New York Times,* September 27, 2007.

179   **Untouchable:** Tania Head's "story" is from Robin Gaby Fisher and Angelo J. Guglielmo, *The Woman Who Wasn't There* (New York: Atria Books, 2013).

179   **People donated so much blood:** "People Are Lining Up to Donate Blood for the Orlando Shooting Victims," *Buzzfeed News,* June 12, 2016.

180   **"There's a window of opportunity":** Michael Thatcher (President and CEO of Charity Navigator), interviewed by Tori Telfer, June 25, 2019.

180   **IRS had to issue a consumer alert:** "IRS Warns on Charity Scams Following Orlando Tragedy," *Forbes,* June 18, 2016.

181   **"Think fast and move":** Michael Thatcher (President and CEO of Charity Navigator), interviewed by Tori Telfer, June 25, 2019.

182   **"Quite well-done":** Pete Gartland (Detective Constable, City of London Police, IFED), interviewed by Tori Telfer, July 9, 2019.

183   **"I suspect we saved the insurance industry several hundred thousand pounds":** This, and other details of the raid, from Pete Gartland (Detective Constable, City of London Police, IFED), interviewed by Tori Telfer, July 9, 2019.

183   **Leaving behind a variety of expensive designer goods:** "Insurance Fraud: Another Grenfell Scammer Jailed," *Insurance Edge*, January 4, 2019.

183   **"She was a quite secretive individual":** Matt Hussey (Detective Sergeant, City of London Police, IFED), interviewed by Tori Telfer, July 9, 2019.

184   **Mitigating circumstances:** "Fraudster Who Made £180,000 Bogus Claims Is Jailed for Three Years," Insurance Fraud News, Coalition Against Insurance Fraud, December 19, 2018.

185   **Nothing popped up:** "Woman Suspected of Fire Donation Scam," *Los Angeles Times*, September 11, 2018, B3.

186   **She had *made it herself*, she insisted:** Ashley Bemis, appearance on *Dr. Phil*, November 1, 2018.

187   **"No words can explain the pain of losing a child!":** "San Clemente Woman Wove Tangled 'Web of Lies' in Faking at Least 3 Pregnancies, Victims Say," *Daily Breeze* (Torrance, CA), September 13, 2018.

187   **Once, she claimed that he, too, had died:** "Woman Suspected of Fire Donation Scam," *Los Angeles Times*, September 11, 2018, B3.

188   **"I get lied to":** This paragraph taken from Ashley Bemis, appearance on *Dr. Phil*, November 1, 2018.

189   **"World Trade Center superstar":** Fisher and Guglielmo, *Woman*, 241.

190   **Never been in the World Trade Center *at all*:** "In a 9/11 Survival Tale, the Pieces Just Don't Fit," *New York Times,* September 27, 2007.

190   **A survivor, but not of terrorism:** Tania's real background from Fisher and Guglielmo, *Woman*.

190 **Most likely:** Technically, September 11 was a school holiday in Spain, so Tania could have hopped on a plane to New York then—but there's no evidence that she did.

191 **Welles Crowther:** "Saved on 9/11, by the Man in the Red Bandana," *New York Times,* September 8, 2017.

191 **"No other event has inspired so many false claims among my patients":** "Another Dark Side of 9/11: Manipulating Trauma for Sympathy," *Psychology Today,* September 24, 2017.

192 **"They get away with it":** Michael Thatcher (President and CEO of Charity Navigator), interviewed by Tori Telfer, June 25, 2019.

193 **"One of the worse kinds":** The comments about Tania are taken from "Tania Head: The 9/11 Faker," topdocumentaryfilms.com, accessed March 25, 2020, https://topdocumentaryfilms.com/tania-head-the-911-faker/.

194 *My husband died on that ship,* **she told people:** Hallie Rubenhold, *The Five* (Boston: Houghton Mifflin Harcourt, 2019), 170–171.

194 **Begged for donations:** "Woman Who Posed as Victim's Aunt, Ran Newtown Fundraising Scam Gets 8-Month Sentence," *CBS New York,* October 15, 2013.

194 **Bullet-ridden body:** "Newton Fraud Investigation," Anderson Cooper 360, December 27, 2012.

194 **"This is so shocking":** Ibid.

BONNY LEE BAKLEY

194 **Alias:** Dennis McDougal and Mary Murphy, *Blood Cold: Fame, Sex, and Murder in Hollywood* (New York: Penguin, 2002), 172, 171, 118, 43.

194 **"Liked to live on the edge":** "Actor's Slain Wife Had Checkered Past," *The News Journal* (Wilmington, DE), May 8, 2001, A8.

195 **"Was not Mother Teresa":** "In Cold Blood," *People,* May 21, 2001.

195 **Stalking rock stars:** "Blake's Wife Had Spotty Past," *The San Francisco Examiner,* May 7, 2001, 5.

196 **The detectives working on her case couldn't help but notice:** "All the detectives remarked on how thoroughly he trashed his dead wife's life and reputation mere hours after her brutal murder." McDougal and Murphy, *Blood Cold,* 251.

196 **"It's kind of unfair":** "Actor's Slain Wife Linked to Sex Scam," *Santa Cruz Sentinel,* May 9, 2001, A6.

196 **Gave three of their children up for adoption:** McDougal and Murphy, *Blood Cold,* 83.

197 **Her father attempted to molest her:** David Grann, "To Die For," *The New Republic,* August 13, 2001.

197 **The tough guys that her mom and grandma were also obsessed with:**

Deanne Stillman, "The Strange Collision of Bonny Bakley and Christian Brando," *LA Observed*, January 27, 2008.

197 **"I'll show them, I'll be a movie star":** David Grann, "To Die For," *The New Republic*, August 13, 2001.

198 **Like she was wearing thrift-store clothes:** Jerry Lee Lewis's road manager said, "She *always* had a bad hair day. She dressed kind of old-timey, like she got her clothes from a thrift store." McDougal and Murphy, *Blood Cold*, 144.

198 **Bonny was hooked:** Ibid., 85.

198 **Climbed over the walls of Elvis's Graceland estate:** Ibid., 119.

198 **"Former girlfriend":** Bonny had a fake photo of herself and Elvis Presley captioned, "Miss Leebonny—Elvis's former girlfriend—to appear in upcoming motion picture." "Actor's Slain Wife Linked to Sex Scam," *Santa Cruz Sentinel*, May 9, 2001, A6.

198 **Neither was true:** "Blake's Wife Had Spotty Past," *The San Francisco Examiner*, May 7, 2001, 5.

198 **"An insult to the intelligence of the audience":** Robert Ebert's review of *Turk 182!*, February 15, 1985, accessed November 8, 2019, https://www.rogerebert.com/reviews/turk-182-1985.

199 **She had him deported:** McDougal and Murphy, *Blood Cold*, 118.

199 **"Bakley had between nine and more than a hundred husbands":** Deanne Stillman, "A Murder in Hollywood: The Robert Blake Affair," *Rolling Stone*, May 23, 2002, 55–61.

200 **"I don't have anyone to spend the holidays with, do you?":** "Actor's Slain Wife Linked to Sex Scam," *Santa Cruz Sentinel*, May 9, 2001, A6.

201 **She might even go ahead and marry him:** Some examples of Bonny's many husbands can be found in McDougal and Murphy, *Blood Cold*, 191.

201 **Shocked to find that he had a "fiancée":** Ibid., 137.

201 **Eight levels:** Ibid, 176.

202 **"Everything she did was crooked":** Ibid., 16.

202 **Racking up a bit of a criminal record:** "'Groupie' Lifestyle Ended in Death," *The Gazette* (Montreal, Quebec, Canada), May 12, 2001, B4.

203 **Two of his wives had died under suspicious circumstances:** "The Sudden Death of Wife No. 5 Confronts Jerry Lee Lewis with Tragedy—and Troubling Questions," *People*, September 12, 1983.

203 **"You can't get pregnant from a blow job":** McDougal and Murphy, *Blood Cold*, 190.

203 **"I like being around celebrities":** "Blake Adds Top Lawyer to His Dream Team," *New York Post*, May 16, 2001.

204 **Put a man on the phone:** "'Groupie' Lifestyle Ended in Death," *The Gazette* (Montreal, Quebec, Canada), May 12, 2001, B4.

206   **"You're lucky, you know"**: "Blake Defense Has Tape of Phone Conversation, *CNN Live Today*, aired August 2, 2002, 13:30 ET.

206   **"Who would you go for? Blake or Christian?"**: McDougal and Murphy, *Blood Cold*, 52.

207   **Blake would sometimes choke her, or try to rip out her hair**: Ibid, 48.

207   **"For the rest of my life I'll never forget it"**: Transcript of a 1999 telephone conversation between Robert Blake and Bonny Lee Bakley, included in a court filing by the prosecutors. Tape no. 270936, p 9, accessed November 8, 2019, http://www.thesmokinggun.com/file/transcript-blakebakley-telephone-talk?page=0.

208   **"I can conceive of *me* killing somebody"**: Lawrence Linderman, "Robert Blake: The Playboy Interview," *Playboy*, June 1977.

209   **Christmas cards**: McDougal and Murphy, *Blood Cold*, 220.

209   **"I'll get someone else"**: Ibid., 239.

209   *2 Shovels, Small Sledge:* From a note found in Caldwell's Jeep, filed during Robert Blake's trial, accessed November 8, 2019, http://www.thesmokinggun.com/file/caldwells-laundry-list-murder?page=0.

209   **"Blake's gonna get you"**: McDougal and Murphy, *Blood Cold,* 60.

210   **"Girl, you better remember who you are fucking with. I'll kill your ass!"**: Ibid., 244.

210   **"Think this guy's going to kill me?"**: Ibid., 222.

210   **"I know he's going to kill me"**: From WDBJ 7 News at 11, April 22, 2002, accessed November 8, 2019, https://scholar.lib.vt.edu/VA-news/WDBJ-7/script_archives/02/0402/042202/042202.11.htm.

211   **Her eyes rolled back in her head**: "Actor Robert Blake's Wife Is Shot to Death," *Los Angeles Times*, May 6, 2001, 11.

211   **She struggled . . . a stranger**: McDougal and Murphy, *Blood Cold*, 250.

211   **Knew her killer**: "The People v. Robert Blake: How DA Team May Raise the Curtain on a Vicious Slay Plot," *New York Post*, April 21, 2002.

211   **Personal documents . . . "The dowdy grifter"**: "Show and Tell," *Los Angeles Times*, May 11, 2001, E2.

212   **Comparisons to the trial(s) of O.J. Simpson**: "Why Robert Blake Isn't O.J. Material," *New York Post*, April 23, 2002.

212   **"I'm still here, you bastards"**: "Robert Blake #2," *20/20*, Season 42, Episode 20, January 11, 2019.

213   **Her sister took . . . her mother signed**: McDougal and Murphy, *Blood Cold*, 254.

LAURETTA J. WILLIAMS

217   **Alias**: Loreta Janeta Velasquez or Velazquez; according to historian William C. Davis, Lauretta favored the first spelling, but used the second in

her memoir *The Woman in Battle* (Madison: The University of Wisconsin Press, 2003). Lieutenant Harry T. Buford, also from her memoir (as well as many newspaper interviews). Ann or Mary Ann Williams, from William C. Davis, *Inventing Loreta Velasquez: Confederate Soldier Impersonator, Media Celebrity, and Con Artist* (Carbondale: Southern Illinois University Press, 2016), 8. Mary Ann Keith, from Davis, *Inventing*, 18. Mrs. M. M. Arnold, from Davis, *Inventing*, 25. Mrs. L. J. V. Beard, from "A Woman's Glorious Dream," New Orleans *Times-Picayune*, October 25, 1900. Señora Beard, from "Many Friends Await Senora Beard's Return," *The Times*, Philadelphia, December 10, 1901. Loretta J. Wasson, from Davis, *Inventing*, 124. Mrs. Bonner, from "The Exploits of Mrs. Bonner," *Atlanta Constitution*, January 15, 1875. Clapp through Roche, from Davis, *Inventing*, 5.

217 **Teenage sex worker:** Davis, *Inventing*, 8–9; also 266, note 11.

218 **"Velazquex":** Ibid., 142.

218 **Ann or Mary Ann Williams:** Historian William C. Davis makes the link between Lauretta and Ann/Mary Ann Williams during her teenage years. When Lauretta was arrested later in New Orleans in 1862, at the age of 20 or so, papers referred to her as Ann Williams, and she also identified herself that way. Ibid., 5, 8, and 29.

218 **"Latin":** For example, in January 1878, a journalist in Washington DC described her as "the dark, Spanish type." Ibid., 181.

218 **The real Lauretta . . . a revelation:** For more on what we know (or rather, don't know) about Lauretta's childhood, see Ibid., 5–8. 1842 was the birth year she used the most.

219 **Rape:** Julie Beck, "Gender, Race, and Rape During the Civil War," *The Atlantic*, February 20, 2014, https://www.theatlantic.com/health/archive/2014/02/gender-race-and-rape-during-the-civil-war/283754/.

219 **"Song of the Southern Women":** Julia Mildred, "Song of the Southern Women," in *Personal and Political Ballads: Arranged and Ed. by Frank Moore* (New York: G. P. Putnam, 1864), 98–99.

220 **Birth certificate:** De Anne Blanton and Lauren M. Cook, *They Fought Like Demons: Women Soldiers in the Civil War* (Baton Rouge: LSU Press, 2002), 27.

221 **"Her dashing manners":** "A Lady, of Romantic Turn . . ." *Richmond Dispatch*, September 27, 1861, 2.

221 **Mary Ann Keith:** Davis, *Inventing*, 16–19.

221 **Curtsied:** John B. Jones, *A Rebel War Clerk's Diary at the Confederate States Capital*, 1:94, November 20, 1861.

222 **"First celebrity":** Davis, *Inventing*, 21.

222 **Prison:** Ibid., 31.

222 A **"wily heroine"**: "The Heroine Again," New Orleans *Daily Delta,* November 15, 1862, 3.

222 **"This celebrated fast one"**: Davis, *Inventing, 32.*

223 **"Altar of her country"**: "Adventures of a Young Lady in the Army," *The Mississippian,* June 6, 1863, republished in the *Natchez Daily Courier,* June 13, 1863.

224 **"The female Lieutenant"**: Lauretta J. Williams to Samuel Cooper, July 20, 1863, Letters Received by Confederate Adjutant-General, July–October 1863, Record Group 109, M474, roll 88, frame 0101, file W1310, NA. Source found in Davis, *Inventing*—he hunted this gem down, not me!

224 **Bundle of letters:** Davis, *Inventing,* 49, 225.

225 **Thomas C. DeCaulp:** Ibid., 52–54.

225 **Blow the whole place up:** Velasquez, *The Woman in Battle,* 447.

226 **"In secret service"**: Pass, January 26, 1864, DeCaulp Provost File, and Davis, *Inventing,* 64–63.

226 **Had her baby:** Davis, *Inventing,* 72, 75.

226 **"Limbs and Lives"**: Flyer, no date [July 1864], DeCaulp Provost File.

226 **Fake personal ads:** Davis, *Inventing,* 91 and 192.

227 **Caroline Wilson:** Kerry Segrave, *Women Swindlers in America, 1860– 1920* (Jefferson, NC: McFarland, 2007), 50.

228 **The *Miami*:** Davis, *Inventing,* 99–100, and "Terrible Explosion," *New York Times,* January 31, 1866.

228 **"Flaxen hair"**: Velasquez, *The Woman in Battle,* 539.

229 **"Unprincipled adventurer"**: "The Exploits of Mrs. Bonner," *Atlanta Constitution,* January 15, 1875.

230 **Knife:** Davis, *Inventing,* 173.

231 **"Incipient mental problems"**: Ibid., 154.

232 **Fact-check:** For a deeper look into the contradictions and mistakes in Lauretta's memoir, see Davis, *Inventing,* Chapter 12.

232 **"Onions"**: Velasquez, *The Woman in Battle,* 550.

232 **Doubt on its truthfulness:** John William Jones, "Book Notices," *Southern Historical Society Papers,* 2, October 1876, 208.

232 **Jubal Early:** Sylvia D. Hoffert, "Heroine or Hoaxer?" *Civil War Times,* August 1999.

233 **"At the very least an opportunist"**: Ibid.

233 **"To date there is still no independent"**: Davis, *Inventing,* 256.

233 **Californian hotel . . . railroad:** To learn more about these schemes of Lauretta's, see Davis, *Inventing,* 216–218.

234 **Wire services:** Ibid., 224.

234 **Comment on it:** Ibid., 49, 225.

234 **"Plausible and fluent"**: "Many Friends Await Senora Beard's Return," *The Times* (Philadelphia), December 10, 1901.

234 **Government Hospital for the Insane . . . obituary:** Davis, *Inventing*, 233–237.

235 **One of the central characters:** American Battlefield Trust, "Biographies," battlefields.org, accessed June 11, 2019, https://www.battlefields.org/learn /biographies.

235 **"Was fictitious":** Velasquez, *The Woman in Battle*, 92.

236 **"Human nature is greatly given to confidence":** Ibid., 363.

MARGARET LYDIA BURTON

237 **Alias:** Some of Margaret's many aliases can be found in "FBI Reveals Story of Mrs. Gray: 18 Years of Crime and 22 Aliases," *The Atlanta Constitution*, August 17, 1957, 1 and 12.

237 **Both of her children were gone, too:** "'Salvation' of Jail Asked for Mrs. Gray," *The Atlanta Constitution*, December 11, 1957, 1.

237 **Rumors swirled:** "She's in $100G Doghouse," *Daily News* (New York, NY), August 25, 1957, 78.

238 **"Plain snippy" . . . "just worked for the fun of it":** The gossipy quotes from Atlanta's fashionable set are all taken from "A Look at Mrs. Gray, Woman Who Got Away," *The Atlanta Constitution*, August 21, 1957, 14.

239 **Airport . . . car trouble:** "$100,000 Missing at Decatur Clinic; FBI, DeKalb Police Hunt Woman," *The Atlanta Constitution*, July 31, 1957, 1.

240 **Unstable:** Details of the McGlashan family's many migrations can be found in "FBI Reveals Story of Mrs. Gray: 18 Years of Crime and 22 Aliases," *The Atlanta Constitution*, August 17, 1957, 1 and 12.

240 **Born:** State of California, *California Death Index, 1940–1997* (Sacramento, CA: State of California Department of Health Services, Center for Health Statistics).

240 **Scottish-born father apparently died young:** 1930 United States Federal Census, New Jersey, Essex, East Orange, District 0411, Enumeration District No. 7–411, Supervisor's District No. 4, Sheet No. 9B.

240 **Likely went to college:** In the 1940 US Census, she claimed to have completed four years of college, and her ex-husband would later refer to her as "well-educated." "'Don't Know the Man,' Candy's Mother Says," *The Atlanta Constitution*, August 23, 1957, 10.

240 **Bookkeeper:** 1930 United States Federal Census, New Jersey, Essex, East Orange, District 0411, Enumeration District No. 7–411, Supervisor's District No. 4, Sheet No. 9B.

240 **Living in Panama:** "FBI Reveals Story of Mrs. Gray: 18 Years of Crime and 22 Aliases," *The Atlanta Constitution*, August 17, 1957, 1 and 12.

240 **Jasper W. Burton:** For information about their marriage, see "Candy's Father, Living in Athens All This Time, Vows to Help Her," *The Atlanta Constitution*, August 22, 1957, 1, 14.

241 **Grand jury:** "FBI Reveals Story of Mrs. Gray: 18 Years of Crime and 22 Aliases," *The Atlanta Constitution*, August 17, 1957, 1 and 12.

242 **Skipped town:** "Mrs. Burton Is Given 240 Days in Jail for Los Angeles Thefts," *The Atlanta Constitution*, October 27, 1959, 17.

242 **Vancouver . . . Norfolk:** "FBI Reveals Story of Mrs. Gray: 18 Years of Crime and 22 Aliases," *The Atlanta Constitution*, August 17, 1957, 1 and 12.

242 **"Numerous":** Ibid.

242 **Johns Hopkins Hospital:** "Skill as 'Actress' Fools Doctors Out of $186,000," *Valley Morning Star* (Harlingen, Texas), April 20, 1958, A11.

242 **Affair:** "Mrs. Gray Seized in Tulsa at Job in Doctors' Office," *The Atlanta Constitution*, August 22, 1957, 8.

242 **If he was still alive:** "Mrs. Gray, Candy Return, Check Into Fulton Tower," *The Atlanta Constitution*, August 29, 1957, 1.

244 **Angry dog owners:** "She's in $100G Doghouse," *Daily News* (New York, NY), August 25, 1957, 78.

244 **Westminster Kennel Club Dog Show in 1954:** "Cocker Spaniel Wins Title in Westminster," *Chicago Tribune*, February 10, 1954.

244 **"Shiney":** "Candy Freed, Leaves in Few Days to Live With Uncle in California," *The Atlanta Constitution*, August 31, 1957, 8.

244 **Absent for most of the year:** "FBI Reveals Story of Mrs. Gray: 18 Years of Crime and 22 Aliases," *The Atlanta Constitution*, August 17, 1957, 1 and 12.

244 **Seemed a little lonely:** "Cocker Club Holds a 'Wake' to Swap Views on Mrs. Gray," *The Atlanta Constitution*, August 22, 1957, 24.

244 **Brisk, efficient work style:** "She's in $100G Doghouse," *Daily News* (New York, NY), August 25, 1957, 78.

245 **Peeled out of the state:** One of Margaret's getaway drivers talked to the press. For the full story of this getaway, see "Atlantan Admits Driving Mrs. Gray's Getaway Van," *The Atlanta Constitution*, August 21, 1957, 8.

245 **"An elephant in a snowbank":** "Suspect, Caravan of Dogs Hunted," *Independent* (Long Beach, California), August 1, 1957, B-5.

246 **Tracked the dogs obsessively:** "Woman Flees, Leaving Accounts $100,000 Shy: FBI Reveals Thousands in Unpaid Bills as It Presses Search for Bookkeeper," *Los Angeles Times*, August 18, 1957, A3.

246 **"Amazing":** "Amazing 'Mrs. Gray' Is Mystery No Longer," *The Atlanta Constitution*, August 17, 1957.

246 **"Audacious":** Ibid.

246 **"Flamboyant":** "Merry Chase for Mrs. Gray," *The Atlanta Constitution*, August 19, 1957, 14.

246 **"Fascinating":** "Hundreds of Visitors Find Mrs. Gray 'Out,'" *The Atlanta Constitution*, August 26, 1957, 1.

246 **Peru:** "Merry Chase for Mrs. Gray," *The Atlanta Constitution*, August 19, 1957, 14.

246 **"She has become a sort of Jesse James–type heroine":** "Amazing 'Mrs. Gray' Is Mystery No Longer," *The Atlanta Constitution*, August 17, 1957.

246 **"Now I hope the FBI isn't going to construe this as un-American":** "Merry Chase for Mrs. Gray," *The Atlanta Constitution*, August 19, 1957, 14.

247 **The Cocker Spaniel Club held a somber meeting:** "Cocker Club Holds a 'Wake' to Swap Views on Mrs. Gray," *The Atlanta Constitution*, August 22, 1957, 24.

248 **Her long run was over:** "Mrs. Gray Seized in Tulsa at Job in Doctors' Office," *The Atlanta Constitution*, August 22, 1957, 1.

248 **Getaway car driver:** "Atlantan Admits Driving Mrs. Gray's Getaway Van," *The Atlanta Constitution*, August 21, 1957, 8.

248 **Clothing store in Atlanta:** "Hundreds of Visitors Find Mrs. Gray 'Out,'" *The Atlanta Constitution*, August 26, 1957, 11.

248 **Hat . . . photographer:** "Conwoman 'Vanishes' from Ga.," *Daily Press* (Newport News, VA), August 18, 1957, 5A.

248 **Two mysterious bouquets:** "2 Bouquets, Note Sent to Accused Pair," *The Austin Statesman*, August 23, 1957, 5.

248 **$40,000 total:** "Mrs. Gray Left Assets Put at Only $40,000," *The Atlanta Constitution*, August 2, 1957, 3.

248 **Everything she owned was auctioned off:** "Mrs. Burton's Belongings Go on Sale," *The Atlanta Constitution*, November 2, 1957, 1.

248 **The American Spaniel Club scraped together $1,555:** "Shepherd Wins Best in Show at Central Indiana Trials," *Muncie Evening Press* (Muncie, Indiana), November 11, 1965, 32.

249 **Drove past Margaret's old house:** "Hundreds of Visitors Find Mrs. Gray 'Out,'" *The Atlanta Constitution*, August 26, 1957, 1.

249 **Jasper Burton:** "Candy's Father, Living in Athens All This Time, Vows to Help Her," *The Atlanta Constitution*, August 22, 1957, 1.

249 **"Quiet, refined and intellectual":** "The Burtons United Here After 18 Years," *The Atlanta Constitution*, August 30, 1957, 13.

249 **"Kind, gentle person who faints":** "Candy Freed, Leaves in Few Days to Live with Uncle in California," *The Atlanta Constitution*, August 31, 1957, 8.

250 **Dropped due to a technicality:** "U.S. Drops Charges, Hands Over Mrs. Burton to DeKalb Today," *The Atlanta Constitution*, October 30, 1957, 1.

250 **Facing charges:** "Freckles Betray Hunted Woman," *The Miami News*, August 22, 1957, 8B.

250 **"Lost [his] faith in humanity":** "'Salvation' of Jail Asked for Mrs. Gray," *The Atlanta Constitution*, December 11, 1957, 1.

250 **Talking about Margaret from the pulpit:** "Medical Examination Ordered for Mrs. Gray," *The Atlanta Constitution*, January 1, 1958, 20.

250 **Top news story:** "Adventures of 'Mrs. Gray' Was Top State News of '57," *The Atlanta Constitution*, January 1, 1958, 16.

250 **Skulking around in pale blue satin pajamas:** "Pale, Tired Mrs. Gray Brightens Cell with Books, Basket of Fruit," *The Atlanta Constitution*, December 30, 1957, 2.

250 **"Slightly pale but chipper":** "Mrs. Burton Likened to Oil Swindler," *The Atlanta Constitution*, February 4, 1958, 1.

250 **She told the courtroom:** "Skill as 'Actress' Fools Doctors Out of $186,000," *Valley Morning Star* (Harlingen, Texas), April 20, 1958, A11.

251 **Suffered from fainting spells:** "Medical Examination Ordered for Mrs. Gray," *The Atlanta Constitution*, January 1, 1958, 1.

251 **"Confidence man in a Texas oil swindle":** "Mrs. Burton Likened to Oil Swindler," *The Atlanta Constitution*, February 4, 1958, 1.

251 **Fainted . . . "actress to the last":** "Skill as 'Actress' Fools Doctors Out of $186,000," *Valley Morning Star* (Harlingen, Texas), April 20, 1958, A11.

251 **It was the first time . . . she hadn't been able to escape:** "Woman's Record Cited in Missing Fund Case," *The Hartford Courant* (Hartford, CT), August 25, 1957, 14D1.

251 **240 days in a county jail:** "Mrs. Burton Is Given 240 Days in Jail for Los Angeles Thefts," *The Atlanta Constitution*, October 27, 1959, 17.

252 **Authorities put her onto an ocean liner called *Bremen*:** "Deported After 2 Jail Terms, Mrs. Burton Sails to Britain," *The Atlanta Constitution*, May 13, 1960, 10.

252 **"Housewife":** The National Archives of the UK; Kew, Surrey, England, *Board of Trade: Commercial and Statistical Department and Successors: Inwards Passenger Lists*, Class: BT26, Piece, 1452.

252 **"The great masquerader":** "Mrs. Burton Is Given 240 Days in Jail for Los Angeles Thefts," *The Atlanta Constitution*, October 27, 1959, 17.

252 **"The remarkable Mrs. Burton":** "FBI Pictures 'Janet Gray' as Con Artist," *The Austin Statesman*, August 17, 1957, 14.

253 **"Heroic and demonic American dreamer":** "American Pseudo," *New York Times Magazine*, December 12, 1999, Section 6, Page 80.

253 **One brief interview:** "Mrs. Gray, Candy Return, Check Into Fulton Tower," *The Atlanta Constitution*, August 29, 1957, 1 and 16.

253 **"She always made a point of staying out of the pictures":** "Oh, How She

Fooled Them," *The Everyday Magazine (St. Louis Post-Dispatch)*, September 1, 1957, 1.

254   **"What ever happened to the Mrs. Gray that had all the dogs":** "The Mysterious Mrs. Gray," *The Atlanta Constitution*, January 19, 1972, 2.

254   **Passed away in 1992:** State of California, *California Death Index, 1940–1997* (Sacramento, CA: State of California Department of Health Services, Center for Health Statistics).

254   **"I want to become 'Miss Anonymous'":** "Candy Freed, Leaves in Few Days to Live with Uncle in California," *The Atlanta Constitution*, August 31, 1957, 8.

SANTE KIMES

255   **Alias:** These are only *some* of Sante's many aliases. From "Blood Ties: The Dark Transformation of Sandy Chambers: Partial List of Aliases," *Reno Gazette-Journal*, 29 October 2000, 14A.

256   **"Soulmate son" . . . "honey bunny":** "A Look at Notorious Mother-Son Killers 20 Years Later," *New York Post*, July 4, 2018.

256   **His mother was the smartest person in the world:** Intro scene is taken from "Kenneth Kimes Tells Jurors His Mother Put Him Up to Murder," *CNN Court TV*, June 18, 2004, and "Son Describes Mother's Orders in Her Murder Trial," *The Signal* (Santa Clarita, CA), June 18, 2004, A10.

256   **Prame Singhrs:** Prame's obituary is full of colorful stories that are extremely hard to believe. "Story of Missed Rajah's Throne Taken to Grave," *The Daily Oklahoman*, June 27, 1940, 21.

257   **That's what her little sister Retha claimed:** Kent Walker with Mark Schone, *Son of a Grifter* (New York: William Morrow, 2001), 492.

257   **Teased her for her name . . . powdering her face:** Ibid., 18, 22.

257   **Closed off:** Jeanne King, *Dead End: The Crime Story of the Decade—Murder, Incest and High-Tech Thievery* (New York: M. Evans & Company, 2002), 39.

258   **"Parting of the ways situation":** Ibid., 37–38.

259   **"Absolute paranoia about being poor":** Ibid., 40.

259   **Catch herself a millionaire:** For more on Sante's, uh, colorful time in Palm Springs, see Walker, *Son*, 40, 53.

260   **The resemblance was so strong:** Ibid., 14.

260   **"Nothing felt as good as basking in the charged warmth of her love":** Ibid., 30.

261   **He'd managed to register as Native American:** Ibid., 60.

261   **She peacocked around him:** Ibid., 41–43.

261   **A decade later:** Ancestry.com, *Nevada, Marriage Index, 1956–2005* [database online] (Provo, UT: Ancestry.com Operations, Inc., 2007).

261   **Buying houses in Honolulu:** "A Family Portrait: A Twisted Tale of Deceit, Fraud and Violence," *New York Times*, July 14, 1998, A1.

261   **Glued a rhinestone to her ear:** Walker, *Son*, 74.

261   **Grilled by the FBI:** "Ambassador . . . ? Who Is That Man?" *The Atlanta Constitution*, March 21, 1974, 1-C.

262   **Bit him on the wrist:** This horrifying scene has to be read in full to be believed—hair plugs, urine, and all. Find it in Walker, *Son*, 129–130.

263   **The next day, he'd be perfectly fine:** "The Story of Sante Kimes: Mother, Murderer, and Criminal Mastermind," *Vanity Fair*, March 2000.

263   **Sante let him shower with her:** "Kimes and Punishment," *Details*, November 2000, 133.

264   **Managed to drag the case on:** Walker, *Son*, 167.

264   **"Peace deprivation":** Kenneth Kimes, as told to Jonna Ivin-Patton, "My Mother Taught Me to Kill," *Narratively*, November 26, 2018.

264   **"TO: KENNETH K. KIMES and SANTE KIMES":** "Legal Notice," *The Honolulu Adviser*, October 16, 1979, 15.

265   **"COUPLE CHARGED WITH SLAVERY":** "Couple Charged with Slavery," *The Californian* (Salinas, CA), August 6 1985.

265   **Turned the case over to the FBI:** FBI agent Gilbert M. Pieper in an article for the Society of Former Special Agents of the FBI, August 2015.

265   **Coat hanger . . . iron:** "Killer Women," *Daily News* (New York, NY), January 27, 2000, 52.

265   **Boiling water:** Alice McQuillan, *They Call Them Grifters: The True Story of Sante and Kenneth Kimes* (New York: Onyx Books, 2000), 78.

266   **"IT IS GOING TO BE A HELL, HELL FOR YOU":** Walker, *Son*, 213.

266   **"CONTROL!":** McQuillan, *They Call*, 85.

266   **"Clinically speaking, this is a person who 'snaps' from time to time":** Ibid., 105.

266   **"Sante Kimes was the cruelest, most self-centered":** FBI agent Gilbert M. Pieper in an article for the Society of Former Special Agents of the FBI, August 2015.

266   **"The best female con I've ever seen":** McQuillan, *They Call*, 108.

267   **Evil ex-wife:** "'Dragon Lady' Leaves a Legacy of Mystery," *Las Vegas Review-Journal*, August 23, 1998, 5B.

267   **Found guilty of:** Ibid.

267   **More than she'd paid her maids, ever:** McQuillan, *They Call*, 96.

267   **Managed to get her insurance company to pay:** "Las Vegas Criminal Defense Attorney Douglas Crawford Represents Dangerous Defendant Sante Kimes," *The Daily Moss*, March 25, 2018.

267   **And a $10 fine:** McQuillan, *They Call*, 130.

268   **Haunting homeless shelters:** Walker, *Son*, 11, 276.

268 **Strangle his mother . . . a copy of *The Anarchist Cookbook* on the counter:** Ibid., 291, 293.

269 **Nonviolent:** "Anna Sorokin: Why Do Con Artists and Fraudsters Fascinate Us?" *BBC News*, May 11, 2019.

270 **Police forced Holmgren to become a double agent:** "Kimeses' Informant Has Disappeared," *The Honolulu Advertiser*, July 16, 1998, A11.

270 **If he didn't get in touch in three days:** Adrian Havill, *The Mother, the Son, and the Socialite* (New York: St. Martin's Paperbacks, 1999), 170.

270 **Kent was positive they were talking about poor Elmer Holmgren:** Walker, *Son*, 285.

270 **His fortune had been frittered away:** Ibid., 338.

271 **Sometimes she'd create a scene:** Ibid., 355.

271 **"Our incredible love affair lives on and on":** King, *Dead End*, 106.

272 **Told the detective:** Walker, *Son*, 3.

272 **He thought they were too shady to do business with:** Kenneth Kimes, as told to Jonna Ivin-Patton, "My Mother Taught Me to Kill," *Narratively*, November 26, 2018.

272 **Threw his body into the ocean:** Details of Ahmed's death from "Banker's Body Down for Counts, *Daily News* (New York), June 23, 2004, 4.

273 **Mother and son would take long midnight drives:** From Kenny's diary entries in "Kimes and Punishment," *Details*, November 2000, 130, 132.

273 **In January of 1998:** Walker, *Son*, 388–389.

273 **"Nice food, cocktails, and fake friendliness":** "Kenneth Kimes Tells Jurors His Mother Put Him Up to Murder," *CNN Court TV*, June 18, 2004.

274 **Flowers:** Details of the killing of David Kazdin from Ibid.

274 **"Mommy and Clyde":** "Kimes Turns on Mom; Killer Grifter to Rat Her Out in Slay," *New York Post*, November 19, 2003.

275 **Worth nearly $8 million:** "Arguments End in Murder Trial of Mother and Son," *The New York Times*, May 13, 2000.

276 **She received a call from someone calling herself "Eva Guerrero":** People v. Kimes, 2006 NY Slip Op 09134 [37 AD3d 1], December 7, 2006.

276 **Like he just got out of jail:** "Trouble in Apt. 1-B," *People*, April 17, 2000.

277 **Convincing a notary public to sign:** People v. Kimes, 2006 NY Slip Op 09134 [37 AD3d 1], December 7, 2006.

277 **"The more morbid-minded we became":** "Murderer Reveals New Details in Slaying of Socialite in 1998," *The New York Times*, June 24, 2004.

277 **Planning to evict "Manny" on Monday:** People v. Kimes, 2006 NY Slip Op 09134 [37 AD3d 1], December 7, 2006.

277 **A sudden, overwhelming sense of evil:** "The Lady Vanishes," *The Sydney Morning Herald* (Sydney, New South Wales, Australia), January 8, 2000, 16.

278   **Began to squeeze:** Irene's murder taken from Kimes, "My Mother Taught Me to Kill," and "'Mom Hit Her in the Head with the Stun Gun. Then Mom Said, 'Do It!'" *Daily News* (New York, NY), June 23, 2004, 5.

278   **Took themselves out for coffee and pastries:** Kenneth Kimes, as told to Jonna Ivin-Patton, "My Mother Taught Me to Kill," *Narratively*, November 26, 2018.

278   **He offered to buy the officers a drink:** "'Mommie and Clyde' Blaze Trail of Deceit and Death Lies Leads to Murder," *The Guardian*, May 13, 2000.

279   **The "Kenny Kimes" he already had in custody:** "The Story of Sante Kimes: Mother, Murderer, and Criminal Mastermind," *Vanity Fair*, March 2000.

279   **Her diminutive corpse never turned up:** "Search Finds No Trace of Missing Widow," *The New York Times*, August 28, 1998, B5.

279   **"I think [my mother] is a beautiful person":** "The Story of Sante Kimes: Mother, Murderer, and Criminal Mastermind," *Vanity Fair*, March 2000.

280   **"What was I supposed to do?":** "Kimes and Punishment," *Details*, November 2000, 133.

280   **Also charged with David Kazdin's murder:** "California Killing Is Added to Charges Against a Mother and Son," *The New York Times*, September 16, 1999, B7.

280   **125 witnesses and 350 pieces of evidence . . . "Your Honor, how can we have fairness?":** "Jury Hears a Murder Defendant's Outburst," *The New York Times*, April 29, 2000, B8.

280   **"I'm afraid of you, I'm afraid of this corrupt system":** "Agitated Murder Defendant Declines to Testify," *The New York Times*, May 6, 2000, B2.

280   **"We're innocent! For God's sake, help us!":** Ibid.

281   **"Performance—I mean, your statement":** "Kooky Kimes Killers Each Get 120+ Years in Prison," *New York Post*, June 28, 2000.

281   **The mountain of circumstantial evidence against her and Kenny was damning:** People v. Kimes, 2006 NY Slip Op 09134 [37 AD3d 1], December 7, 2006.

281   **An ominous folder:** "Mother and Son Guilty of Killing a Socialite Who Vanished in '98," *The New York Times*, May 19, 2000, A1.

282   **"Virtual roadmap":** People v. Kimes, 2006 NY Slip Op 09134 [37 AD3d 1], December 7, 2006.

282   **"Mom, it'll be okay":** "Mother and Son Guilty of Killing a Socialite Who Vanished in '98," *The New York Times*, May 19, 2000, A1.

282   **"Bizarre, rambling and sometimes vulgar":** "Mother and Son Are Given Life Sentences," *The New York Times*, June 28, 2000, B6.

282   **"Rambling, bitter and sometimes comical":** "Kooky Kimes Killers Each Get 120+ Years in Prison," *New York Post*, June 28, 2000.

282   **"Mom, don't talk!":** "Grifters get 245 years," *Daily News* (New York, NY), June 28, 2000, 5.

283   **"Worst, unjust mistake in the history of the United States":** "Convicted Murderers Sante and Kenneth Kimes Profess Their Innocence," *Larry King Live Weekend*, aired March 25, 2001, 9 PM ET.

283   **Demanding that Sante not be extradited:** "Kenneth Kimes Takes Reporter as a Hostage," *The New York Times*, October 11, 2000, B1.

283   **Kenny wept as he testified against his mother:** "Son Describes Mom's Orders in Her State Murder Trial," *The Desert Sun* (Palm Springs, CA), June 18, 2004, A12.

284   **"Broke him":** "Sante Kimes Denies 1998 Slaying," *The Los Angeles Times*, June 22, 2004, B4.

284   **"Tortured and coerced":** "'Mom hit her in the head with the stun gun. Then Mom said, 'Do it!'" *Daily News* (New York, NY), June 23, 2004, 5.

284   **"Just spent the last ten minutes vomiting":** Kenneth Kimes, as told to Jonna Ivin-Patton, "My Mother Taught Me to Kill," *Narratively*, November 26, 2018.

285   **"It's important how I look in the interview":** "Killers' Motto: 'No Body, No Crime,'" *The Los Angeles Times*, May 22, 2014, A5.

285   **"Moral compass":** Kenneth Kimes, as told to Jonna Ivin-Patton, "My Mother Taught Me to Kill," *Narratively*, November 26, 2018.

285   **Full-length memoir:** Email correspondence between author and Ivin-Patton, March 25, 2019.

285   **His daughter's obituary was full of darker compliments:** "Sante Kimes Dies in Prison at 79; Killed and Swindled with Her Son," *New York Times*, May 21, 2014.

286   **When she was in a good mood:** Walker, *Son*, 13–15, 112.

286   **"What was real and what wasn't real":** "'Dragon Lady' Leaves a Legacy of Mystery," *Las Vegas Review-Journal*, August 23, 1998, 5B.

286   **"She was known by every name there ever was":** "Suspects in a Disappearance Have Been Running for Years," *The New York Times*, July 10, 1998, A1.

CONCLUSION: CONFIDENT

287   **Listed on Wikipedia as a serial killer:** From Wikipedia, "List of Serial Killers in the United States," accessed March 30, 2020, https://en.wikipedia .org/wiki/List_of_serial_killers_in_the_United_States.

288   **Don't come forward at all:** "The Mind of the Mark," *NPR*, August 7, 2019.

ABOUT THE AUTHOR

Tori Telfer is the author of *Lady Killers: Deadly Women Through-out History* and the host of the podcasts *Criminal Broads, Why Women Kill: Truth, Lies, and Labels* (CBS All Access), and *Red Flags* (Investigation Discovery). She lives in New York City with her husband and son.